CHILD VERSUS CHILDMAKER

D0878617

Studies in Social, Political, and Legal Philosophy
General Editor: James P. Sterba, University of Notre Dame

This series analyzes and evaluates critically the major political, social, and legal ideals, institutions, and practices of our time. The analysis may be historical or problem-centered; the evaluation may focus on theoretical underpinnings or practical implications. Among the recent titles in the series are:

Citizenship in a Fragile World
   by Bernard P. Dauenhauer, University of Georgia
Critical Moral Liberalism: Theory and Practice
   by Jeffrey Reiman, American University
Nature as Subject: Human Obligation and Natural Community
   by Eric Katz, New Jersey Institute of Technology
Can Ethics Provide Answers? And Other Essays in Moral Philosophy
   by James Rachels, University of Alabama at Birmingham
Character and Culture
   by Lester H. Hunt, University of Wisconsin–Madison
Same Sex: Debating the Ethics, Science, and Culture of Homosexuality
   edited by John Corvino, University of Texas at Austin
Approximate Justice: Studies in Non-Ideal Theory
   by George Sher, Rice University
Living in Integrity: A Global Ethic to Restore a Fragmented Earth
   by Laura Westra, University of Windsor
Racist Symbols and Reparations: Philosophical Reflections on Vestiges of the American Civil War
   by George Schedler, Southern Illinois University
Necessary Goods: Our Responsibilities to Meet Others' Needs
   edited by Gillian Brock, University of Auckland, New Zealand
The Business of Consumption: Environmental Ethics and the Global Economy
   edited by Laura Westra, University of Windsor, and Patricia H. Werhane, University of Virginia
Child versus Childmaker: Future Persons and Present Duties in Ethics and the Law
   by Melinda A. Roberts, College of New Jersey

CHILD VERSUS CHILDMAKER

Future Persons and Present Duties in Ethics and the Law

Melinda A. Roberts

ROWMAN & LITTLEFIELD PUBLISHERS, INC.
Lanham • Boulder • New York • Oxford

ROWMAN & LITTLEFIELD PUBLISHERS, INC.

Published in the United States of America
by Rowman & Littlefield Publishers, Inc.
4720 Boston Way, Lanham, Maryland 20706

12 Hid's Copse Road
Cumnor Hill, Oxford OX2 9JJ, England

Copyright © 1998 by Rowman & Littlefield Publishers, Inc.

All rights reserved. No part of this publication may be reproduced,
stored in a retrieval system, or transmitted in any form or by any
means, electronic, mechanical, photocopying, recording, or otherwise,
without the prior permission of the publisher.

British Library Cataloguing in Publication Information Available

Library of Congress Cataloging-in-Publication Data

Roberts, Melinda A., 1954–
    Child versus childmaker : future persons and present duties
in ethics and the law / Melinda A. Roberts.
        p.   cm. — (Studies in social, political, and legal
philosophy)
    Includes bibliographical references and index.
    ISBN 0-8476-8900-X (cloth : alk. paper). — ISBN
0-8476-8901-8 (pbk. : alk. paper)
    1. Human reproductive technology—Moral and ethical aspects.
2. Cloning—Moral and ethical aspects.   I. Title.   II. Series.
RG133.5.R62   1998
176—dc21   98-13911
                                                                CIP

Printed in the United States of America

♾ ™ The paper used in this publication meets the minimum requirements of
American National Standard for Information Sciences—Permanence of Paper
for Printed Library Materials, ANSI Z39.48–1984.

*To Annabel, Tommy, and
Alan, and to my father, with love and gratitude.*

Contents

Preface

I am enormously indebted to Eva Bodanszky, who commented on and supported this project at every step of the way. I also owe warmest thanks to Gerald Barnes, Cynthia Cohen, and Fred Feldman, who gave extremely useful comments on earlier drafts. Still others—Torin Alter, Earl Conee, Judith DeCew, Christoph Fehige, Douglas Husak, Gareth Matthews, Peter Pruim, Michael Robertson, Don Vandegrift, Mort Winston, and Clark Wolf—offered acute criticism and advice at important points. Clare Reimers and Waldo Wakefield answered critical questions regarding cloning and DNA, and took the time, in addition, to let me check some of my ethical intuitions about specific cases against theirs. I thank Keith Krabill and Bonnie McMichael as well for their extremely useful professional advice regarding some of my medical examples.

I appreciate the thoughtful responses that John Broome gave to my queries. His arguments regarding person-affecting theories directly led me to propose an alternative approach. I also thank Jefferson McMahan, whose expertise in the issues I address in this book is second to none, for his extremely useful assessments of some of my thinking along the way.

The book itself crosses the disciplines of law and philosophy. I want especially to thank Fred Feldman, who did the best that he could to keep me on the path of the straight and narrow, and Gareth Matthews, who kept me on the path, of the Department of Philosophy at the University of Massachusetts at Amherst. My debt to John Robertson of the University of Texas School of Law is beyond estimation. For one thing, it was he who, as teacher and scholar, made the connection for me between the nonidentity problem, wrongful life, and the new reproductive technologies. Even more importantly, it was Robertson's formidably creative approach to analyzing the harm to offspring issue in connection with the new reproductive technologies that forced me to revise my own estimation of person-affecting theories and to take a new look at the nonidentity problem. So, though I may sometimes disagree with Robertson on the details, in a very real sense I owe the big picture to him.

A handful of people have given support over the last year and a half that has been absolutely essential to this project. I am especially indebted to Kristin and Bob Clouser, whose generosity and kindness have been beyond parallel. I also thank Pam Betterton, Kit Jahn, Donna Sesee, Gail Lyon, Janet Williams, and others at the University League for their patience and good sense of what comes first.

I am extremely grateful to Joanne Cantor for her ability and conscientiousness in helping me to prepare (more than once) the manuscript.

I am also grateful to The College of New Jersey, which has been unstinting in the research leaves it has provided, and to the remarkable law firm of Cleary, Gottlieb, Steen & Hamilton, which gave me the time, the support, and a good bit of the training that I needed to do much of the work for this book.

Finally, I thank Fay Roberts Crane, Melissa Dooley, and, especially, my mother, Jane Roberts Wood, and my sister Susan Roberts Read, for their lasting enthusiasm for my projects and for me.

Acknowledgments

The author acknowledges permission to use previously published material in connection with this book.

Portions of chapter 3 are reprinted from "Present Duties and Future Persons: When Are Existence-Inducing Acts Wrong?" *Law and Philosophy* 14 no. 3/4 (1995): 297–327. Copyright © by Kluwer Academic Publishers. Reprinted by kind permission.

Portions of chapter 4 are reprinted from "Distinguishing Wrongful From 'Rightful' Life," *Journal of Contemporary Health Law and Policy* 6 (1990): 59–80. Reprinted by kind permission.

Portions of chapter 5 are reprinted from "Human Cloning: A Case of No Harm Done?" *Journal of Medicine and Philosophy* 21, no. 5 (1996): 537–554. Copyright © by The Journal of Medicine and Philosophy, Inc. Reprinted by kind permission.

The front cover photograph is reproduced by kind permission of Pryde Brown Photographs, Princeton, New Jersey.

(We) dwell in Possibility—

E. Dickinson

Chapter 1

What Is the Person-Affecting Intuition?

1.1 The Basic Idea

In this book, I will investigate an idea about moral obligation known as the "person-affecting intuition."[1] It is hard to find sense in these three words strung together in this particular order. One reader of an early draft of a part of this book (a relative, actually) asked whether the basic idea was that affected people were intuitive. Or was it that intuitive people were affected? Or was I saying I had some moral problem with intuitive, affected people in general?

Clearly, there is a need to say what the person-affecting intuition is. Describing the intuition as I understand it is the aim of this chapter. But it is surely desirable for the reader to have some idea of what the person-affecting intuition is up front and not just upon completion of the entire chapter. So very briefly, the basic idea of the person-affecting intuition is that the morally significant aspect of how we conduct ourselves as agents lies in the consequences our conduct has for each and every person who ever lives.[2] Thus, as I interpret it, the intuition is a form of, or constraint on, consequentialism. But, as I interpret it, the intuition extends beyond the Sidgwickian thesis that consequences that do not make some person's life better do not add to the moral value that a world has. The person-affecting intuition goes further than this, focusing on people as *distinct* from one another in a way that more traditional forms of consequentialism do not. Like most forms of consequentialism, the person-affecting intuition requires that agents bring about the greatest amount of the good that they can bring about. Where person-affecting consequentialism, as I will interpret it, distinguishes itself from the competition is in considering the good that is to be maximized—not the *total* good that, whether in accordance with the

1

Sidgwickian thesis or not, inheres or is contained in the entirety of things, that is, the world—but rather, for each and every person who ever lives, the good that is accorded to that person as an individual. As we will see, this will mean, among other things, that where other forms of consequentialism identify conduct that is wrong *simpliciter*, the person-affecting intuition takes the view that to do something wrong is always a matter of, and ultimately explicable in terms of, wronging *some person*.

One reason that I am interested in the person-affecting intuition is that the intuition seems to provide a plausible treatment of procreative choice—the choice, that is, whether to produce a child. It says that we have no obligation to have children, or more generally to bring new people into existence, when our doing so would not be good for, or would be bad for, others who do or will exist, including ourselves. The intuition also seems to provide insight into the obligations that we as "childmakers" have with respect to the children we may one day produce. It says that the choices we make today must be made with a view toward the new people we ultimately bring into existence. Many theorists agree that these tenets seem plausible. But many of these same theorists take themselves to be forced to reject the person-affecting intuition on grounds that are, I believe, inadequate. For these reasons, among others, I believe that the person-affecting intuition is worth further study.

In this chapter, I will first talk in a general way about the person-affecting intuition (parts 1.2–1.7). I will then briefly introduce each of the topics of the four following chapters (parts 1.8–1.11).

A main goal of this chapter will be to say more about how the person-affecting intuition, as I interpret it, is distinct from more traditional forms of consequentialism and from other person-affecting approaches (parts 1.2–1.4). I will consider the implications the intuition has for three collections of people: those who exist now, or *"existing"* people (part 1.5); those who could but in fact will never exist, or *"merely possible"* people (part 1.6); and those who will but do not yet exist, or *"future"* people (part 1.7). In calculating wrongdoing at a given time, the person-affecting intuition considers only how well people who exist or will exist relative to that time fare. Other things being equal, the intuition thus considers irrelevant how merely possible people might or would have fared had they existed. It is this aspect of the intuition, as we will see, that enables it to provide a plausible account of procreative choice when more standard forms of consequentialism do not.

But it is critical that the person-affecting intuition maintains its concern with future people as well as existing people. For the intuition—and surely any other theory—loses any plausibility it might otherwise have if it cannot be understood to include, as our obligees, not only people who exist now but also people who are temporally heading our way. We need a theory, in other words, according to which facts about future people place moral constraints on how we conduct ourselves today (part 1.7.1). Under the assumption that determinism is false, who these people are and how many there will be are not yet settled matters. Is it problematic, then, to assert that, for the sake of this seemingly ill-defined class of individuals, to avoid wrongdoing tomorrow we must act in a certain way today? I argue that it is not (parts 1.7.2–1.7.4).

In chapter 2, I address one of two important objections that have been raised against the person-affecting intuition. This is the argument that the intuition is inconsistent. In the context of examining this argument, I take the opportunity to provide a more formal and precise statement of the intuition.

In chapter 3, I address a second important objection to the person-affecting intuition. This is the "nonidentity problem." Described by one theorist as "the alpha and the omega" of any theory of population ethics, the nonidentity problem probably accounts for a good bit of entrenched doubt about the person-affecting intuition. But as I formulate the intuition, the nonidentity problem is not, or so I will argue, a clear objection to the intuition. It is in the context of discussing the nonidentity problem that we will see precisely how the intuition supports the notion that facts about future people place moral constraints on how we conduct ourselves today.

In chapters 4 and 5, I apply the intuition to a handful of practical problems in ethics and the law. In chapter 4, the focus will be the problem of "wrongful life." One issue here is whether it can ever coherently be said that there are circumstances in which an existing person would have been better served by never having been brought into existence to begin with. I argue that claims of wrongful life can quite coherently be made and should be given legal recognition. In chapter 5, the focus will be the new reproductive technologies, in particular, human cloning. Here the primary issue will be whether human cloning and other new reproductive technologies can by their nature harm those individuals they bring into existence. Unless the existence is less than one worth having, how can the application of a technology that brings someone into existence also harm that person? My aim in chapter 5 is to explain, in person-affecting terms, just how and when such a thing can happen.

1.2   What Matters?

We begin with two basic questions about the person-affecting intuition: *what* matters, morally, according to the intuition, and *who* matters, morally, according to the intuition.

I have noted that I will understand the person-affecting intuition as a form of, or constraint on, consequentialism. Consequentialist theories aim to evaluate acts in light of their consequences. Consequentialists maintain that we can compare, in respect of their goodness, the consequences of one act that an agent might at a given time perform against the consequences of each alternative act open to the agent at that time. The act that the agent *ought* to perform is just that act that has the *best* consequences. More precisely, the agent ought to perform some act the consequences of which are *at least as good as* the consequences of any other act.³

Consequentialists thus generally share the tenet that agents ought to bring about the greatest amount of good that they can. They ought, that is, to *maximize* the good.⁴ But consequentialists do not rigidly adhere to any single concept of the good. Thus, the form of consequentialism embraced by John Stuart Mill—utilitarianism—provides that happiness is the greatest good.⁵ But not all consequentialist theories rest with the view that the good consists in conscious, pleasant states of mind. The views that the good consists in education, autonomy, or wealth are equally consequentialist.⁶ And G. E. Moore argues that, though "that which is good" may include pleasure or intelligence, the property or characteristic that makes such mental states good is itself "indefinable."⁷ Moreover, although the usual consequentialist supposition is that the good that is to be maximized has something to do with what is good *for people*, even this supposition is not affirmed by all consequentialists. Comparing an "exceedingly beautiful" unpopulated world with the "ugliest world you can possibly conceive," also unpopulated, Moore thus argues that it is rational to think that it would be "better" for the beautiful world to exist than the ugly.⁸ Sidgwick takes the other side. According to Sidgwick, goodness exists only in "relation to human existence, or at least to some consciousness or feeling."⁹

Consequentialist theories thus vary in what they take the nature of the good that is to be maximized to be. For purposes of this present work, I leave this question open. I will focus on a distinct issue that must be faced when the claim is made that agents ought to maximize the good. This is the issue of *what* good—or equivalently the good of *what*—is to be maximized.

Many answers to this question might be given. Before turning to the answer given by the person-affecting intuition, let us first note how two more traditional forms of consequentialism answer this question. Most contemporary forms of consequentialism take the view that the good that is to be maximized is the good *of*, or contained *in*, or displayed *by*, the *entirety* of things. As among all the "ever so many ways that a world might be"¹⁰—as among, that is, all the "possible worlds"—we ought to bring about that way or world that contains the greatest *total* amount of good that we can. More precisely: we ought to bring about some world than which none is better. If one accepts the usual consequentialist supposition that total good accrues as a function of specific facts *about people*, then an obvious mechanism for calculating the *total* good of any world is simply to aggregate, or sum up, all the individual parcels of good—or equivalently, we will say, all the *"well-being"*—that each person who ever lives at that world enjoys or possesses.

Mill's utilitarianism can be understood as aggregative in this sense. Thus, we can say that for Mill the good that is to be maximized—the total good—is simply the aggregate of individual happiness.[11] But not all views so directly connect total good and individual well-being. As Broome observes, a world's total good could in theory be made a function of the net aggregate amount of individual well-being along with the extent to which some independent set of values—such as the extent to which well-being is equally, or justly, distributed among people—is reflected in the world.[12]

Just as consequentialist theories vary in what they take the good that is to be maximized to be, they also vary in what they take individual well-being to be. For example, if total good is what we are to maximize, and if total good is understood simply to be the aggregate of individual well-being, it is clear that figuring out what individual well-being consists in will automatically determine a theory of what total good is. And vice versa: if we happen to know what total good is and think that total good is simply the aggregate of all individual well-being, we can work our way backward to a theory of individual well-being. But if one takes total good to be something more complex, then figuring out what individual well-being consists in will not by itself determine a theory of what total good is. One will need to bring in additional values (e.g., equality or justice). But however complicated the relationship between total good and individual well-being, it seems a sensible approach to *start* with the task of figuring out individual well-being. For this latter task seems at an intuitive level the more feasible. Thus, we might start with the idea that well-being is that which makes life "worth living" and, from the point of view of the one who lives, gives value to life.

But the question of what it is that makes life worth living and valuable is, of course, a point on which theorists disagree. In Mill's view, well-being consists in happiness; for Bentham, it is pleasure. Other theorists take other views. Just as consequentialists do not feel constrained to think that the good to be maximized consists in any conscious, pleasant state of mind, neither do they feel constrained to think that well-being consists in any conscious, pleasant state of mind. Thus, one might theorize that individual well-being consists in education, autonomy, or wealth.[13] As noted earlier, I leave open the question of what the overall good is for purposes of this present work. I likewise leave open the question of what individual well-being is.

The variations on consequentialism that we have just mentioned take the bottom line to be *total good*. Individual well-being is pertinent only to the extent that it determines, or is a factor in determining, the total good. The good that is to be maximized—the good that moral law requires agents to maximize—is total good. But there are other views on what good is to be maximized. Thus, a second consequentialist approach provides that the good that is to be maximized is the greatest *average* good *per person*.[14] According to this form of consequentialism, we must still calculate the total good, but the bottom line is obtained by dividing the total good by the number of all the people who ever live. It is this *average* that we are to maximize. More precisely, we ought to bring about some world than which none has a greater *average* amount of the good.

As I interpret it, the person-affecting intuition denies both these forms of consequentialism, which we will call, respectively, *totalism* and *averagism*.[15] Collapsing the distinction between the good that is to be maximized and individual well-being, the intuition provides—with restrictions to cover the case where one person's well-being can be increased only at a cost to someone else—that, for each and every person who ever lives, agents ought to bring about the greatest amount of good they can for that person. The good that is to be maximized, according to this intuition, is thus not total good, or average good, but personal good or, equivalently, individual well-being. We will understand this basic idea to include, among other things, that any person whose well-being has been maximized has not been wronged and that, with restrictions, people whose well-being we have failed to maximize sometimes *have* been wronged.

The person-affecting intuition, or, as interpreted in what follows, *personalism*, is not intended as a complete theory of all that we ought to do.[16] It is, rather, a way of locking the consequentialist imperative to maximize the good into a particular domain. Totalism and averagism strive to define a pairwise comparison of all possible worlds that agents can at a given time bring about. Having ranked worlds in respect of their total or average goodness, as the case may be, such theories then obligate agents to bring about some world or another than which none is better. In contrast, the pairwise comparisons of worlds appealed to within personalism are always *in respect of particular people*. Thus, worlds are understood to be ordered relative to each person who exists at any time in respect of how good they are for that person, and the basic betterness relation, under personalism, is always a three-place relation ("*X* is better for *s* than *Y* is"), rather than the usual two-place relation ("*X* is better than *Y* is").[17] And since often agents cannot maximize the good for each and every member of any collection of real people, the part of personalism that directs that the good is to be maximized must leave open many questions of how agents' obligations are to be discharged. I am not suggesting that personalism obligates us to undertake both of two inconsistent courses of action or that personalism denies that there is, in every case, an answer to the question of what ought be done. Rather, at defined points—particularly, when agents cannot maximize the well-being of each of two or more individuals—personalism hands the choice of what ought to be done over to theories that operate *independently* of the imperative to maximize the good.[18]

In view of the fact that personalism does not settle every question of moral obligation—or even every important question of moral obligation—that comes its way, what reason is there even to bother thinking about personalism?[19] For one thing, the consequentialist notion that we ought to bring about the most good that we can—that to do this is to do the *best* that we can—seems a truly important, even profound, insight regarding moral law. I, at least, find approaches that abandon maximization difficult to understand, often ad hoc and broadly indeterminate, and occasionally based on grating religious doctrine. (I am thinking of, respectively, deontic theories, rights theories, and some divine command theories.)

Of course, totalism and averagism preserve this insight as well as personalism does. But both these forms of consequentialism seem vulnerable to serious challenges. For one thing, both totalism and averagism face the familiar—and, it seems, compelling—objection from justice. The best of the examples that pose the objection from justice capture a single idea. This idea is that it is difficult to see why it is *always* morally impermissible to shift well-being to someone who has less from someone who has more in any case in which doing so reduces total, or average, well-being.[20] Totalism often condones, indeed, requires, a shifting of resources from one who has more to one who has less on the grounds that a given unit of resources will produce, at the margin, more well-being in the hands of one who has less than in the hands of one who has more. Thus, an extra loaf of bread produces more well-being for the poor family than it does for the well-off family. But condoning a shift of resources in this context hardly solves the objection from justice. For there is no *necessity* that such a shift in resources will not decrease total good.

Rawls, it seems, accurately diagnoses the problem with totalism—and perhaps averagism as well.[21] According to Rawls, totalist forms of utilitarianism do "not take seriously the distinction between persons."[22] Personalism, in contrast, does take seriously the distinction between persons and, without abandoning the basic consequentialist insight, opens the door to the project of finding a response to the objection from justice. Personalism itself is incomplete. It provides a particular conception of the imperative to maximize the good and does not include a theory of justice. But unlike totalism and averagism, personalism leaves room for such a theory. In what follows, I speculate about what such a theory might be (part 2.7.4). But I do not defend any particular theory. Rather, I simply refer to the *correct* theory—whatever that theory might be—with prejudice but without loss of generality as a "theory of fair distribution" or simply "fairness."

Procreative choice raises a second problem for totalism and averagism. We will be addressing the broad issue of the obligations that we, as "childmakers"—as parents, obstetricians, infertility specialists, embryologists, lab technicians, lawyers negotiating commercial surrogacy arrangements, or policy makers determining future population growth—have in respect of the children we may or may not bring into existence. And one question that we will therefore be addressing is this: how ought we conduct ourselves *now* in respect of any new person we at some *later* point bring into existence? But a second question, and the one I want to focus on for the moment, is this: under what circumstances ought we bring a new person into existence to begin with? The answers that totalism and averagism give to this latter question seem very implausible. Both views require the production of new people in some cases in which this choice is bad for the agents themselves or for others and good for no one other than (perhaps) the new people themselves. I find deeply implausible any view that requires us to have yet another baby when doing so will make things worse for the babies (two? four? one who is ill? one who has special needs?) we already have, or even for ourselves, and better for no other existing or future person. Personalism gives a distinct, and I think more plausible, analysis of procreative choice. As we shall see, personalism implies that we have no obligation to have children, or more generally to bring new people into existence, when our doing so would be bad for ourselves or for others and good for no one (other than, perhaps, the new person) or, indeed, when our doing so would not be positively good for others. Personalism thus endorses a concept of procreative freedom when other theories do not.[23] We will be comparing the personalist account of procreative choice to the totalist account in a variety of contexts—including in connection with the issue of whether to produce a child to begin with (part 3.8.2) and the distinct issue of whether to produce the "lesser" or the "better" child (part 3.8.3).

A related problem for totalism, though not for averagism, is the "repugnant conclusion." According to this objection, totalism implies the intuitively false result that a world containing a vast number of people whose lives are just barely worth living, whose well-being is in each case just barely in the positive range, may be better than a world containing a more manageable number of much more well-off people and thus that, as between just these two worlds, agents are obligated to choose the former over the latter.[24] In contrast, personalism, with its focus on how well off each individual is rather than on the undifferentiated total aggregate well-being, avoids at least the most "repugnant" forms of the repugnant conclusion. We will be talking more about personalism, totalism, and the repugnant conclusion in part 3.11.

In contrast to totalism, averagism nicely sidesteps the repugnant conclusion. But averagism appears otherwise defective. As Parfit puts it, averagism implies that whether the birth of any child

> would be bad . . . depends on facts about all previous lives. If the Ancient Egyptians had a very high quality of life, it is more likely to be bad to have a child now. It is more likely that this child's birth will lower the average quality of the lives that are ever lived. But research in Egyptology cannot be relevant to our decision whether to have children.[25]

Parfit's point seems right. Whatever our problems with totalism, averagism is no solution.

I do not mean to suggest that the points I have raised regarding totalism and averagism refute these forms of consequentialism. For one thing, there are just too many ways of reformulating these views. We will be considering later on, for example, Feldman's totalist reply to the repugnant conclusion (part 3.11.5). And perhaps averagism should just exclude from its calculation the levels of well-being of those who no longer exist. For another thing, there are too many unsettled moral intuitions about some very hard issues floating around. Thus, some theorists may not consider, for example, the objection from justice a genuine problem for totalism and averagism at all. Still, though the basic consequentialist insight—that moral obligation lies in maximizing the good—seems entirely beguiling, totalism and averagism do not. It is therefore, at a minimum, nice to have a third way of preserving this important insight. This fact alone justifies our thinking further about the person-affecting intuition.

1.3   What Else Matters?

As part of his description of the person-affecting intuition, Narveson writes that "[w]e are in favour of making people happy."[26] It is this sentiment that I have just begun to interpret. Narveson focuses on happiness, but we need not. We can thus say that, according to the person-affecting intuition, what matters is, with restrictions, that, for each and every person who ever lives, agents maximize the good for that person. But as another part of his description of the intuition, Narveson notes that we are "neutral about making happy people."[27] It is this second notion, also critical to the person-affecting approach, that I want to emphasize now.

Parfit expresses the notion, which he then rejects, this way: "what is bad must be bad *for someone.*"[28] And Temkin, who is more sympathetic, puts it as follows: "[o]ne outcome is worse than another only if it affects people for the worse."[29] This point can equally well be expressed as one of closure. Personalism maintains that agents, having discharged their obligations toward people, have thereby entirely discharged their obligations *simpliciter.* There is, in other words, no further overlay of moral law beyond that which governs obligations toward people. Having attended to the needs and interests of each and every person in a prescribed manner, agents have satisfied their obligations and done their duty. Thus, agents who have wronged no one cannot have at the same time done something wrong.

This feature of personalism has been extravagantly criticized by, among others, Parfit. For it is this feature of personalism that leads to the nonidentity problem, which, as noted, will be a main concern in this present work (chapter 3).

1.4   Who Matters?

This question can be understood as a question about the relationship between one's temporal status and one's moral status.[30] Does one affect the other? Do we owe existing people—people who exist now—more than we owe future people—those who will but do not yet exist?[31] Do we owe them less? What do we owe existing people in the way of bringing, or not bringing, additional people into existence? And how, if at all, do the interests of these additional people figure in the moral equation? Do we ever wrong people by bringing them into existence? Is it possible to wrong merely possible people by, say, having failed to bring them into existence?

As I will construe it, the person-affecting intuition takes a position on all these issues. Briefly, it says that the people who matter now are all those who now exist and all those who will ever exist—that is, all existing and all future people. Future people do not by virtue of their not yet existing have any lesser moral status than do people who already exist. The fact of future people, like the fact of existing people, thus constrains our conduct now. And a future person's claim to our good behavior is as strong as is any existing person's. The intuition also implies that we sometimes wrong people by bringing, and sometimes by failing to bring, other people into existence. At the same time, it implies that we cannot wrong those whom we refrain from ever bringing into existence.

Thus, as I interpret the person-affecting intuition, it implies, with restrictions, that, for each person who now exists or who now *will* exist, we ought now act in such a way as to bring about the greatest amount of good that we can for that person. In assessing agents' conduct, what is important is the extent to which agents manage to confer well-being on *these* people. In cases in which the level of well-being accorded to any person is less than maximal, then what is important is whether the lower level of well-being can be justified on independent grounds—such as by appeal to the theory of fairness that we have already said personalism leaves room for.

Three further points should be clarified here. First, when I say that we should "bring about" the most good for people, I do not imply that it is *only* by doing some positive or affirmative good-promoting act that we satisfy the obligations that we have. We might in some cases bring about the most good by not doing anything at all. And in other cases we bring about the most good by preventing some bad thing from happening. Thus, I am making no fine, and I think ultimately groundless, distinctions between acts and omissions, or between acts or omissions that promote the good and those that prevent the bad.[32]

Second, I have not included, among those who matter now, those who once existed. I have taken it that the fact of people's past existence does not in itself morally constrain how we conduct ourselves today. Accordingly, my more formal statement of the intuition (in chapter 2) will exclude past people from those "who matter" now. But depending on what we take well-being to be, this formal exclusion might not be necessary. *If* we define well-being in terms of having a good reputation or being remembered, then it would follow that well-being could be conferred on the dead as well as the living. But on other theories of well-being, including some that do not define well-being in terms of some pleasant, conscious state, a person's well-being is something that is unalterable upon that person's death. I think that it is very likely that this latter is the more plausible way of understanding well-being. For if we take the other view, then we seem to be countenancing the notion that agents may undo what would otherwise count as wrongs done to people during their lives at some time *after* those people have died. And this result seems excessively permissive. The better view, it seems to me, is that our obligations can be discharged only to the extent that we confer well-being on people during their lives. If we blow it then, then we have blown it forever.

Finally, when I say that the people who matter include all existing and future people, I do not mean to propose that the people who exist or will exist at any one world also matter at any distinct world. Rather, those people who matter at any distinct world—those who constrain how agents conduct themselves *there*—will be just those people who are at *that* world existing or future. Thus, Chelsea Clinton matters, for purposes of assessing conduct at the actual world, since she actually exists. But it does not follow that agents (e.g., Bill and Hillary) might have wronged her had they never brought her into existence to begin with. This is true, despite the fact that as a nonexistent person her level of well-being would have been significantly lower than it in fact is.[33]

1.5   People Who Now Exist: "Existing" People

The person-affecting intuition as interpreted by one and all implies that we have obligations toward people who now exist—that is, toward our contemporaries. Thus, the intuition bars the extreme and uninteresting view that the good of a couple who choose to bring a child into the world must be entirely sacrificed for the good of the child. Even parents count.

A somewhat more common, though equally uninteresting, view barred by personalism is the view that the good of the child may be entirely sacrificed for the good of the parent. According to this view, the child has obligations toward the parent—perhaps as quid pro quo for the "gift of life"—but not the other way around. Personalism might mistakenly be thought to generate this false result. It is true that, according to personalism, the choice to have a child will usually be made independently of how good existence will be for the child and rather on the ground of whether bringing the child into existence will be good or bad for other people, including, perhaps especially, the parents.[34] But it does not follow from this fact that personalism favors the child's parents, or any other elders, over the child who is brought into existence. *All* existing people matter, according to personalism, even our own children.

1.6   People Who Never Exist: "Merely Possible" People

1.6.1   The Choice Not to Reproduce: A First Test Case

Personalism distinguishes itself from totalism and averagism by providing an alternative means of factoring into the moral analysis how the contrary-to-fact choice to produce additional people would have affected those people. Let us first note that only the most eccentric theorist—and not, for example, the normal totalist—would propose that we have obligations toward, or can wrong, people who remain at all times merely possible. But the theorist who believes that such possibilia and the kinds of lives that they might lead are morally relevant is extremely common. Indeed, the view is essentially endorsed by any totalist or averagist account. According to both totalism and averagism, the fact that people who might be brought into existence would have a good life if they were to exist matters. Thus, both approaches sometimes require that we bring new people into existence even if doing so would be bad for, or not good for, others. Personalism, compellingly, avoids this implication. We prefer a view that requires us to provide "aid and succor to those who are needy and miserable" over a theory that would allow us to "counterbalance their misery and destitution by bringing more happy people into existence."[35]

Suppose, for example, that we have chosen not to have children. We think, correctly, that having children would be bad for us and that avoiding parenthood altogether will make our lives better. Suppose that it does not matter to anyone else whether we have children. Finally, suppose that, if, contrary to fact, we had chosen to have children, we would have been very, very good to those children, and they would have had wonderful lives. Depending on the numbers, both totalism and averagism, but not personalism, imply the intuitively false result that we have done something wrong in choosing not to have children. But surely if "having a child would be bad for the couple themselves, even to a small degree, that is a sufficient reason for them not to have one."[36]

This distinction repeats itself in cases in which it is not our own well-being (self-indulgent beasts that we are!) that is at issue but rather someone else's. Thus, depending on the numbers, totalism and averagism both sometimes imply the intuitively false result that we do something wrong when we, to provide better care for one child, choose not to bring a second (or third, or fourth, or tenth) child into existence. Typically, a second child is a great benefit to a first child, or at least not a net burden. And even if burdensome to the first child, a second child might still be good for the parents. But the case at issue here has neither of these two features. In the case at issue here, the first child is better off without the second child, and it makes no difference to us, as the parents, and presumably no difference to anyone else, whether we opt to take better care of the first child or produce the second child.[37] In this context, the implication from totalism and averagism that we *must* bring a second child into existence seems false. Personalism, in contrast, avoids this implication. It offers no excuse for our choosing to treat an already existing child less well than we might, or badly, to make a second child well off whom we have yet to—and may just as well not ever—bring into existence.

1.6.2   A "Weakly" Person-Affecting View

Views other than the one I focus on here have been described as "person-affecting." According to one such view, which I will call a "weakly" person-affecting view, whether we wrong is entirely a function of some fact about whether our acts are, or would be, good or bad for people, including, had they existed, merely possible people, and not a function of any other sort of fact.[38] According to this view, whether an agent has a good character, or whether an agent's act conforms to some Kantian maxim (e.g., "Never lie") or respects a right (e.g., the right to "property" or "liberty") the validity of which derives from some source other than how the act affects people, or whether an act promotes beauty that does not somehow translate into a better life for people, is morally irrelevant.

But the weakly person-affecting view is not equivalent to personalism. In assessing the alternatives, most forms of totalism and virtually all forms of averagism take into account the kinds of lives merely possible people might have had had they been brought into existence. In this way, both totalism and averagism manage to comply with the weakly person-affecting view. In contrast, according to personalism the kinds of lives merely possible people might have had is, in the usual case, morally irrelevant (the exception being the case in which the life is *less* than one worth living). By screening out the extent to which our producing new people might have been good for *those people*, personalism achieves a distinct, and I think more plausible, set of results than totalism or averagism in the context of, for instance, reproductive choice.

1.7   People Who Will But Do Not Yet Exist: "Future" People

1.7.1   Choices That Affect Future People's Lives: A Second Test Case

The person-affecting intuition fails if we do not or cannot understand it to protect future as well as existing people. Thus, if the claim that we *now* have obligations in respect of future people is demonstrably false or inconsistent with some other part of personalism, or if it is incoherent in some way and we *cannot* have such obligations, then we must reject personalism. For it seems clear that moral law must take into account, in assessing the choices we make, how those choices affect the lives of unknown, unnamed, seemingly indistinct, and possibly distant future people.

This point might be made another way. We think that we have some duty to save—some duty, for example, to conserve resources and to protect the environment. According to the person-affecting intuition, this duty must derive from obligations that we have to behave well *toward people*. But does it derive solely from obligations we have relating to people who now exist? Or does it also derive from obligations we have relating to future people? If the former, the duty is less stringent. Much of what we do now, even if harmful over the long-term, will present few risks to even the youngest of our contemporaries. I believe that it is clear that our duty is more stringent than this. Thus, for the person-affecting intuition to maintain any plausibility, it must be understood to protect future as well as existing people.

The person-affecting intuition implies that those who now exist— our contemporaries—matter. The fact of the *current* existence of others constrains how we conduct ourselves today. As I will interpret the person-affecting intuition, the fact of the *future* existence of others places a further constraint on how we conduct ourselves today. Just as, according to personalism, I ought not carelessly engage in conduct that is likely to injure the baby in my lap, so too, other things being equal, I ought not carelessly engage in conduct now that is likely to injure some future baby whose conception is moments or months away.

But the notion of present obligation toward people who do not yet exist might be considered problematic. Since personalism is not a plausible moral theory if this notion cannot be made to work, we should consider carefully why someone might find the notion of obligations toward future people problematic.

1.7.2   How Can We Have Obligations Toward People Who Do Not (Yet) Exist?

One might think that relations cannot obtain at a time at which one or another relatum fails to exist. Thus, the two-place relation, "*x* hugs *y*," cannot obtain between two people at any time at which they do not both exist. If this view is correct in general, then, since future people by definition do not yet exist, we cannot now have obligations toward them. But it is plausible that not all relations have this existence requirement. For example, it seems that the relations "*x* remembers *y*" and "x is an ancestor of y" may obtain even at times at which one or both relata do not exist. Thus, we might propose that "x has an obligation toward y" can likewise obtain at a given time even though y does not exist until some later time.

But a critic might then object that "x has an obligation toward y" implies, if not that y *does* exist, at least that y *will* exist. And this implication may seem problematic if we think that the future existence of any given person is not a matter that is *now* settled or decided.

We can address this worry by specifying more clearly what it is to have obligations "toward," or, perhaps better, "in respect of," future people. No one, I think, contests the fact that an act can be performed at an earlier time and, at some much later time, have its effect on a person who did not exist at the earlier time. And it is surely coherent to suppose that some theories of personal wronging can count a human action that eventuates in a given bad effect on some later-born person as a wrong to that person. This is so, even though it is plausible to understand that the wrong does not occur (or, we might say, is not completed) until all of its elements occur—until, among other things, someone both exists and is affected badly by the earlier act. But the very fact that what we do today may wrong someone tomorrow places a moral constraint on how we conduct ourselves today. It means that we must take steps today to avoid wronging anyone who does happen tomorrow to pop into existence. People who never exist cannot be wronged by *anything* we do today; and if no one pops into existence tomorrow, what we have done today is not wrong at all—assuming, of course, that it does not wrong some already existing person—and we are, morally, off the hook. But if there is some later born person—if someone does pop into existence—then that person will then be perfectly vulnerable to being hurt by, indeed, wronged by, conduct that we engage in today. It is in this sense that facts about future people constrain how we conduct ourselves today.

As an analogy, consider a bill that, if passed by Congress and signed by the president, would retroactively impose liability on conduct we engaged in, say, last year. If the president vetoes the bill and it never becomes law, then we are off the hook, legally, with respect to the conduct in question. Otherwise, we are liable. Was our conduct all along illegal? No. Our conduct becomes illegal only when and if the bill becomes law (just as the wrong is completed only when and if the future person both exists and is adversely affected). Does the president's signing the bill "change the past"? No, it just makes illegal now conduct that was not illegal at the time performed. We might debate the morality of ex post facto law but not its coherence.

1.7.3 How Do We Distinguish Between Future People and Other Possible People?

Another kind of worry might arise depending on how we understand the concept of a future person. In describing personalism, I have relativized to time. Thus, necessarily a person who is now a future person will be at some later time an existing person and therefore at that time *not* future. A problem might arise if we do not also understand the concept of a future person to be implicitly world-relative as well as time-relative. For suppose that we understand things otherwise. Then, we eliminate the distinction between those who, at a time, *will* exist and those who, at that time, *might* exist. But without this distinction all that we say about "future people" will be hopelessly confused. On the other hand, the concept of a future person, understood to be relative to a particular world and time, is perfectly clear. Future people, relative to a world X and a time t, are just those people who at t do not yet but will exist in X. According to personalism, it is in respect of how well the people who exist, or will exist, at X fare that agents' conduct at X is to be assessed.

1.7.4 If Determinism Is False, Then How Can We Meaningfully Assert Obligations Toward Future People?

As just noted, the distinction between future people and possible people is important to personalism. But in making the distinction we did not thereby imply that who or how many people will exist is now a settled fact. Suppose that if an agent does one thing in a moment or two, say, at t, a population consisting of $s_1, \ldots, s_m$ will exist. And suppose that if the agent does something else at t, a distinct population consisting of $s'_1, \ldots, s'_n$ will exist. Finally, suppose that it is not prior to t settled whether the agent will do the one thing or the other at t. Then, prior to t it is not settled whether $s_1, \ldots, s_m$, or alternatively $s'_1, \ldots, s'_n$, will exist. But this means that prior to t there is no unique class of people who do not *now* exist such that we can say that we have obligations to the members of *that class*.

No matter. Without it being settled who or how many people will come into existence, agents' choices can still be assessed in respect of how well off those people are who *do* come into existence, whoever they may be. Thus, if the agent does one thing, $s_1, \ldots, s_m$ will exist, and conduct engaged in now can affect, and perhaps wrong, $s_1, \ldots, s_m$. If the agent does another thing, $s'_1, \ldots, s'_n$ will exist, and conduct engaged in now can affect, and perhaps wrong, $s'_1, \ldots, s'_n$. According to personalism, how our acts affect the people who will exist, *whoever they turn out to be*, determines, together, of course, with how our acts affect existing people, the extent to which we have discharged the obligations that we have.[39]

It may be that, through no fault of anyone's, no one who does not already exist *will* exist—that there will be no future people. In this case, with respect to any *prima facie* bad-seeming conduct the agent engages in today, the agent is "off the hook," morally, with respect to those who exist (just) tomorrow. Perhaps the agent's questionable conduct wrongs some *existing* person; but it will not wrong any future person. But from the fact that *if* no future person exists, then no future person is wronged, it clearly does not follow that, unconditionally, no future person is wronged. If future people do come into existence, then simply given the way the natural universe works—namely, that acts performed today can have effects tomorrow—those individuals will be vulnerable to being hurt by any risky conduct the agent engages in today.

Is it a problem that we do not *know* who or how many will exist? Epistemically, future people are at best smudges on the lenses through which we view the horizons of our own lives. But then so are the nursery school children who play behind me on those mornings when I am the helping parent and suffer to wash dishes and paintbrushes. My lack of consciousness regarding whom precisely I must not bump into or step on does not affect the children's moral status with respect to me.[40]

1.7.5 Heyd's Narrow "Person-Affecting" Approach

Heyd, who also describes what he calls a "person-affecting" approach, takes a position opposite my own on the question of whether conduct we engage in today can wrong those who exist tomorrow. In Heyd's view, the fact that an agent *controls*, in some sense, whether a given future person exists (none, of course, exist necessarily) obviates any duty that agent might otherwise have toward that person. The implication of Heyd's narrow view is that we are obligated to behave well toward many fewer than *all* future people whom our acts affect.[41] Moreover, those future people whom we need not behave well toward include people—particularly, our own children—toward whom it might seem obvious that we *do* have rather stringent obligations. Suppose that a couple correctly judge that their bringing a new person—exactly one new person—into existence will be generally good for themselves and for other already existing people. According to Heyd's narrow view, the couple who aim to produce a new person become obligated to constrain their conduct insofar as it might one day affect the new person only *after* he (say) begins to exist. *Prior* to that point, Heyd categorizes the new person, relative to the couple who control his existence, as a merely "potential" person. As such, relative to the couple, the new person has, according to Heyd, "no moral status of any kind, not even a weak one."[42]

> Only [people other than potential people] have moral standing, that is, rights, claims to being morally considerable, a status of belonging to the moral community, or to the class of those whose welfare or utility is to be taken into account. Potential people have no such standing.[43]

Heyd's narrow view is problematic. I claimed earlier that the person-affecting intuition fails if it is understood in such a way that it does not protect future as well as existing people.[44] As Heyd interprets it, the person-affecting intuition fails for this very reason. It deems morally irrelevant the obvious truth that people have some needs and interests that can be adequately provided for only *prior* to their coming into existence. Planting a giant sequoia the day the child is born will do nothing to satisfy the child's interest in the spectacle of nature. And it will not do to think about the consequences a polluted environment will have for the next generation only after these individuals, their organs riddled with toxins, begin to exist. We cannot, likewise, wait until infants are born starving to address food shortages or intellectually impaired to address substance abuse. Moral law, surely, *requires* that we plan ahead, even when the children we hurt are our own and thus ones we *might* have chosen never to bring into existence at all.

In contrast to Heyd's narrow view, personalism implies that the fact of a future person always begins to constrain an agent's conduct *prior* to the point at which that future person comes into existence, independently of whether his or her existence is within the agent's control. If the couple's present conduct projects, like an arrow through time, a risk of a bad effect, which plants itself in the back of any new person this couple subsequently bring into existence, the basis for a claim of personal wronging is established.

We made the supposition that the new person in fact comes into existence. But no one exists necessarily. Suppose that the couple reconsider and decide not to have a child after all, or that for some reason or another their intention to bring a new person into existence is not realized. Then, according to personalism there would be no basis for the claim that their questionable act, aimed, as it were, toward the future and not toward any existing person, wrongs anyone or is wrong.

The arrow through time, if the future person *never* exists, lands in no-body's back. The never completed wrong is not in fact a wrong at all.

Because Heyd relativizes the notion of a potential person to an agent (my future children are potential with respect to me but not with respect to you), in many cases the "counterintuitive" implications of the narrow view are, he believes, "mitigated."[45] Like slightly less obvious forms of nepotism, obligations to future generations, according to Heyd, run diagonally downward from one family tree to another. Thus, my obligation to conserve natural resources is owed not to my own child but to yours, and yours not to your own child but to mine. Assuming we both discharge our respective obligations, in the end neither child faces a shortage since each escapes potentiality with respect to *some* elder if not with respect to his or her own parent.

But the extent to which Heyd's notion of relativized potentiality mitigates the ocean of counterintuitive implications his narrow person-affecting view produces is really very slight. For one thing, the narrow view implies that people who will be born more than a generation or two from now will almost certainly be wholly "potential," since in Heyd's view their existence will in some sense be controlled by us.[46] As merely potential people, these future generations have, in Heyd's view, "no moral status of any kind, not even a weak one."[47]

But problem cases also arise much closer to home, indeed, in our own backyards. Thus, the narrow view implies that my neighbor's future child, but not my own, has a claim to my good behavior. Suppose that I now bury some glass in a shallow bed beneath the swing set in the back yard. Suppose that I bury this glass to the benefit of no one, even myself. Suppose that I then have a child and that, once this child exists, I cannot undo the hazardous condition I have created (perhaps I die). Suppose that in three years my *neighbor's* two-year old is badly hurt by what I have done; according to Heyd, it is at least possible that I have wronged *that* child.[48] Now suppose that in three years the same bad thing happens to my own two-year-old whose existence I controlled rather than my neighbor's. Then, according to Heyd, I have not wronged *this* child and thus have done nothing wrong.

Perhaps this account of the case misses Heyd's point about relativized potentiality. Thus, Heyd might suggest that the harsh result according to which I have not wronged my own child is mitigated by the fact that in burying the glass I at least risk wronging my *neighbor's* child and thus at least risk doing something that is wrong *simpliciter*. Heyd's view would allow us to say this much, even as it deems my own hurt and bleeding child not to have been wronged at all. But this tactic does not create the genuine security for my future child that she (say) deserves. By building a high fence around my own property, including the swing set, I can eliminate any risk to my neighbor's child. And then we would have no basis, according to the narrow view, for the conclusion that I have even risked doing something that is wrong. But surely I have.

What justifies the sharp distinction Heyd makes between the moral status of potential people and that of other future people? According to Heyd:

> We cannot *harm* "the first person born in London in January 2015" if it is we who are going to decide whether any such individual is going to exist at all and whether he or she will have properties that would make him or her susceptible to such harm. Only if the individual denoted by this description is someone whose existence and identity lie beyond our control, can such an assignment of harm be coherently made.[49]

Why is this? According to Heyd, the "problematic status [of potential people] in moral reasoning is not due to lack of sharpness in the contours of their existence and identity, but to the *logical dependence* of their existence on our choice."[50] Heyd thus seems to want to say that we cannot harm and thus cannot wrong those whose existence we control. But the quoted passages do not explain *why* we cannot wrong these individuals. If we "control" our victims' existence, then presumably we can always opt *not* to bring them into existence and always thereby avoid wronging *them*. But why, if we do permit their existence, can we *not* wrong them? How precisely does the supposed "logical dependence of [the potential person's] existence on our decision" give rise to that person's morally "problematic status"? (And why, by the way, does Heyd imagine that the relationship between the potential person's existence and the agent's decision is one of "logical" dependency to begin with?)

I will not try to evaluate Heyd's argument. Perhaps he has some of the worries that we have already addressed. Or perhaps he accepts the implications of the nonidentity problem (which we will briefly describe in this chapter and discuss in detail in chapter 3) but does not think these implications represent a defect.[51] Perhaps, indeed, this is just his understanding of what the person-affecting intuition amounts to: that existing and future people matter, except for merely potential future people.

But no plausible theory can sustain this view. Thus, I want to distinguish it from the interpretation of the person-affecting intuition that I aim to give here in the form of personalism. The intuition, as I interpret it, rejects Heyd's narrow view and embraces the claims of both the neighbor's child and my own child to my good behavior. Neither child exists, of course, at the time the glass is buried. But in the story told earlier they both, as future people, eventually do come into existence. And my own child is hurt by the glass I have buried. There being no good excuse for what I have done (e.g., the world is not somehow saved by my burying the glass), my act thus wrongs my child.

1.8   Broome's Inconsistency Argument

My aim in the preceding discussion has been to provide some sense of one way of understanding the person-affecting intuition. In large part, this has been a matter of situating personalism vis-à-vis other forms of consequentialism (totalism and averagism) as well as alternative person-affecting tenets (the "weakly" person-affecting view and Heyd's "narrow" view). My aim in this part and what follows will be to give some sense of two objections that have been raised against the person-affecting intuition and how I will be responding to them.

   In chapter 2, we take up the first objection, an argument from Broome. Broome sweeps away person-affecting approaches as inconsistent, writing that they are "doomed to fail."[52] Broome begins by advancing a principle that he takes to represent the person-affecting intuition and then argues that this principle leads to contradiction—or at least to trouble. I have no serious objection to his derivation of the contradiction. Rather, I argue that the principle from which he begins does not adequately express the person-affecting intuition. His argument thus forces us not, I maintain, to reject the intuition but, usefully, to restate it. And I restate it along the lines suggested earlier. I take the basic person-affecting relation not to order pairs of worlds in respect of their goodness *simpliciter* but rather to order pairs of worlds in respect of how good they are for *each person*. Appealing to this latter sort of relation, I give a partial theory of the conditions under which a person has been wronged. I then understand what it is to do something wrong in terms of wronging people.

1.9   The Nonidentity Problem

1.9.1   What Is the Problem?

   In chapter 3, we will take up what Parfit calls the "nonidentity problem." The nonidentity problem is really a nest of viperous cases that seem to challenge some of our most deeply held, person-affecting, intuitions about moral obligation.[53] It is this fascinating problem that leads Parfit, among others, to abandon the person-affecting approach altogether. Thus, he writes that we need a

> principle I call Theory X. Only X will fully solve the Non-Identity Problem. . . . We can predict that Theory X will not take a person-affecting form. The best theory about beneficence will not appeal to what is good or bad for those people whom our acts affect.[54]

The buried glass example introduced earlier can be adapted as a nonidentity problem. We need just to add a couple of additional suppositions.

To convert the original buried glass example to a nonidentity case, we need to suppose that, had I not buried the glass under the swing set, the child I in fact produced—the child in fact hurt by the glass—*would never have existed at all*. We can suppose, had I not buried the glass, I would have produced some distinct child (hence the name "nonidentity") who would have fared better than the actual child in view of my not having buried the glass.

What gives this counterfactual claim its plausibility? What could the burying of the glass possibly have to do with whether one child exists rather than another? Those riveted by the nonidentity problem, as I am, know well the answer to this question. It has to do with what Kavka calls the "precariousness" of existence.[55] Under any plausible theory of personal identity, virtually *any* variation in the course of events that in fact constitutes one's own life might well affect the identity of one's children. Conceiving a child one month rather than another (thus a child who develops from one ovum rather than another), even, perhaps, one day, hour, or minute rather than another (thus conceiving a child who develops from one sperm rather than another), will very likely cause one to produce one child rather than another. Timing is, though not everything, a major factor in determining *which* child the parent ultimately produces. And any little thing—even taking a few minutes to bury some glass under a swing set—can affect the timing of conception.

We need to add a second supposition to the original buried glass example to generate the nonidentity problem. We must also suppose that the child who in fact exists is not *badly* hurt by the glass. Thus, the child's flawed existence is not *so* burdensome to her (say) that her own interests would have been better served had she never existed at all. Despite its special burdens, her life represents a net good to her—a positive level of well-being. Using Parfit's term, we can say that her life, despite its flaws, is a life "worth living."[56]

And, finally, we suppose that no one else is affected by my burying the glass under the swing set.

We can now state the nonidentity problem. Had I not buried the glass, *this* child would not have existed at all. And her existence is, from her own point of view, a good, or at least not a bad, thing. Hence, my burying the glass does not make this child's situation worse than it would otherwise have been. It might even be argued that my burying the glass makes things better for the child, since she is now able to enjoy the benefits of existence.[57] But if I have not made this child's situation *worse*, it seems that I cannot have wronged her. And if I have not wronged *her*, then, on the assumption that I have wronged no one else, personalism implies that I have *done nothing wrong*. It is against this implication that Parfit's intuitions—and my own—rebel.[58]

Parfit, at least provisionally, thus rejects personalism in favor of a yet to be identified, impersonal "Theory X." One approach that has the capacity to imply that a wrong has been done even in contexts in which no one has been made worse off is totalism. According to totalism, the fact that I could have produced a greater good by not burying the glass and producing some other child in place of the child I in fact produce implies that what I have done is, though worse for no one, wrong. Totalism thus avoids the nonidentity problem by shifting the focus from the consequences of each of the various alternative acts I could have performed *for the very child I in fact produce* to the consequences of each of the various acts I could have performed *for the total good*.[59]

1.9.2   A Person-Affecting Reply to the Nonidentity Problem

I will argue, however, that the nonidentity problem does not provide a good reason to reject personalism. I will argue, in particular, that personalism avoids the implication that burying the glass does not wrong the child. To show this point, I must give an account of how it is that the child can be wronged when my burying the glass gives her an existence that is, while flawed, worth living, perhaps well worth living, when otherwise she would have none.

In my view, the nonidentity problem, at least as I have just stated it, errs by failing to take into account my capacity as agent to bring it about that the very same child—the numerically identical child—who is in fact hurt both exists and is *not* hurt. It is the fact that I could have improved *this* child's lot but did not that I believe grounds the position that my burying the glass wrongs the child. Thus, a main tenet of personalism is that no one whose well-being has been maximized has been wronged. But it seems clear that the well-being of the child in question has *not* been maximized. The laws of neither nature (assuming determinism false) nor logic preclude my taking steps to bring about a world that is better for this very child. No agent acts outside my control to thwart my efforts to bring about some better-for-*this*-child world. Nor are there any independent moral obstacles to my bringing about this world. This is not the sort of case in which I *must* bury the glass to, for example, save all the rest of humankind.

The notion of accessibility can help us put this point more clearly.[60] I will not define this notion, but it is, I think, an intuitive one. A world is *accessible* at a time if it is then within the capacity, or ability, of agents (acting in concert or as individuals, jointly or severally) to bring about. And we can say, derivatively, that a given situation, or state, or outcome, is accessible at a time just in case it is included in a world that is then accessible.

Not all *possible* worlds are accessible to agents at a given time. Worlds where cures for cancer are readily available are possible worlds but not, now, accessible. Worlds where gravity fails will presumably never be accessible. Thus, accessible worlds are limited to those that agents have the capacity or ability to bring about. This is not to say, however, that accessible worlds are necessarily worlds that agents have the capacity or power to ensure. Thus, prior to a fair coin toss, we cannot ensure that, say, heads will turn up. Nonetheless, worlds that include heads turning up are accessible to us before the toss. Despite the lower odds, so is rolling a six.

The concept of accessibility is of critical importance to any moral judgment. We rely on this notion when we conclude that a doctor wrongs no one by failing to produce a "miracle cure." And it is our firm grasp of this notion that leads us to hold the Nuremberg defendants responsible for the atrocities they committed, notwithstanding the defense that they were "required" by law or by order of a superior or by a principle of self-preservation to do what they did.

We can use the notion of accessibility to express the relevant sense of the claim that I *could* have done better for the child than I in fact did when I buried the glass. Thus, we may say that a world where I do not bury the glass yet produce the very same, numerically identical child who then plays unscathed on the swing set was *accessible* to me, as agent, just prior to the point at which I buried the glass. That such a better-for-the-child world was accessible implies that I have not, in fact, maximized the child's well-being when I bury the glass, even though, by hypothesis, the child's life is worth living. Under these circumstances, nothing in personalism implies that the child has not been wronged. Indeed, given the suppositions we have made about this case, personalism implies, as we will see, that the child *has* been wronged.

A critic might object that the personalist solution to the nonidentity problem that I have just sketched overlooks the fact that we are in some instances excused from taking steps to achieve better worlds if those worlds are, for one reason or another, highly *improbable*. In view of the "precariousness" of existence, it does seem clear that any departure from the course of events that as a matter of fact produced a particular child, such as my *not* burying the glass, would have made *that* child's existence highly improbable. But the critic who tries to make anything of this point is, I think, not going to succeed. The "precariousness" of existence is the idea that, had any little thing *e* that happened in the course of events in fact leading to the existence of any particular person *s not* happened, that person *s* may very well have not existed at all. This seems correct. But it does not follow from this point that the fact that *e* happens makes the existence of that same person *s* any *more likely* than would some little substitute thing *e'* happening instead of *e*. And it is this principle that the critic needs, I believe, to get the probabilistic version of the nonidentity problem off the ground.

We can put this point in another way (and we will come back to it again in chapter 3). Suppose that the child's existence *is* highly improbable given that I do not bury the glass just when I do. This point does not by itself get us very far in excusing my conduct unless we *also* think that the child's existence is more probable given that I *do* bury the glass. But it isn't. There are just too many contingencies between the moment at which I bury the glass and the moment at which the particular child is conceived. The child's existence remains highly improbable at the critical time, even if at that time I do bury the glass. But is the child's existence *less* highly improbable if I do bury the glass than if I do not bury the glass? Not necessarily. It depends on *how* I go about not burying the glass. Suppose that instead of burying the glass I have a cup of tea and then proceed to the business of conceiving a child—at exactly the same time and under exactly the same circumstances as I do in the original case. Then, it seems that whichever act I perform during the ten minutes in question—burying the glass, having a cup of tea—the particular child's existence remains equally highly improbable. So the appeal to probabilities does not seem to work as a way to argue that the burying of the glass is, in any important sense, what is best for the child or what maximizes her well-being (or, we might say, her *expected* well-being).

According to the person-affecting analysis I will propose, the truth of the counterfactual supposition—to the effect that had I not buried the glass, this child would never have existed—is irrelevant to the moral question whether my burying the glass wrongs the child. Thus, my person-affecting solution to the nonidentity problem need not deny that the child is, in some sense, benefited by her flawed existence, or at least not made worse off than she *would* have been had I not buried the glass. Moreover, we need not deny that, as between a flawed existence and none at all, plausibly the former is better for her than the latter. (And, by implication, we need not deny that these kinds of comparisons—between existence and nonexistence—can coherently be made.) But this is only the beginning of the account that I will propose. The rest of the account, according to personalism, is that among the array of possibilities accessible to me at the critical time, at least one was *better still* for this very child. Personalism takes this fact to be, from a moral point of view, highly significant. It is this fact that allows us to avoid the implication that what I have done does not wrong the child. And it is this fact, along with the other suppositions that we have made about the particular case, that allows us to reach the further implication that what I have done *does* wrong the child.

1.9.3 Another Version of the Nonidentity Problem: A Third Test Case?

It might be argued that the statement of the nonidentity problem that I have just given is inaccurate.[61] Consider two types of cases. In cases of both types, a particular person *s* as a matter of fact has an existence that is flawed in some way. And in cases of both types, among the alternatives to *s*'s flawed existence is the state of nonexistence; *s* *need* not, that is, ever have been brought into existence to begin with. But in cases of one type but not the other, at least one world accessible to the agent is a world where *s* exists and is better off than *s* is in *s*'s actual, flawed world. We will call "type 2-alt" (for "two-alternative") those cases in which there is no such better-for-*s* world. And we will call "type 3-alt" (for "three-alternative") those cases in which there is at least one such better-for-*s* world.

The buried glass example is a clear type 3-alt case. But type 2-alt cases arise as well. We do not, for example, now have the medical wherewithal in many instances to ensure the "normality" of chromosomes or genes or, in most instances, to repair those abnormalities, such as Down's syndrome, that we can detect. In cases of this sort, worlds that are better for the children who suffer as a consequence of such abnormalities are, though clearly *possible* in a logical or metaphysical sense, not *accessible* to us. Personalism implies, on the assumption that these children's lives are worth living, that they have not been wronged by having been brought into existence. I am not denying, of

course, that in other cases we *do* have the wherewithal to avoid imposing chromosomal, genetic, or other serious abnormalities. Consider,
for example, the current debate regarding whether thalidomide should
be approved for treating leprosy and some other diseases. Thalidomide causes profound birth defects. To the extent that children are ex-
posed in utero to the drug and are born with missing and stunted
limbs, their suffering will have been entirely avoidable. This avoidabil-
ity means that personalism will not excuse the use of thalidomide
where that use leads to babies being born with missing and stunted
limbs and other abnormalities that diminish their level of well-being.[62]
Personalism, regarding such cases, will not provide a decision. The
issue will be referred, according to the scheme I am suggesting, to an
independent theory, such as fairness, in which the critical facts will
presumably include how fairly well-being has been distributed between the children who suffer the effects of the drug and the adults
who reap the benefits of the drug.[63]

Thus, in the thalidomide case, we *can* do better for the child than we
have in fact done. But the focus here is on those cases in which we
cannot do better for the child. And the interpretive question that arises
is whether the nonidentity problem involves type 3-alt cases, as we
supposed earlier, or rather type 2-alt cases. If Parfit means to suggest
that it is type 2-alt cases that give rise to the nonidentity problem, then
he will certainly think that my statement of the problem is inaccurate.
But if it is the type 2-alt cases that Parfit thinks challenge the person-
affecting intuition, then he must believe that, even when agents have
done all that they can for a person whose life is, though flawed, one
worth living, a wrong has still been done.

Here my own intuitions are quite distinct from Parfit's. I agree that
personalism implies that in type 2-alt cases no one has been wronged
and no wrong has been done. But I do not see at any intuitive level
that any wrong *has* been done. If we have done the best that anyone
could have done for a particular child and have maximized that child's
well-being, and if we have therefore avoided wronging the child, then
assuming we have wronged no one else—including ourselves—where
is the wrong?

Suppose a couple choose to have a child whom they know in advance will in all likelihood have Down's syndrome. Suppose that the
couple had the alternative of having ova screened for the chromosomal
abnormality that causes Down's syndrome. Had the couple opted for
screening, they might then have rejected the defective ovum in favor of
one that did not carry the abnormal chromosome. Thus, the couple
might have conceived a child—though a distinct child—without
Down's. Suppose that it makes no difference to the parents, any sib-

lings, or anyone outside the family unit which child is produced. Suppose that the Down's child will have somewhat less well-being than a "normal" child would have had, simply because of the shorter life span she (say) will have as part of the syndrome. But the parents will be very, very good to the Down's child, and her well-being will have been maximized. Personalism implies that the couple's choice to have the Down's child is not wrong.

As we test our intuitions in the context of hypothetical cases, we need obviously to avoid any rosy pretense that all is well with the child and his or her primary caregiver. In real life, the couple's choice to produce a Down's child might deeply affect the couple, other children in the family, and perhaps the community. At the same time, given the suppositions we have made here, it is very hard for me to see that this case marks a clear problem for personalism. Indeed, it seems to me at least as plausible that it is personalism—and not totalism or averagism—that analyzes this case correctly. We will consider this issue, and the nonidentity problem generally, in chapter 3.

1.10   Wrongful Life

We turn to tort law—in particular, the law of negligence—in chapter 4. The law of negligence contains person-affecting elements. To take just one example, to recover in negligence a plaintiff must establish, among other things, that he or she has suffered *legal harm*. Thus, it is not enough for the plaintiff to show that, had the defendant exercised due care, the total, or average, quantity of the good in the world would have been greater than it in fact is. Negligence law rather demands a concrete, existing human victim—a complainant who suffers harm as a consequence of someone else's careless or reckless conduct. Personalism likewise requires a victim, since wrongdoing, under personalism, requires the wronging of some person.

Wrongful life, a cause of action in negligence, presents a context in which the infant-plaintiff suffers as a consequence of the defendant's negligence yet is typically unable to convince judges that he or she has been *legally harmed*. The twist of the wrongful life action is that an obstetrician or other health care personnel, as defendant, is claimed to have negligently failed to prevent not the underlying medical condition that gives rise to the child's suffering but rather the child's very *existence*. Thus, in wrongful life cases the defendant is not charged with any ordinary, garden-variety medical malpractice. It is not as though the defendant has administered a drug that has given rise to a birth defect or failed to prescribe prenatal vitamins or watch for signs of placenta previa or toxemia. The underlying condition that causes the child to suffer is, rather, a genetic or chromosomal defect, and the child's claim is that the defendant has harmed the child by failing to prevent the child from coming into existence to begin with.

Thus, suppose that a surgeon negligently performs a vasectomy in a man at risk of producing children with a particular genetic defect.[64] Suppose that as a consequence of the surgeon's negligence the man unintentionally fathers a child who suffers as a result of the defect. The issue of wrongful life, then, is the issue of whether, independently of any claim of negligence that the child's *parent* might make against the surgeon, the *child* may also seek damages on the grounds that the child's very existence constitutes a harm to the child.[65] It is at this point that judges have traditionally balked, querying how life itself, however flawed, can constitute a harm to the one who lives.

In cases in which the child's life, despite its flaws, remains worth living, personalism suggests a powerful *moral* defense against actions for wrongful life. Personalism in effect categorizes such cases as type 2-alt nonidentity problems.[66] The most expert and most cautious doctor does not have the medical wherewithal to bring it about that the child who is a plaintiff in a wrongful life action both exists and escapes the genetic or chromosomal defects that give rise to his or her suffering. A better-for-the-plaintiff world is, in other words, not one that is accessible to any agent. A healthier, happier child might have been produced in the one child's stead had the doctor not been negligent. But a healthier, happier child would have been a *distinct* child. Thus, though the child undeniably suffers as a function of the fact that he or she is alive and burdened by a genetic or chromosomal disorder, according to personalism the doctor—who has, however unintentionally, maximized the child's well-being—cannot have wronged the child.

But personalism does not provide an *automatic* defense against wrongful life actions. For it suggests an analysis very different from the one just sketched in cases in which the child's flawed existence is *less* than one worth living—in cases, for example, in which the child's life is so full of pain and suffering that the child's own best interests would have been better served had the child never existed at all. Personalism does not, in such cases, hold the defendant responsible for doing what he or she *cannot* do—for failing, for example, to correct a genetic defect. Rather, it holds the defendant responsible for not doing something well within the defendant's power—that is, for not having taken greater care to avoid bringing the child into existence to begin with.

The personalist account of wrongful life just sketched is a *moral* account. But we need a legal account too, one that demonstrates how it is that one might be *legally harmed* by having been brought into existence.

The first effort in defining a test of legal harm must be to locate the moral concept of well-being within the law of negligence. Well-being, in other words, must be reworked to comprise those values that the law of negligence recognizes. It might be objected that the law of negligence, which focuses generally on the bad things that happen to people, in fact does not recognize any positive values at all. But if this objection were correct, then it would follow that judges are mistaken ever to object to wrongful life claims on the grounds of the plaintiff's inability to establish legal harm. For if judges are not entitled to recognize offsetting positive aspects of the plaintiff's life, the harm analysis would be complete once it is noted that the plaintiff in fact suffers as a consequence of the underlying defect. However, the law of negligence appears, at least implicitly, to recognize positive values. For example, not every patient who has open heart surgery possesses a viable claim against his or her surgeon. We think, rather, that the pain and suffering that accompany open heart surgery are acceptable *because* they are necessary, or probably necessary, to achieve a certain good end. But were there not at least some likelihood of achieving this good end, the burdens of surgery would *not* be acceptable. Thus, the patient who is conscious but whose death from, say, liver failure, is known to be imminent might well have a legitimate claim against the medical team who insists that the liver patient undergo open heart surgery. What positive values, then, does the law of negligence recognize? Clearly, the law of negligence protects against such losses as physical or emotional pain and suffering, or the loss of life, limb, liberty, property, or reputation. In a more general way, we might speculate that, for purposes of the law of negligence, well-being consists in a complex of values, including good health, the capacity for pleasure, happiness, autonomy, social interaction, and intellectual development.

Since all claims in negligence assert harm, we have a better idea of the negative values recognized by the law of negligence than the positive values. Plausibly, pain and other forms of suffering—together with limitation, discomfort, and indignity—can be collected, among others, as forms of negative well-being, or "ill-being." Room must be made in the analysis for a rule of offsetting. Even a substantial amount of ill-being can be offset if it *must* be endured to achieve sufficient levels of well-being; thus, we will gladly endure, for example, temporary indignities to gain the lasting capacity to, say, read and write. Likewise, the life "worth living" for purposes of the moral analysis is one that constitutes a *net* good for the one who lives, a *net* positive level of well-being.

Assuming in hand a reconception of well-being suitable for purposes of the law of negligence, we can then distinguish between those cases in which the wrongful life plaintiff has been legally harmed and those cases in which he or she has not. To begin, we can take harm roughly to be any diminution in well-being from one's maximal level of well-being. We can then say that the child who has been negligently brought into existence suffers no legal harm *if* his or her actual level of well-being is at least as great as it is in each other accessible world, including those worlds in which the child does not exist, where, I will suppose, the child's level of well-being is simply none at all, or a "zero" level. Thus, if the child's well-being has been maximized, in other words, the child has not been harmed.

When, then, has the wrongful life plaintiff—the child—been harmed? We may say that legal harm is imposed on the child by the defendant's negligent act in all those cases in which the child's actual level of well-being is negative. Legal harm is imposed, in other words, if the child's actual level of well-being is less than that level of well-being the child has in a world in which the child does not exist. It would be nice if such cases never arose—if no life were ever less than one worth living. But I do not see how any court can fairly make the supposition that such cases never arise.

The wrongful life claim of harm has been challenged on a number of grounds. Thus, it has been questioned whether existence can ever have a negative value from the point of view of the one who exists, and whether we can consistently and cogently assert that in some instances an existing person would have been "better off" never having been brought into existence to begin with. I will address this challenge, among others, in chapter 4. But the broader aim of chapter 4 is to show that the person-affecting account of wrongful life produces a set of results that is consistent with the legal account and thus supports the view that wrongful life claims should receive legal recognition.

1.11   Human Cloning and Other New Reproductive Technologies

In chapter 5, we turn to what Robertson calls the "new reproductive technologies."[67] Personalism can shape our discussion of the new technologies in ways that I believe are productive.

A wonderful thing about the new technologies is that they give babies to people who want them. In cases of male infertility, the technology of donor insemination allows couples to have children who are genetically related to at least the woman. Donor insemination is a routine, accepted, and low-cost treatment for infertility. Women whose fallopian tubes are scarred or damaged can through the technologies of egg extraction and in vitro fertilization (IVF) give birth to children who are genetically their own. Once a matter of controversy, IVF is now, like donor insemination, a routine and accepted, though very costly, procedure.

Reports of ever more advanced reproductive technologies—culminating, at the time I write this, with the prospect of cloning both early undifferentiated human embryos as well as adult human beings—stirs ever more fury within the media and among commentators. Will the fury inevitably spend itself and human cloning come to be seen, like IVF and donor insemination, as both routine and right? In my view, we should resist looking at the new reproductive technologies as all of a piece, and we should reject the notion that it is just their newness that gives rise to some deep irrational angst that will inevitably subside, at which time reason will again be permitted to prevail. Perhaps it takes more time than we have yet given the matter to clarify our thinking about cloning. But it hardly follows from this fact that there are no good arguments to be made for or against it.

I want to acknowledge that I owe my understanding of the interrelatedness of the nonidentity problem, wrongful life, and the new reproductive technologies to Robertson as exemplary teacher and theorist. To my knowledge, he nowhere expressly accepts the person-affecting intuition. Indeed, as a constitutional law scholar, Robertson's basic conjecture is that "procreative liberty is a negative right against state interference with choices to procreate or to avoid procreation."[68] And as ethicist, Robertson suggests that a "person violates no moral duty in making a procreative choice, and that other persons have a duty not to interfere with that choice."[69]

But in any traditional liberal view, including Mill's, the right of liberty applies strictly to "self-regarding" conduct and does not include the right to hurt or "definitely damage" *others*.[70] Robertson, who consistently raises and addresses the question of harm to offspring, seems to adopt something like the Millian scheme:

> Determining the scope of procreative liberty requires some standard or method for balancing reproductive choice with the competing interests that it affects. . . . I propose that procreative liberty be given presumptive priority in all conflicts, with the burden on opponents of any particular technique to show that *harmful effects* . . . justify limiting procreative choice.[71]

Thus, to know whether we have reached the limits of the liberty principle in any given case, we must be able to discern whether the agent's conduct harms another. And in Robertson's view what we discern on careful examination is that the new reproductive technologies in fact have no significant harmful effect.

In the case of harm to children and with respect to some of the new technologies, I find Robertson's reasoning compelling. Imagine a couple who want a child but are infertile as a consequence of the man's low sperm count. The couple would like to solve their problem by making use of donor insemination. Is their choice a morally acceptable one? Some ethicists, concerned about the child, might focus on the "possibility of adverse effects from deliberate separation of . . . elements" of "[g]enetic and biological ties."[72] But this moral worry is, I think, soundly defeated by Robertson's defense of donor insemination. He writes:

> [E]ven if . . . offspring have difficulties adjusting to the fact of donor . . . assistance, it does not follow that collaborative assistance should be discouraged in order to prevent harm to offspring. But for the technique in question, the child never would have been born. Whatever psychological or social problems arise, they hardly rise to the level of severe handicap or disability that would make the child's very existence a net burden, and hence a wrongful life.[73]

Thus, the ethicist who purports to be concerned about the child produced by donor insemination cannot persuasively challenge the very technology that makes the existence of the child possible. In the absence of donor insemination, *this* child would not, *could* not, not even probably, have existed. If donor insemination imposes a risk of psychosocial distress, the risk is one that is unavoidable if the child is to exist at all. The child therefore would seem not to be harmed in a way that has any constitutional or other legal or moral significance. If anything, the child seems to have been benefited by donor insemination. IVF could be viewed analogously, along with drug therapies that, while imposing some risk, allow a woman to become pregnant or to carry a fetus to term when she otherwise could not.

Robertson is clear that the defense he suggests would not be applicable in a case in which the child suffers so badly that the life is one that is *less* than worth living—in a case, that is, in which the child's life is, as Robertson puts it, genuinely "wrongful" or in which, we might say, the child's level of well-being is negative. But, as Robertson suggests, the technologies introduced to date seem simply not to have the capacity to produce suffering on this order.[74] In the case of donor insemination, for instance, the worry would be that the child would suffer some mild psychosocial distress, perhaps as a result of discovering that his or her father is not, in fact, a genetic forebear. But such distress will hardly render a life *less* than one worth living.

Robertson's analysis of whether it can plausibly be claimed that IVF and donor insemination harm, in any significant sense, the offspring they produce closely tracks a person-affecting analysis. The worlds in which the children born of these technologies are accorded more well-being than they in fact enjoy are simply not ones that are accessible to any agent. IVF and donor insemination were these children's only paths into existence. Assuming that their well-being falls in the positive range—that is, that their lives *are* worth living—such children are thus in the same position as the child-plaintiff who brings an action for wrongful life or the child-victim of the type 2-alt nonidentity problem. The best that can be done for all of these children *has* been done. This is the case, even if they do suffer some emotional or physical trauma as a consequence of the application of the new technologies. The children's well-being having been maximized, personalism implies that they have not been wronged.

But the personalist analysis just sketched also allows us to see very clearly the precise scope of its exculpatory force. Suppose that, in a given case, a world that is better for the flawed children than their actual world *is* one that is accessible. Suppose, in other words, that agents in fact had the capacity to bring some of the very children whose existence is to some degree flawed by the new technologies into an *unflawed* existence. In such a case, the children's well-being has not been maximized, and the best that *can* be done for them will *not* have been done for them. The exculpatory provisions of personalism will simply not apply to any such case.

In chapter 5, I will argue, contrary to Robertson, that cases of human embryonic cloning, in which the early, undifferentiated human embryo is split into two or more genetically identical embryos, and in cases of somatic cloning, in which the differentiated organism is cloned through a technique of cell fusion, lie beyond the exculpatory scope of personalism.[75] I will argue, in other words, both that unrestricted cloning causes a diminution in the cloned child's level of well-being and that a world better for the child is one that is perfectly accessible to the parents, doctors, and technicians whose concerted action leads to the child's diminished existence. Clearly, the child of cloning cannot exist absent the cloning technology; equally clearly, the child of cloning will have a life worth living. But it is not the prospect of the child's being hurt by the cloning per se that we should worry about. Rather, we should worry about the child's being hurt by the combination of multiple clonings *and* transfers of genetically identical embryos. It is this combination of technologies, not cloning in isolation, that has the capacity to lower the child's well-being. Just as we surely think our lives will be better if we are permitted tight control over our own individual genetic identities, the lives of future people—the children we aim to bring into existence—will likewise predictably be better if we ensure—since they cannot do it for themselves—similar tight control over their genetic identities.

It might be objected that agents can improve one child's life according to the scenario I suggest only by refraining from bringing into existence other, genetically identical children. This is true, but so what? We cannot wrong those who never exist. What we must do, rather, is the best we can for those who do, or will, exist.

Personalism thus does not support the conclusion that the children produced by the unrestricted use of the cloning technologies have *not* been wronged. Should we therefore conclude that the children of cloning *have* been wronged? Not as a general matter, I think—not yet, anyway. For there are parties other than the child who have interests at stake. Thus, within the scope of this work, I reach the more limited result that the moral issues presented by human cloning are more complex than they initially seem to be and can in some cases be resolved only by a fair balancing of the conflicting interests of child and childmaker.

Notes

1. See generally Derek Parfit, *Reasons and Persons* (Oxford: Clarendon, 1984) (hereinafter, *RP*), 351–441. For a clear statement of the person-affecting intuition—and one that shows why the intuition is so difficult to part with—see John Broome and Adam Morton, "The Value of a Person," *Proceedings of the Aristotelian Society* supp. 68 (1994): 167, 167–68.

2. I want to note earlier rather than later that my use of the term *person* should not be taken to be necessarily limited to human beings. I see no reason to think that moral theory should categorically exclude animals from its scope.

3. This latter is the better way of making this particular point, since two acts may have consequences that are equally good. In such cases, neither act could then be the *best*, and it is enough to require that agents perform some act than which none is better.

4. A classic statement of utilitarianism, a form of consequentialism, is provided by John Stuart Mill in "Utilitarianism," in *The Collected Works of John Stuart Mill*, ed. John M. Robson (Toronto: University of Toronto Press, 1969), 205–59. See also G. E. Moore, *Principia Ethica* (Cambridge: Cambridge University Press, 1971), 148, defining "duty" as "that action, which will cause more good to exist in the Universe than any possible alternative."

Whether consequentialist theories necessarily involve maximization is somewhat controversial. Thus, Michael Slote proposes a form of "satisficing" consequentialism in *Beyond Optimizing: A Study of Rational Choice* (Cambridge, Mass.: Harvard University Press, 1989).

5. See Mill, "Utilitarianism," 234–39.

6. I follow John Broome, whose work I discuss in detail in what follows, in leaving the question of the nature of the good that is to be maximized unanalyzed. See Broome, *Counting the Costs of Global Warming* (Cambridge: White Horse, 1992), 41–44. Thus, I leave open in what follows whether the "overall good" consists of (1) net aggregate well-being, a concept I introduce later and that itself might consist of happiness, pleasure, preference satisfaction, autonomy, income, wealth, education, or, according to Sen (see below), "capability to achieve functionings" or (2) some other property or complex of properties that includes, alongside aggregate "well-being," such attributes as equality and justice. See also Partha Dasgupta, *An Inquiry into Well-Being and Destitution* (Oxford: Clarendon, 1993), 3–131; Amartya Sen, *Inequality Reexamined* (Cambridge, Mass.: Harvard University Press, 1992), 1–55 and especially 4–5 (sketching his notion of well-being as a "person's capability to achieve functionings [which] can vary from most elementary ones, such as being well-nourished, avoiding escapable morbidity and premature mortality, etc., to quite complex and sophisticated achievements, such as having self-respect, being able to take part in the life of the community, and so on"); and Ronald Dworkin, "What Is Equality? Part I: Equality of Welfare," *Philosophy & Public Affairs* 10, no. 3 (1981): 185–225, and "What Is Equality? Part II: Equality of Resources," *Philosophy & Public Affairs* 10, no. 4 (1981): 283–345 (comparing alternative theories of equality, including versions of equality of welfare and equality of resources). Another possibility is that the concept of the good is, as Moore suggests, unanalyzable.

7. Moore, *Principia Ethica*, chap. 1, § 9. Goodness is thus for Moore a simple, unanalyzable characteristic of objects or states. See generally Moore, *Principia Ethica*, chap. 3 ("Hedonism") and chap. 6 ("The Ideal").

8. Moore, *Principia Ethica*, 83–85.

9. Henry Sidgwick, *The Methods of Ethics* (Chicago: University of Chicago Press, 1962), 113.

10. David Lewis, *On the Plurality of Worlds* (Oxford: Blackwell, 1986), 2.

11. Fred Feldman provides a contemporary statement of the aggregative approach to defining total good. But Feldman, like Moore, leaves open whether total good accrues as a function of specific facts about people. See Feldman, *Doing the Best We Can: An Essay in Informal Deontic Logic* (Dordrecht: Reidel, 1986). Partly to avoid some of the formal problems that beset "act" and "rule" forms of totalism, Feldman proposes that "we morally ought to do what we do in the intrinsically best possible worlds still accessible to us," where the value of each world is to be determined by a principle that sums up the intrinsic values of certain states within that world (*Doing the Best We Can*, xi, 30–36). For casual statements that expressly apply totalism to issues regarding future generations, see R. I. Sikora, "Is It Wrong to Prevent the Existence of Future Generations?" in *Obligations to Future Generations*, ed. R. I. Sikora and Brian Barry (Philadelphia: Temple University Press, 1978), 112–66, and L. W. Sumner,

"Classical Utilitarianism and the Population Optimum," in *Obligations to Future Generations*, ed. Sikora and Barry, 91–111.

12. Broome, *Counting*, 41. See also Sen, *Inequality Reexamined*, 136–38.

13. As noted earlier, I leave it open here whether well-being is best understood to consist in any of, or some combination of, happiness, pleasure, education, autonomy, wealth, preference satisfaction, income, or, according to Sen's proposal, "capability to achieve functionings." See note 6.

14. For a discussion of the relative merits of averagism, see John Rawls, *A Theory of Justice* (Oxford: Oxford University Press, 1972), 161–75.

15. I owe the concise terminology of "totalism" and "averagism" to Feldman. For a clear description of both these forms of consequentialism, see Feldman, "Justice, Desert, and the Repugnant Conclusion," *Utilitas* 7, no. 2 (Nov. 1995): 189, 190–93. The person-affecting intuition would also deny some other forms of consequentialism (e.g., egoism).

16. The term *personalism* has been used to name views other than the one I describe here. According to one such view, "we are essentially persons." See Ingmar Persson, "Genetic Therapy, Identity and Person-Regarding Reasons," *Bioethics* 9, no. 1 (1995): 18. The term also names a view associated with some of the Transcendentalists. See Bernard Schmidt, "Bronson Alcott's Developing Personalism and the Argument with Emerson," *American Transcendental Quarterly* 8, no. 4 (1994): 311. I do not mean to invoke either of these views here. Rather, I use *personalism* to distinguish the view I describe from other forms of consequentialism, including totalism and averagism, and other ways of understanding the person-affecting intuition.

17. Others have associated "person-regarding reasons" with an appeal to a three-place relation of the kind I describe here. See, for example, Persson, "Genetic Therapy," 27, and Robert Elliot, "Contingency, Community and Intergenerational Justice," in *Contingent Future People: On the Ethics of Deciding Who Will Live, or Not, in the Future*, ed. Nick Fotion and Jan C. Heller (Dordrecht: Kluwer Academic, 1997), 162.

18. See part 2.7.4 ("Theory of 'Fair Distribution' ").

19. Tyler Cowen suggests that the incompleteness I am proposing for personalism is problematic ("What Do We Learn from the Repugnant Conclusion?" *Ethics* 106 [July 1996]: 754, 757–60):

> [W]e wish to avoid moral theories which beg agnosticism instead of facing up to unappealing conclusions. I use this axiom to force moral theories to rank the [r]epugnant [c]onclusion against alternatives. Admittedly, moral theory may not be able to rank a variety of outcomes, but if we place the hard cases in this category, we give up the search for a normative population theory. . . . [W]e might as well admit that consequentialism has failed.

Cowen suggests that a view that does not rank all outcomes, and thus fails to comply with what he calls the axiom of "universal domain," implies that "consequentialism has failed" ("What Do We Learn from the Repugnant Conclusion?" 760). This conjecture is suspect. Moral theories should provide accounts of some hard cases. From this it does not follow that any moral theory that fails to rank all outcomes is inadequate.

20. Excellent discussions of the objection from justice are included in Broome, *Counting*, 41–44, and Parfit, "Overpopulation and the Quality of Life," in *Applied Ethics*, ed. Peter Singer (Oxford: Oxford University Press, 1986), 161–64. See also Richard B. Brandt, *Ethical Theory* (Englewood Cliffs, N.J.: Prentice Hall, 1959), 407–32, 480–96; and John Rawls, *A Theory of Justice* (Cambridge, Mass.: Harvard University Press, 1971), 22–33.

21. Larry S. Temkin makes this point in connection with averagism; see *Inequality* (New York: Oxford University Press, 1993), 102.

22. Rawls, *A Theory of Justice*, 27; also see generally 22–33.

23. When our having children *would* be good for ourselves or others, personalism treats the matter differently, in some cases *requiring* procreation. See part 3.8.2.

24. Parfit's statement of the "repugnant conclusion" is most well known; *RP*, 381–90. The totalist calculation produces the intuitively false result only in cases in which the less well-off population is sufficiently larger than the more well-off population. Cowen describes the repugnant conclusion as "the most serious obstacle which normative population theories must face" ("What Do We Learn from the Repugnant Conclusion?" 754). Feldman outlines a totalist response to the repugnant conclusion in "Justice, Desert, and the Repugnant Conclusion," 190–93. Denying that all values necessarily "lay on the same scale," Parfit outlines his own "perfectionist" response to the repugnant conclusion. See his "Overpopulation and the Quality of Life," 160–64. For a critique of Parfit's view, see Jesper Ryberg, "Parfit's Repugnant Conclusion," *Philosophical Quarterly* 46, no. 183 (April 1996): 202–13. I briefly discuss Parfit's perfectionism in part 2.11 and Feldman's theory in part 3.11.5.

25. Parfit, *RP*, 420; see also Feldman, "Justice, Desert, and the Repugnant Conclusion," 192–93.

26. Jan Narveson, "Moral Problems of Population," in *Ethics and Population*, ed. Michael D. Bayles (Cambridge, Mass.: Schenkman, 1976), 73. See also Narveson, "Future People and Us," in *Obligations to Future Generations*, ed. R. I. Sikora and Brian Barry (Philadelphia: Temple University Press, 1978), 38–60.

27. Narveson, "Moral Problems of Population," 73.

28. Parfit, *RP*, 363.

29. Larry S. Temkin, "Intransitivity and the Mere Addition Paradox," *Philosophy and Public Affairs* 16, no. 2 (Spring 1987): 138, 166.

30. The question of who matters is potentially much broader. Thus, other issues that might be understood to fall under the heading of "who matters" include whether family members have a greater claim to our behaving well than do, say, strangers, or whether members of our own species have any sort of moral priority over orangutans or macaws, or whether we owe the human infant more than we owe the human zygote. Though these are extremely important issues, I do not address them here.

31. Future people, together with existing and even past people, are sometimes said to exist "tenselessly." But for purposes here I will understand "existing people" to designate people who exist at a given time—which time, unless otherwise indicated, will be the present. Thus, the descriptions "exist-

ing people," "currently existing people," and "people who exist now" all designate the same class of individuals. Correspondingly, I will understand "future people" to designate people who do not exist at a given time—which time, unless otherwise indicated, will be the present—but will exist at some later time.

32. Earl Conee made this point to me.

33. Eva Bodanszky and Conee suggested the need for this clarification. An equivalent way of putting this point is just to say that "existing people" and "future people" are not terms that rigidly designate those individuals who, as a matter of contingent fact, exist and will exist in the *actual* world. Thus, when I say that personalism implies that all existing and future people matter, I am not suggesting that each person who happens in fact to exist matters morally, and can be wronged, in those other worlds where he or she does not exist. In a sense, of course, the nonexistent "can" be wronged: were they to exist, we could wrong them. But this is consistent with the personalist tenet that people cannot be wronged in any world where they do not and will not exist.

34. The exception to the usual case will be where the child's existence itself is so full of unavoidable misery, or more generally ill-being, that it would have been better for the particular child never to have been brought into existence to begin with. In this circumstance, and depending on other facts, the child's suffering, I will argue, forms the basis of the legal action known as "wrongful life" (chap. 4).

35. Clark Wolf, "Social Choice and Normative Population Theory: A Person Affecting Solution to Parfit's Mere Addition Paradox," *Philosophical Studies* 81 (1996): 265.

36. Broome and Morton, "The Value of a Person," 167–68. This judgment, it seems, assumes that the couple's producing the child is important to no one else (e.g., an older or future younger sibling).

37. Thus, suppose an agent has just two options. He (say) can either (A) feed a child who will then enjoy only a moderately high level of well-being but avoid outright hunger or (B) allow the very same child to go hungry from time to time, thereby causing her to have modestly less well-being than she would otherwise have, while tomorrow creating a *second* child who will have a very high level of well-being. It does not matter to anyone else, including the agent, whether he chooses A or B. Suppose the agent chooses A. Depending on the numbers, totalism and averagism—again, in contrast to personalism—would both declare the agent to have done something wrong, since he could have, but did not, implement B.

38. Parfit describes this notion in *RP,* 394–401. Here we are referring back to the Moore-Sidgwick debate and can identify the "weakly" person-affecting approach with the Sidgwick position.

39. It could happen that new people continuously come into existence throughout eternity, in which case it would never be "settled" whether one population rather than some other would constitute the class of future people. This would mean that there would be no particular time when a hypothetical future morals tribunal would be able to render an assessment of conduct we

engage in today. But this unsettledness should be distinguished from any conceptually problematic indeterminacy. Even in the infinite case, it is true that anyone who ever exists will come into existence at a particular time. So if the claimed justification for diminishing a child's well-being today is that otherwise some future child will be much worse off, either this claim will be true given that the world is a certain way at some future time, or it will be false given that at no time is the world ever the particular way it needs to be for this claim to be true. Either way, the conditions for permissibility are determinate. We might just note that, if the class of future people is infinite, so be it; we are "on the hook," morally, with respect to them all.

40. Persson suggests that, since future people can be harmed or benefited by being brought into existence, they fall within the scope of principles that are person-affecting; Persson, "Genetic Therapy, Identity and Person-Regarding Reasons," 27–30. I agree with both these points but do not propose that they are related in the way that Persson suggests. Rather, in my view, though people can be, in a sense, benefited by having been brought into existence, they can never be wronged by having not been brought into existence; and person-affecting principles, to be plausible, must be formulated to have application to future as well as present people.

41. David Heyd, *Genethics: Moral Issues in the Creation of People* (Berkeley: University of California Press, 1992).

42. Heyd, *Genethics*, 99.

43. Heyd, *Genethics*, 106.

44. See part 1.7.1 ("Choices That Affect Future People's Lives: A Second Test Case").

45. Heyd, *Genethics*, 193ff.

46. Heyd, *Genethics*, 198.

47. Heyd, *Genethics*, 99.

48. I here use a case described by Parfit, *RP,* 356.

49. Heyd, *Genethics*, 105.

50. Heyd, *Genethics*, 99, emphasis added.

51. I will just note that the nonidentity problem does not *categorically* deny the moral status of what Heyd calls "potential people" altogether. Rather, it challenges the claim that an act can properly be said to have harmed, or wronged, a person in a case in which his or her very existence in some sense "depends" on that act being performed.

52. Broome, *Counting*, 125.

53. Parfit, *RP,* 351–79.

54. Parfit, *RP,* 378.

55. Gregory Kavka, "The Paradox of Future Individuals," *Philosophy and Public Affairs* 11, no. 2 (1981): 93.

56. See Parfit, *RP,* 359 (describing the life of a "young girl's child").

57. Parfit discusses this question at length, *RP,* 487–90 (app. G: "Whether Causing Someone to Exist Can Benefit This Person"). He concludes that the belief that causing to exist can benefit is "defensible" (490).

58. Not all theorists will necessarily agree that this implication is clearly

false or that some wrong or another has been done. Heyd, as we have seen, endorses this implication (even in the absence of the additional suppositions, which provide that the child would otherwise have been worse off). Moreover, in connection with the question of our adopting public policies (such as a "more or less laissez-faire policy") that would impoverish "our distant descendants," Thomas Schwartz takes the view that we are not obligated *not* to adopt these policies since they wrong no one; "Obligations to Posterity," in *Obligations to Future Generations*, ed. Sikora and Barry, 3, 10–12.

59. Parfit hardly rests content with traditional formulations of totalism in view of the fact that they give rise to a challenge that at least equals the nonidentity problem, in the form of the repugnant conclusion. Thus, specifications for the Theory X that Parfit seeks include that it address both the nonidentity problem and the repugnant conclusion.

60. Feldman designates the accessibility of worlds as a primitive concept, and I follow suit here. "Loosely," Feldman writes, "a world is accessible to an agent at a time if and only if he still can see to it that that world occurs, or is actual" (*Doing the Best We Can*, 18). For Feldman's more detailed account of accessibility, see generally *Doing the Best We Can*, 16–25.

61. The version of the nonidentity problem I have just given parallels Kavka's "slave child" case. For his note on the unlikelihood of the slave child's existing as a nonslave, see "The Paradox of Future Individuals," 100, n.15.

62. I make a handful of suppositions about personal identity in this paragraph. In suggesting that it is possible to repair some genetic or chromosomal defects to the benefit of the very child whose existence is flawed, I make the supposition that it is possible that in *some* instances genes, or even chromosomes, can be repaired or replaced without any alteration in the *identity* of the child. This supposition is, I think, extremely plausible. Surely one might have existed and had eyes slightly lighter in color than one in fact has. Moreover, when an environmental toxin or a drug, such as thalidomide, damages an embryo or fetus, I make the supposition that this change does not necessarily mark a shift in personal identity. Thus, it seems to me that, in at least many instances, a new person is not created in lieu of the undamaged original when thalidomide is ingested and its damage done. Rather, one and the same person, the original person, suffers the ill effects of the drug. Or, more precisely (since there is no reason to suppose that the very early fetus is a person at all), in at least some cases, the person who is ultimately produced and suffers the effects of thalidomide is identical to the person who would have been produced had the thalidomide never been ingested to begin with. Related issues involving personal identity are outlined in chap. 5, note 37.

63. The thalidomide case is in fact one with respect to which totalism and personalism, coupled with fairness, may imply distinct results. If *many* adults show modest increases in their levels of well-being as an effect of the drug, and if only a few children are born showing the ill effects of thalidomide, then totalism may imply that there is nothing objectionable about the drug even if the cost to these few children in terms of well-being is massive. But, assuming that fairness has something to do with a fair distribution of well-being and

that fair distribution has something to do with equal distribution, fairness may imply that the children have been wronged. See part 2.7.4 ("A Theory of 'Fair Distribution' ").

64. This unlikely example is from an actual case. In this same case, once the couple learned that the vasectomy had failed and that a pregnancy had resulted, the woman made arrangements to have an abortion. But the abortion also failed, and the child was born with neurofibromatosis, or "elephant man's disease." See *Speck v. Finegold*, 497 Pa. 77, 81–82 n.2, 439 A.2d 100, 112 n.2 (1981).

65. The parents' independent cause of action, which is, unlike wrongful life, widely accepted, is known as "wrongful birth." See part 4.3.2 ("Examples of Wrongful Life Claims").

66. A person's good, or well-being, remains unanalyzed here, as earlier. Perhaps it is happiness; perhaps it is autonomy; I do not try to say here.

67. See John A. Robertson, *Children of Choice: Freedom and the New Reproductive Technologies* (Princeton, N.J.: Princeton University Press, 1994). Robertson provides detailed descriptions of IVF, donor insemination, and other new technologies, catalogues their usefulness, and discusses both the legal and moral issues to which these technologies give rise (*Children of Choice*, 97–145).

68. Robertson, *Children of Choice*, 23; and, generally, chap. 2 ("Procreative Liberty"), 22–42.

69. Robertson, *Children of Choice*, 23.

70. See, e.g., John Stuart Mill, *On Liberty* (New York: Appleton-Century-Crofts, 1947), 78 ("Acts injurious to others require a totally different treatment"); and, generally, chap. 4 ("Of the Limits to the Authority of Society over the Individual"). There is for Mill an exception to the exception: where the harm produced is "merely contingent, or, as it may be called, constructive," and the conduct itself "neither violates any specific duty to the public, nor occasions perceptible hurt to any assignable individual except himself," the conduct is considered to be self-regarding and thus protected by the individual's right of liberty (*On Liberty*, 82).

71. Robertson, *Children of Choice*, 16, emphasis added.

72. Robertson, *Children of Choice*, 121.

73. Robertson, *Children of Choice*, 122, citation omitted.

74. See, e.g., Robertson's discussion of the kinds of harmful effects human cloning is most likely to produce (*Children of Choice*, 168–69).

75. I have elsewhere argued that commercial surrogacy and postmenopausal pregnancy also lie beyond the exculpatory scope of Robertson's argument. See Melinda A. Roberts, "Good Intentions and a Great Divide: Having Babies by Intending Them," *Law and Philosophy* 12 (1993): 287–317; and "A Way of Looking at the Dalla Corte Case," *Journal of Law, Medicine & Ethics* 22 (1994): 339–42.

Chapter 2

Is the Person-Affecting Intuition Inconsistent?

2.1 The Intuition

The person-affecting intuition has many admirers but few defenders. Rough statements suggest a view so beguiling as to be utterly without content. Parfit puts it this way: "what is bad must be bad *for someone*."[1] Temkin phrases it another way: "[o]ne outcome is worse than another only if it affects people for the worse."[2] And most famously Narveson writes, "We are in favour of making people happy, but neutral about making happy people."[3] Who could disagree with these sentiments? And how could such near platitudes contribute in any meaningful way to our understanding of moral law?

In fact, the upside of the person-affecting intuition is considerable. Perhaps most significantly, the intuition coincides with our views about common matters like whether a couple is morally obligated to have a child whom they do not particularly want but would be good to. "If having a child would be bad for the couple themselves, even to a small degree, that is a sufficient reason for them not to have one."[4] More generally, we prefer a view that requires us to provide "aid and succor to those who are needy and miserable" over a theory that would allow us to "counterbalance their misery and destitution by bringing more happy people into existence."[5]

Perhaps more insistently than anyone else, Parfit has argued that, whatever the perceived upside of the person-affecting intuition, we are compelled to reject it. The intuition's defect is revealed, Parfit thinks, in what he calls the "nonidentity problem." This problem is really just a series of puzzle cases about which we feel compelled to say, according to Parfit, that what has been done is *bad for no one* but is nonetheless *bad*.[6] In need of a theory that embraces both these results, we must, he

45

thinks, abandon our person-affecting sentiments. The "best theory about beneficence," he writes, "will not appeal to what is good or bad *for those people whom our acts affect.*"[7]

The nonidentity problem will be considered in the next chapter, where I will argue that the person-affecting intuition does not in fact support the clearly counterintuitive results that Parfit and others have ascribed to it and that the results that the intuition *does* support are in fact plausible. But charges even more serious than the nonidentity problem must first be addressed. Broome, for instance, argues that the intuition is inconsistent. I turn to his argument now.

2.2   Broome's Teleological Approach

In a monograph, Broome considers some of the ethical and policy implications of global warming. A primary value of his work is that it sets out an analytical framework for approaching what he takes to be the critical question of "how benefits and harms coming at one time are to be weighed against benefits and harms at another."[8] This question includes, among others, such issues as obligations toward future generations, discounting, and the "demographic effects" of global warming.[9]

Broome assumes a "teleological," or, he says, "consequentialist," view of moral obligation.[10] Teleology, he thinks, "can be identified by its *structure.* . . . [I]t has a maximizing structure."[11] He writes:

> When there is a range of alternative actions, one of them will turn out to be the best, after weighing up goods and bads (or perhaps several might be equally best). It is natural to suppose that this is the one that ought to be done (or that one of the equal best ought to be done). Teleology assumes that the right action—the action that ought to be done—is necessarily the best of the alternatives available.[12]

Several issues arise. Broome here suggests that the kinds of entities that are better or worse than others are "actions." But he later refers to people existing "in" actions and switches to talk of comparing, with respect to their "overall goodness," what he calls "outlooks."[13] But what is an "outlook"? And what is "overall goodness"?

Though Broome does not expressly say, it seems fair to think of outlooks as possible worlds. However, not all possible worlds count as outlooks. According to Broome, an outlook is a way the "world will progress."[14] Though in some worlds Lincoln was never assassinated, those worlds are not ways the world could *now* progress and so are not now outlooks. Suppose that an enormous meteorite is discovered to be hurtling toward Earth. The idea that we might stop the meteorite—by, say, waving our arms and converting it into a feather—involves no logical inconsistency. Equivalently, we might say that there is some possible world where we stop the meteorite by waving our arms. But this world does not appear to be an "outlook" for Broome. According to Broome, outlooks are a function of (1) a "state of nature," one of which "will occur" and each of which itself contains "all the other things that will happen apart from our action," and (2) our own action, which we "choose amongst a range of alternatives."[15] But we cannot "choose" the "alternative" of converting the meteorite into a feather. Thus, the world where we convert the meteorite into a feather is not, for us in our present circumstances, what Broome considers an outlook.

A Broomeian outlook would seem to be what was described in chapter 1 as a world that is *accessible* at a time—that is, a world, among many possible worlds, that agents at a given time, acting individually or in concert, have the *capacity* to bring about.[16] I earlier said that it does not follow from the fact that a world is accessible to us that we can, if we choose, *ensure* that that world comes about. Worlds where we get to school safely in the morning are very likely accessible to us before we start out from home. But whether any such world actually comes about will depend on, among many other things, how other drivers behave themselves on the road. This feature of accessibility is reflected in Broome's notion of an outlook: we might choose to drive carefully, but whether we get to school safely will depend not just on this choice but also on which "state of nature," among many possibilities, will in fact occur.

Given this understanding, we can express Broome's teleological assumption as a principle governing moral permissibility (P). Where a world *X* is accessible to agents at a time *t*,

P: *X* is permissible for agents at *t* *if and only if*, for each world *Y* accessible to agents at *t*, *X* is at least as good as *Y* in respect of "overall goodness."[17]

X is thus permissible—involves, in other words, no wrongdoing—if it is, to quote Broome, among the "equally best."[18]

Left open is the question of what "overall goodness" is. But Broome's aim is not to define or defend any "particular notion of the good."[19]

The notion of good can include many ethical values. For instance, it can include the value of equality. . . . If equality is a good thing, then that good can be put together with other goods, such as the total of people's wellbeing, to determine *overall good*. So a teleologist can aim to maximize overall good, taking equality into account.[20]

Broome's interest, rather, is in the relationship between the overall good and what he calls a "person's good," or "well-being." "I shall assume," he writes, "that a distribution of well-being contains all the information necessary to determine how good the outlook is."[21] The question then is "*how, exactly*" the overall goodness of a given world is "determined by the distribution of well-being."[22]

A "person's good," or equivalently, "well-being," also remains undefined.[23] Thus, well-being might be a matter of experiencing a certain amount or degree of pleasure or happiness, or it might be a matter of taking a certain amount of satisfaction in the achievement of one's own goals and ambitions or in having one's own preferences met. Alternatively, well-being might consist in characteristics that individuals are unaware of or do not appreciate. Thus, key concepts, in defining well-being, might include one or more of income, consumption, net worth, education, autonomy, and perhaps capabilities.[24]

Broome's ultimate goal is to describe the "value function" from a given distribution of well-being to the "overall goodness" of any world that manifests that particular distribution of well-being.[25] The "structural" nature of Broome's approach clearly makes his view more congenial than it might otherwise be to a wide range of philosophers, legal theorists, and economists who may be unprepared to come to consensus on any particular theory of the overall good or of well-being. And it seems likely that the implications of multiple, inconsistent axiologies will converge as a matter of fact: the person whose income is reasonably high will also both have a good education and experience a significant degree of satisfaction in achieving his or her aims and goals in life. If these correlations remain consistent across a broad segment of the community, and if we accept Broome's description of the relationship between the overall goodness of a world and the distribution of well-being within that world, we are, in view of principle P, clearly well on our way to a mutually satisfactory, if partial, account of what is morally permissible.

2.3 Broome's Formulation of the Person-Affecting Intuition

Within this analytical framework, Broome considers how the person-affecting intuition "might . . . be formulated as a condition on the value function."[26] He writes:

Suppose that we have to compare two alternative actions. Suppose one contains a certain number of people, and the other contains all the same people, and some more as well. This, for instance, is the choice facing a couple wondering whether to have a child. Then the condition is that one alternative is at least as good as the other if and only if it is at least as good for the people who exist in both.[27]

Taking note of the equivalence between well-being and a person's good, we can extract from Broome's discussion a ranking principle that reflects his understanding of the person-affecting intuition. Where at least one person (the same person) exists in both worlds X and Y, at least one person exists in one world but not the other, and anyone who exists in one world but not the other there has a "good life":

BPAR: X is at least as good as Y *if* for each person s who exists in both X and Y, s has as much well-being in X as s has in Y.[28]

According to BPAR, then, from a moral point of view the "well-being of the person who exists only in [one of the two worlds] does not affect the comparison."[29] By implication, the fact that a given world contains extra people does not make that world either better or worse than the other.

2.4   Broome's Inconsistency Argument

Suppose that three people, s_1, s_2, and s_3, have the levels of well-being indicated in the following table in each of three worlds, A, B, and C. The significance of each numerical assignment, for purposes here, "lies entirely in its ordinal properties."[30] To show that s_3 does not exist at all in A, I make no entry at all at that position. No one other than s_1, s_2, and s_3 ever exists in any of the three worlds, and each world, and no other, is accessible at the relevant time to the pertinent agents.

Case 1, Deprived Example

	A	B	C
s_1	5	5	5
s_2	5	5	5
s_3		6	1

In this scenario, s_1 has exactly the same level of well-being in each of A, B, and C, and s_2's level of well-being is the same throughout as s_1's.

But, as noted, s_3—whom I will henceforth call "Deprived"—does not exist at all in A. In B, Deprived enjoys a somewhat higher level of well-being, and in C a much lower level of well-being, than s_1 and s_2 do anywhere.

From BPAR, Broome infers that

    (i) A and B are equally good,

and

    (ii) A and C are equally good.

From BPAR, Broome also infers that

    (iii) B is better than C.

But BPAR does not quite support this conclusion. BPAR is restricted. It does not apply to "same people" cases, just to "extra people" cases. The ranking that BPAR provides is thus merely partial and (iii) does not fall within its scope. Nonetheless, (iii) seems independently plausible. *Denying* (iii) at this stage will very likely lead to trouble when we arrive at any complete theory. It is hard to think of any plausible theory that ranks worlds in respect of betterness, including any person-affecting theory, that would deny (iii).

Finally, given the transitivity and symmetry of "equally good," (i) and (ii) imply that

    (iv) B and C are equally good,

which contradicts (iii).

The contradiction might be avoided by denying the transitivity that leads to (iv). But Broome rejects this solution as implausible—which it would seem, at least facially, to be.[31] Another assumption embedded in this argument is that if X is at least as good as Y, and vice versa, that X and Y are equally good, and that if X is at least as good as Y, but not vice versa, then X is better than Y. But these assumptions also seem plausible. Thus, Broome is led to reject BPAR. According to him, the person-affecting intuition "seems doomed to fail."[32]

2.5   A Problem with Broome's Formulation of the Person-Affecting Intuition

In comparing worlds, BPAR takes into account only facts about the people who exist in both. We can put our finger on a *part* of why Broome needs this restriction if he is to capture the person-affecting intuition. According to the intuition, it does not make Y better than X, where X and Y are otherwise alike, that Y but not X includes an extra person who all in all has a good life in Y. Rather, the existence of this extra person is, according to the person-affecting theorist, "morally neutral."[33]

So far, so good. We can understand why the person-affecting theorist thinks that the claim that Y must be better than X simply because Y contains an extra person whose life is worth living is false, and so we can understand that BPAR's spotlighting just those people who exist in both worlds accurately captures this part of the person-affecting intuition. The problem is that BPAR, by spotlighting just those people who exist in both worlds, jettisons a second claim as well—a claim that seems to be equally a part of the intuition. Were the only issue "Does the existence of the additional person make X *better?*" we would be done. But in fact a second, independent issue arises: "Does the existence of the additional person make X *worse?*"

BPAR denies that the existence of an additional person might make things worse. But discarding this claim seems contrary to the person-affecting notion that *all* people who do, or will, exist, count for moral purposes. Deprived exists in C; why, then, should how well off Deprived is in C *not* be considered pertinent to the overall evaluation of C?

Broome interprets the intuition to imply that the existence of an extra person is morally neutral. Thus, if, on the best statement of the intuition, the existence of an extra person *ever* is *not* morally neutral—if it *ever* makes things worse—then we should reject BPAR as a statement of the intuition.

In fact, it seems that the person-affecting theorist can quite coherently take the view that the existence of an extra person never makes things *better* (assuming it makes things better for no one else) but may make things *worse.*[34] Existence usually, though I think not always, creates positive well-being for the person who exists.[35] But even teleological purists—those Benthamites and positivists and simple welfarists who think we can very nearly measure whatever it is that gives rise to the good—deny outright that *any* given quantity of well-being, or the good, will *by itself* decide *any* question of moral obligation. The fact that *tons* of good have been created does not by itself imply that the act creating all this good is not wrong. Rather, we must, according to the teleologist, consider not just how much good has in fact been created but also how much good *could have been* created. If accessible worlds contain *twice* tons, creating mere tons is wrong—a morally impermissible act.

I do not mean to suggest here that Broome does not consider alternate possibilities to be relevant to questions of obligation. I have understood him, as a teleologist who presupposes that morality has a maximizing structure, to assert that they are. Thus, I attributed to him P, according to which a world is permissible if and only if that world is, in terms of overall goodness, among the best. What I want to suggest, rather, is that the person-affecting theorist need not follow Broome in limiting questions about alternate possibilities to P. There is no reason why the person-affecting theorist cannot, good consequentialist that he or she is, take alternate possibilities—what *could* have been—into account at another stage of the analysis as well.

In particular, it seems that the person-affecting theorist can take "what could have been" into account within the criterion for when a person has been wronged. A person-affecting theorist might posit that Deprived is wronged in *C* because, in view of *B*, Deprived could have been accorded more well-being than he has been in *C* at no cost to anyone else. In virtue of there being someone in *C*, but no one in *A*, who has been wronged, such a theorist might then judge that *C is* worse than *A*. On these grounds the person-affecting theorist may reject Broome's (ii) as false, even though all the people who exist in both *A* and *C* are as well off in *C* as in *A*. Having avoided (ii), the person-affecting theorist also avoids Broome's inconsistency charge.

Thus, the person-affecting theorist explains how it can happen that the existence of an additional person, though it will never make things *better*, in some cases makes things *worse* and why it is that BPAR errs in spotlighting only those individuals who exist in each of the two worlds to be compared. In spotlighting only those individuals, BPAR fails to attend to the plight of some actual person—in particular, to the fact that that person, Deprived, has been wronged in *C*—and thus fails to recognize as morally relevant a fact that the person-affecting theorist would seem perfectly free to bring into the analysis.

2.6   A Person-Affecting Sense of "*X* Is at Least as Good as *Y*"?

Having rejected Broome's BPAR, we might consider adopting, in its place, some superior person-affecting ranking principle PAR*. Such a PAR* would provide, among other things, that *X* is at least as good as *Y* if no one is wronged in *X* and someone is wronged in *Y*. Having ranked worlds by appeal to PAR* rather than BPAR, we might then step back in line behind Broome and use P to determine moral permissibility. But there is a dreadful awkwardness to this approach. It maximizes *twice*: once in deciding whether someone has been wronged (Deprived is wronged, I said, because he could have been accorded more well-being than he was at no cost to anyone else), and then all over again, when deciding whether a wrong has been done (*C* is not permissible, since *C* is not at least as good as either *A* or *B*).

But once is enough, at least for the purpose of addressing Broome's argument. If we think that the criterion for when a person has been wronged includes a maximizing component, then we can perfectly well address the case of Deprived without appealing to a criterion for wronging *simpliciter* that likewise includes a maximizing component.

This point requires elaboration. Broome assumes that a person-affecting theorist's aim is to provide an ordering of worlds, governed by BPAR or some other such principle, for the purpose of determining, under P, when a *wrong has been done*. But it seems that, contrary to Broome's assumption, the aim of a person-affecting theorist might rather be that of ordering worlds for the purpose of determining not when a wrong has been done but rather when *a person has been wronged*. If this is correct, then such a theorist might simply abandon the task of defining a person-affecting sense of "*X* is at least as good as *Y*," not as doomed to fail, or as necessarily incoherent, but simply as inessential to the person-affecting project.

To maintain that we might do without a person-affecting sense of the two-place relation "*X* is at least as good as *Y*" is *not* to say, of course, that we might do without the three-place relation "*X* is at least as good *for s* as *Y*," or, equivalently "*s* has at least as much well-being in *X* as *s* has in *Y*." We do need the three-place relation—as, of course, does Broome. But the three-place relation is not one that causes any particular difficulty for the person-affecting view. Well-being is not a point of dispute between Broome and the person-affecting theorist. Though Broome does not attempt to define well-being, he takes it for granted that the notion can be filled out in some coherent way. We can do the same for purposes here.

Suppose, then, that we may appeal as needed to the three-place relation, and suppose that we simply abandon the task of defining the two-place relation as inessential to the person-affecting project. A critic might suggest at this point that the person-affecting theorist has leaped from the frying pan into the fire. For, if we jettison BPAR *and* PAR*—if we abandon altogether the task of defining a person-affecting sense of "*X* is at least as good as *Y*"—then we will be left with no means of applying the ubiquitous and seemingly innocuous P, a principle that generates results *only* in the presence of an ordering of worlds in respect of their overall goodness. But in fact the person-affecting theorist can do perfectly well without P, by virtue of the intuition's central thesis that links wronging *simpliciter* and wronging *persons*. P, in other words, gives way to a person-affecting principle of moral permissibility (P*):

P*: *X* is permissible for agents at *t if and only if* no person who exists at or after *t* in *X* is wronged at or after *t* in *X*.

We do *wrong*, in other words, by and only by wronging *people*. If what we do wrongs no then existing or future person, then what we do is not wrong at all.

I think the way Broome goes about things is this: P provides him with a criterion of when a wrong has been done. Then, his theory of when a person has been wronged (should he need one; he may not) would involve (among others) the requirement that a wrong has been done and has had a defined adverse effect on that person. The suggestion that I make here is that we instead understand the person-affecting intuition to proceed from the other direction. It settles first whether someone has been wronged. It then on this basis settles whether a wrong has been done.

Of course, this person-affecting scheme requires a theory of when a person has been wronged—a theory, we might say, of "personal wronging." But there is no good reason to think that a plausible theory of personal wronging cannot be worked out. To be of interest in the current context—to fit within the framework of Broome's argument—such a theory must remain "teleological" or consequentialist. For Broome does not suggest that a rights based person-affecting approach, for example, leads to contradiction. With this restriction in mind, we can begin to speculate here as to the rudiments of such a theory.

2.7   Personal Wronging

In what follows, the first goal will be to begin to sketch a theory of personal wronging, the basic theme of which is that moral law imposes on agents at any time the obligation, with restrictions, for each and every then existing or future person, to bring about the most good that they can for that person. I will first sketch the pertinent principles in a general way in parts 2.7.1–2.7.3 and then sum up the view in part 2.7.6. This theory, which includes the principle P* but excludes PAR* as otiose, provides, as an alternative to Broome's, a new interpretation of the person-affecting intuition. For convenience, I call this alternative interpretation "personalism." Personalism is, as we will see, perfectly competent to address Broome's inconsistency argument and to analyze his problem case (the case of "Deprived"). But we will also see that the set of "maximizing for each person" principles that constitute personalism do not provide a complete theory of personal wronging. Thus, along the way, in part 2.7.4, I will say something about what kind of theory might step into the breach in those cases in which a given issue of personal wronging is left undecided by personalism.

2.7.1 Failing to Maximize Is Sometimes, But Not Always, a Sufficient Condition for Personal Wronging

We do not think that failing to maximize a person's well-being is a *sufficient* condition for personal wronging. Sometimes, there are "trade-offs"—situations, that is, in which one person's well-being can be increased only by way of decreasing someone else's well-being. Suppose, for example, Bill's well-being is maximized in *A* but not *B*, and Paula's in *B* but not *A*. Suppose no one else exists in *A* or *B*, and that no other worlds are accessible to the agents. The theory must not imply, in such a case, that agents are required to maximize the well-being of *both* Bill *and* Paula to avoid wronging them. Joint maximization of well-being on these facts is not an option, and any theory that requires us to do what we cannot do is false. Personalism does not make this mistake. Instead, as noted, at defined points, including with respect to some trade-off situations, personalism hands issues off to an independent theory.

Surprisingly many situations, however, do not involve trade-offs. Suppose that we can but do not increase the well-being of a person *s* at no cost to anyone else. Then, failing to increase *s*'s well-being is merely gratuitous; it serves no purpose. And it is avoidable, given the accessibility of the better-for-*s* world. In this case, it seems plausible that we have wronged *s*. How often we think that such cases arise, of course, will depend on what we take well-being to consist in. Consider, for example, the mother on the subway who is hitting her child. It seems to me that, on any plausible theory of well-being, this situation does not involve a trade-off. The child's well-being might have easily been increased without decreasing the mother's well-being, on any plausible theory of well-being, an iota.

A retributionist, or an equalist, would probably disagree with the view that we wrong someone when we can but do not increase his or her well-being at no cost to anyone else. I will consider their objections in part 2.7.5.

There is one other point that I should make here, a point that will be put to use in chapter 3. I said earlier that a person whose well-being has been avoidably, gratuitously decreased has been wronged. Where, in other words, we can but do not increase a person's well-being at no cost to anyone else, we have wronged that person. What I want to note here is that this principle also applies to the case in which we can but do not increase one person's well-being by refraining from bringing others into existence. Thus, my suggestion is that, with restrictions, we wrong someone if we can but do not increase that person's well-being by refraining from bringing some others into existence to begin with.

2.7.2   Failing to Maximize as a Necessary Condition of Personal Wronging

Though failing to maximize well-being is not a sufficient condition for personal wronging, it is a plausible necessary condition. The contrapositive of this principle provides, of course, a nice, clear defense against certain charges of personal wronging. Agents who have conferred a maximal level of well-being on any person—agents who have, that is, done the best that they could for that person—have not wronged that person. By way of anticipation, I note that in some instances (or so I shall argue in chapter 4 in connection with wrongful life) we can only maximize someone's well-being by *not* bringing that person into existence to begin with. Thus, this exculpatory principle cannot be used to justify imposing on anyone a life that is less than one worth living.

It should be noted that the reference to a person's level of well-being in this context is not merely to a person's well-being *at a time*. Clearly, maximizing a person's well-being at a single moment of that person's life sets too low a standard for exculpation, and maximizing well-being at every instant sets too high a standard. The principle must rather appeal to some notion of how well the person has fared *over the course of his or her entire life*. Lifetime well-being may not be a simple summation of the amounts of well-being accorded to someone during the discrete, finite temporal intervals during which that person lives. Perhaps density of well-being is important; perhaps the well-being at the end of life should be weighted more heavily than earlier well-being. But these are not issues I will be investigating. It is enough here to note that the exculpatory principle refers not to well-being at any, or at every, time, but rather to well-being over the course of a person's entire life.

2.7.3   Wronging the Nonexistent?

Though I do not take up the issue of whether we can wrong a person by bringing him or her into existence until the discussion of wrongful life in chapter 4, this issue can be distinguished from the much easier question, which can be quickly dispensed with here, of whether we wrong those who do not and never will exist. We cannot. Perhaps merely possible people could have had more well-being than they in fact have. Perhaps it is even true that, when we refrain from bringing merely possible people into existence, we opt to accord them less well-being than they might otherwise have. Perhaps, in some sense, not bringing into existence those who never exist at all might be said to *harm* them.[36] But we can distinguish between according to a given person a lower level of well-being when we might have accorded to that person a higher level of well-being—that is, *harming* that person—and *wronging* that person. And I cannot see that we ever wrong someone, by leaving them out of existence or otherwise, who never exists.[37]

Totalism implies that we are morally required in some cases to bring additional people into existence, even in cases in which doing so is bad for others, if doing so creates a greater total net amount of good. But even totalism does not suggest that, when we fail to comply with this moral demand, the wrong that we have done is done to the people whom we ought to have brought into existence. Rather, according to totalism, the wrong is done though no one has been wronged.

2.7.4   Theory of "Fair Distribution"

In some trade-off situations personalism hands over to an independent theory the issue of whether someone whose well-being is avoidably low has been wronged. I refer to this independent theory as a theory of "fair distribution," or "fairness," and understand it to settle issues of personal wronging only in cases in which personalism itself is silent.[38] And, though I won't provide an account of fairness here, I will make a couple of suppositions about it. For one thing, it seems that a suitable theory of fairness may well be person-affecting in nature, in which case it will, like personalism proper, include P*. If this is correct, then the theory will not attempt to settle questions of wrongdoing independently of questions of personal wronging. Rather, the question of personal wronging will come first, and the question of whether a given person has been wronged will be settled by reference to whether that person has been treated fairly. For another thing, it seems that a suitable theory of fairness may have something to do with equality.

I will say something more about equality later. But first let us see how a theory of fairness might apply in a simple trade-off situation. Suppose that in *A* Bill's level of well-being is very high and Paula's very low. In *B*, Paula's level of well-being is greater than it is in *A*, and Bill's level of well-being, though still high, is more nearly equal to Paula's. The higher level of well-being Paula enjoys in *B* is made possible by Bill's *not* leading in *B* quite such a grand existence. Suppose that no other alternatives are available. Personalism proper will then imply that no wrong has been done to Bill in *A* or to Paula in *B*, their well-being having been, in those alternatives, respectively maximized. At the same time, personalism proper leaves open both the issue of whether Paula has been wronged in *A* and the issue of whether Bill has been wronged in *B*. We might nonetheless believe that Paula, having been dealt with unfairly in *A*, has been wronged in *A* and that Bill, having been dealt with fairly in *B*, has not been wronged in *B*. An adequate theory of fairness might be expected to confirm this belief.[39]

Does the fact that personalism is incomplete—and thereby leaves room for an independent theory, such as a theory of fairness—reveal a defect in personalism?[40] I think not. Totalism and averagism are not similarly incomplete. But these more traditional forms of consequentialism are vulnerable to the objection from justice. Thus, according to the totalist view one world is better than another just in case the total good contained in the one world is greater than the total good contained in the other. But it is difficult to see why it is *always* morally impermissible to shift well-being to someone who has less from someone who has more in any case in which doing so reduces total well-being. Thus, the enslavement of individuals, or the prosecution and punishment of a known innocent to quell the fears of a nervous community, will decrease the well-being of some people while, perhaps, increasing the well-being of other people. And there is no guarantee that situations cannot arise in which the morally questionable act—the enslavement of individuals or the ill treatment of the known innocent—will not sometimes produce *more* total well-being than will any alternative act. In such cases, the usual formulations of totalism imply that the morally questionable act is itself morally *obligatory* and that any alternative act is morally *forbidden*.[41] Both these implications seem extremely implausible.[42] In contrast, by remaining silent, personalism leaves room for a more intuitively plausible theory of these cases.

As noted, I will not give an account of fairness in this present work. Nor do we need such an account to address Broome's inconsistency argument. But I do note that it seems plausible that fairness will have something to do with equality. Very roughly, I propose that, in those trade-off situations in which personalism is itself silent, the alternative that creates or magnifies an inequality in well-being wrongs anyone left with less.

A hard case for any "fairness as equality" view is one in which adherence to equality implies that individuals must sacrifice large quantities of well-being. Consider case 2:

Case 2, Efficiency Problem

	X	Y
s_1	2	1
s_2	2	1000

For this distribution of well-being, personalism implies that s_1 is not wronged in X and that s_2 is not wronged in Y (their well-being having been respectively maximized). But personalism is silent on the issue of whether s_1 is wronged in Y or whether s_2 is wronged in X. Personalism turns these issues over to an independent theory, such as a theory of fairness. A fairness as equality view will presumably imply that s_1 is wronged in Y but that s_2 is not wronged in X—*despite* the enormous decrease in well-being s_2 suffers in X. No doubt the huge numeric difference will give us pause, but is this implication obviously false? I think actually not. The burden of proof lies with the proponent of inequality, even in this case. How can it be *obviously* morally preferable that one person should be martyred so that another person may be made extraordinarily well off?

Since perfect equality is not always an alternative, a fairness as equality view will be required to measure degrees of equality. In some instances, it is clear when one alternative better complies with equality than another. Consider case 3:

Case 3, Imperfect Equality

	X	Y	Z
s_1	1	2	3
s_2	6	4	5
s_3	8	9	7

Case 3 represents a trade-off situation, and personalism therefore only partially analyzes it, implying that no subject has been wronged in any alternative in which that subject's well-being has been maximized. Moreover, perfect equality of well-being is not an alternative. Nonetheless, Z would seem, based on any theory of equality, to make individuals more nearly equal than do either X or Y. On these grounds, a fairness as equality view might conclude that, although individuals are wronged in both X and Y, no one is wronged in Z and thus, under P*, that Z alone is permissible.

In case 3, it seems clear which alternative better complies with equality. But there are far more subtle cases.[43] Until we have at hand a consistent and otherwise suitable theory of fairness, personalism remains a kind of conjecture, one whose ultimate acceptance awaits inclusion in a more complete moral theory. At the same time, I note that some usual worries about equality lose their edge when equality is given the limited function that I am suggesting for it here. Thus, Sen writes that "equality is not the only social charge with which we have to be concerned, and there are demands of efficiency [and other aggregative considerations] as well."[44] But personalism *does* value efficiency, in the sense that it demands that we maximize well-being for people in the various ways I have described. The demand for equality comes into play *only* at that point at which personalism proper does not determine whether a given person has been wronged. Thus, in many cases a system of incentives is one vehicle by which the well-being of all, or many, may be increased at a cost to none.[45] According to personalism, we *must* opt for such a system of incentives, even if it produces significant inequalities.

A critic might note that many incentive systems *do* involve a cost to some. Within such systems, it is in part the prospect of having to pay that cost that creates the incentive to work hard. Since some individuals in a free society will undoubtedly opt to forgo incentives available to everyone, the following type of case arises, where the ellipses indicate an indefinite number of people:

Case 4, Incentive Problem

	X	Y
s_1	2	1
s_2	2	5
. . .	2	5
s_n	2	5

Thus, individuals $s_2, \ldots, s_n$ each possess more well-being in Y than they do in X. Personalism, again, only partially analyzes this case. It must therefore turn some issues over to a theory of fairness. But we might anticipate that any fairness as equality view would declare s_1 to have been wronged in Y. And this result might seem objectionable, at least in the case in which it is s_1's own choice not to put forth a certain amount of effort that leads to a decrease in the level of well-being that s_1 has in Y. In view of the benefits the incentive system of Y makes available to all those who do participate in the system—if s_1's hardship is self-inflicted—it is hard to see how s_1 is wronged in Y.

But as described case 4 is a bogus case. If s_1's hardship in Y is self-inflicted, and if this fact is supposed to excuse s_1's lower level of well-being in Y, with the implication that s_1 has not been wronged in Y, then we should be presented with a third alternative—some Z—in which s_1 works *and* achieves the level of well-being that the incentive system is designed to provide to those who work. But we are not. There is no such Z. This means that s_1's participating in the incentive system is not, in fact, an alternative for s_1. Thus, s_1 is more *disabled* than disinclined.

But once we conceive the case along these lines, it becomes far less clear that any valid justification exists for choosing *Y* over *X*.

It is important to note also that, while the fairness as equality view rules out some incentive systems, personalism will itself require other such systems, in particular those that increase the well-being of all, or even some, at a cost to none—those, that is, that do not impose the kind of trade-off we see in case 4. Moreover, it should be kept in mind that even an incentive system that would, unblunted, give rise to trade-offs may be modified so as to provide compensation to those who would otherwise suffer. Then, individuals for whom the incentive system is, for whatever reason, unavailable could be compensated by those who have gained by virtue of their participation in the incentive system.

Equality is a deceptively simple matter, and there is no certainty that personalism's handing off of significant moral issues to a theory of fairness as equality—or any other theory of fairness—will work until we have some consistent and otherwise suitable theory at hand. My intention here has not been to present such a theory but, rather, to point out that personalism, although incomplete, is on the face of it capable of being supplemented in a satisfactory way. Its incompleteness, therefore, at this juncture is far from fatal.

2.7.5 Retribution and Equalization

The view that we wrong someone when we can but do not increase his or her well-being at no cost to others might be considered controversial. Thus, a retributionist might argue that a convicted, incarcerated criminal's low level of well-being is *deserved*, even in cases in which increasing the criminal's well-being could be achieved without decreasing the well-being of anyone else. If the criminal deserves his (say) lower level of well-being, then opting not to increase his level of well-being, the retributionist might claim, does not wrong the criminal. In other cases, an equalist might argue that moral law requires the downward adjustment of one fortunate soul's well-being to a point within range of the well-being experienced by others, even in cases in which such an adjustment helps no one. Such an adjustment, the equalist might claim, does not wrong the person who is avoidably, gratuitously made less well off than he or she might otherwise have been.

It should be obvious that these additional principles of retribution and equalization are *far* more controversial than the approach to fairness that I have just discussed.[46] The theory of fairness, as I have described it, applies *only* in trade-off situations—that is, in situations in which one person's well-being *must* be decreased so that someone else's well-being can be increased. In contrast, claims of retribution and equalization can be raised even in cases in which no trade-off is necessary—in cases, that is, in which the joint maximization of well-being *is* accessible. And it is not at all clear that morality requires retribution, or equalization, when retribution and equalization make *no one* better off.

Broome suggests that the individual theorist has the option to "put together" goods such as "equality" and well-being to determine "overall goodness."[47] Such a theorist might equally "put together" retribution, equalization, and well-being to determine whether a person has been wronged. But for purposes here I will assume that these controversial principles of retribution and equalization are false. If I am incorrect on this point, then a clear accounting of these principles will have to be given another time.

2.7.6   Summing Up Personalism

We can pluck from the foregoing discussion those principles, and some others, that we will need to address Broome's inconsistency argument. For one thing, we cannot wrong anyone who never exists (N*). Where *s* is any person and *X* any world:

N*: *s* is not wronged by agents in *X if s* never exists in *X*.

There is, of course, no implication here that, where *s* ultimately *does* come into existence, conduct engaged in *prior* to *s*'s coming into existence cannot ultimately wrong *s* (though we will want to say that any wrong that is done to *s* is not completed until a time at which *s* exists). Rather, N* merely implies that a wrong to *s* does not occur at all if *s* never exists.

Moreover, a person whose lifetime well-being has been maximized has not been wronged (M*). To establish this condition, we must compare how well *s* fares in the world in question with how well *s* fares in any distinct accessible world. Thus:

M*: *s* is not wronged by agents in *X if*, for each world *Y* accessible to such agents, *s* has at least as much well-being in *X* as *s* has in *Y*.

I should note that I am setting aside here and throughout, as Broome does, the problem of evaluating a particular agent's conduct at a particular time. Of course, the circumstance of every agent acting at every time to maximize well-being over a subject's entire lifetime hardly ever happens in the real world. And thus, in the real world, the conditions of M* will rarely be satisfied. One might propose as a real world analogue of M* something like: an act which, for an agent at a time, produces consequences that are at least as good for a given subject as does any other act available to that agent at that time does not wrong that subject. A difficulty for this formulation is that an agent's conduct may produce better or worse results depending on how other agents conduct their affairs and, perhaps, on chance. But this is not the problem I want to focus on here. Thus, for purposes here, I put aside the issue of how blame is to be allocated and refer simply to the conduct of agents, who, either acting in concert or on their own (jointly or severally), will either maximize or not the well-being of some subject. This approach will be adequate, given the schematic nature of the examples we will be examining. At the same time, these examples, though schematic in nature, will be adequate for making the various points that need to be made.

These two principles, N* and M*, provide sufficient conditions for a person's *not* being wronged. As a final matter, the conditions under which a person *is* wronged need to be stated. Sometimes, but not always, failing to maximize a person's well-being wrongs that person. The "but not always" restriction is needed to avoid an implication of personal wronging in cases in which a theory of fairness will likely excuse an avoidably less-than-maximal level of well-being. Consider D*, which incorporates such a restriction:

> **D*:** *s* is wronged by agents in *X* if *s* exists in *X* and there is some world *Y* accessible to such agents such that:
> (i)   *s* has more well-being in *Y* than *s* has in *X*;
> (ii) for each person *s'* who ever exists in *X*, *either s'* has at least as much well-being in *Y* as *s'* has in *X* or *s'* never exists in *Y*; *and*
> (iii) for each *s'* who ever exists in *Y*, *s'* exists at some time in *X*.

This principle implies that we wrong a person when we can but do not increase that person's well-being if we can do so under two conditions: first, without decreasing the well-being of others or, alternatively, without bringing those others into existence to begin with and, second, without bringing any additional, non-*X* people into existence. The reason for the latter condition is that, although we might well be able to increase *s*'s well-being by bringing additional non-*X* people into existence and according to them a very low level of well-being, our choice *not* to create people whom we then exploit for the benefit of *s* clearly does not constitute a wrong to *s*.[48] Thus, the population of *Y* will be either identical to the population of X or a pared-down version of X. Everyone who exists in Y exists in X, but perhaps not vice versa. When such a Y makes s better off than X does, then, so long as no one who survives the paring down—that is, exists in Y—is worse off in Y than in X, D* implies that s is wronged in X. By earlier assumption, no principle of retribution or equalization excuses our conduct. Thus, D* says, among other things, that the avoidable, gratuitous imposition of misery wrongs the person made miserable.

A handful of restrictions *not* imposed in M* and D* should be noted—not to address Broome's inconsistency argument but rather to address the problem of wrongful life in chapter 4. First, in applying M*, we must review not just those worlds in which s exists but also those worlds in which s does *not* exist; and we must ask with respect to each such world whether s is better off there than in X before we are entitled to infer from M* that s is not wronged in X. I am thus supposing that it is at least possible that s has more well-being in a world in which s does not exist than s actually has. Suppose s's existence in X is unavoidably *less* than one worth living (i.e., is "wrongful") and that s has, in any world in which s does not exist, a zero level of well-being. Under these conditions, s's level of well-being at zero is actually *greater* than s's well-being in X, which is negative. Thus, M* avoids the implication that the person whose life is less than one worth living has *not* been wronged.

A parallel point can be made regarding D*. Depending on other facts, if s's existence in X is *less* than one worth having, so that avoiding s's existence to begin with would have in effect *increased* s's level of well-being, we may infer from D* that failing to do so wrongs s.

The three-place relation expressed by "s has at least as much well-being in X as s has in Y," though not completely defined, has the logical properties one intuitively expects, including transitivity (so that if s has at least as much well-being in X as in Y, and at least as much well-being in Y as in Z, then s has at least as much well-being in X as in Z) and linearity (so that if s has at least as much well-being in X as in Y and at least as much well-being in Y as in X, then s has exactly as much well-being in X as in Y).

I have already noted P*, which links personal wronging with wrongdoing:

P*: X is permissible for agents at t *if and only if* no person who exists at or after t is wronged in X at or after t.

Principles N*, M*, and D*, together with P*, constitute what I will call "personalism" (or sometimes "personalism proper," to clarify a reference to these principles stripped of any fairness doctrine). It seems that, in addition, some other principles may also plausibly be considered components of the basic person-affecting intuition.[49]

2.8　Is Deprived Deprived in *C*?

This statement of personalism can be applied to the example that Broome thinks demonstrates the inconsistency of the person-affecting intuition—that is, the case of Deprived. N* implies that the nonexistent hordes of *A* and *B*, whose numbers in *A* include Deprived, are not wronged in either *A* or *B*. M* implies that no one who exists in *A* or *B* is wronged, since each such person's well-being is there maximized. Finally, since Deprived has more well-being in *B* than in *C*, each other person in *C* is at least as well off in *B* as in *C*, and each *B*-person is also a *C*-person, D* implies that Deprived is wronged in *C*.

This point can be summed up graphically. For any level of well-being *n* that we suppose any person to have at any world, I write "*n**" when personalism implies that the indicated person is *not* wronged at the indicated world, and "*n!*" when personalism implies that the indicated person *is* wronged at the indicated world. Finally, I write "***" when the indicated person never exists at the indicated world and is, in virtue of N*, not wronged at that world. Thus we have:

Case 1, Deprived Example, Annotated

	A	B	C
s_1	5*	5*	5*
s_2	5*	5*	5*
s_3	*	6*	1!

Since no one has been wronged in *A* or *B*, P* implies that *A* and *B* involve no wrongdoing and are permissible. *C*, in contrast, involves a wrong to Deprived and thus under P* is impermissible. Clearly, there is no contradiction. At no point do we find that a world both is and is not permissible, or that a person both is and is not wronged.

Personalism thus supports a set of intuitions Broome lauds.

> [T]he basic intuition says it does not matter whether or not the parents have a child. However, the intuition also says that if they do have a child, they should make sure she is as well off as possible. Put generally, it does not matter morally whether we add a new person to the population (provided her life will be good), but if we do add one, we must do our best for her.[50]

He just thinks we cannot coherently maintain these intuitions, whereas I have argued that we can.

Still, the fact that personalism nicely analyzes a single case does not count much in its favor. Let us consider how personalism addresses two additional cases and then turn to a series of objections.

2.9　Two More Cases

2.9.1　Complex Reproductive Trade-Offs

Part of the Deprived hypothetical was that changes in Deprived's situation from one alternative to the next do not force changes in anyone else's situation. But often this is not the case. Producing another child might be a bad thing for his (say) parents unless they exploit that child in some way. Or producing another child might be a bad thing for an already existing child unless the younger child donates bone marrow to the older child and thereby improves her (say) chances of surviving leukemia. Do these complex reproductive trade-offs raise difficulties for personalism?

Broome suggests that they do.

> Think of this as a problem facing parents who already have one child . . . and are wondering whether to have a second. . . . If they do, they can divide their resources between the children either equally or unequally.[51]

Let us suppose that each of three worlds, A, B, and C, contains both a couple, s_1 and s_2, and their first child, s_3. The first child's well-being, but not her (say) parents', is sensitive to whether a second child, s_4, is produced. And s_4's well-being is in turn sensitive to how his (say) parents and s_3 conduct themselves toward him.[52] Thus:

Case 5, Reproductive Trade-Offs

	A	B	C
s_1	3	3	3
s_2	3	3	3
s_3	5	6	4
s_4		1	4

Broome argues that the person-affecting intuition generates problematic results when applied to this case. Since all those who exist in both A and B are at least as well off in B as in A, but not vice versa, BPAR, taken together with some additional principles that Broome finds plausible, implies that B is at least as good as A. Similarly, A is at least as good as C, since A is likewise at least as good for all those who exist in both. Assuming transitivity, we can also infer that B is at least as good as C. But this result seems false. Independently of BPAR, "it is very plausible to assume [that C is better. C] has more well-being in total, and it has it equally distributed between the two children."[53]

I have disputed Broome's claim that BPAR correctly formulates the person-affecting intuition. Nonetheless, if given the facts of Broome's case personalism taken together with other plausible principles produces a contradiction, then I have a problem. Does it?

First, some quick person-affecting inferences. N* implies that s_4 is not wronged in A since s_4 does not exist in A. Since s_3's well-being has been maximized in B, M* implies that s_3 is not wronged in B. The same is true for s_4 in C. Summing up:

(i) s_4 is not wronged in A.
(ii) s_3 is not wronged in B.
(iii) s_4 is not wronged in C.

Personalism is silent about whether s_4 is wronged in B. But it seems clear that an adequate theory of fairness—and in particular a theory of fairness as equality—would have something to say on this point. Since personalism leaves room for fairness, we can appeal to fairness and assert that:

(iv) s_4 is wronged in B.

Someone having been wronged in B, P* rules B out as a permissible option. We are left, then, with A and C.

First, consider C. We already know that s_4 has not been wronged in C. But what of s_3?[54] D* implies, among other things, that if we can make one person better off while at the same time making no one *who exists* worse off, then we must do so. More precisely: since s_3 has more well-being in A than she does in C, s_1 and s_2 are each as well off in A as they are in C, and s_4 does not exist in A, D* implies that s_3 is wronged in C. Thus we obtain that:

(v) s_3 is wronged in C.

P* thus rules out C as a permissible alternative.

Consider, then, A. It would be a problem for personalism if personalism implied that s_3 is wronged in A and that A—our last remaining option—is impermissible as well as B and C. Personalism, however, avoids this result. D^* does not imply a wrong to s_3 in A, even though her well-being is higher in B. This is because a condition of D^*'s application is that each person—including s_4—who exists in the better-for-s_3 world—B—must also exist in A. And s_4 does not. So D^* does not apply. This restriction is hardly ad hoc: we do not think that we wrong someone s by causing s to have less well-being when the only way we might create more well-being for s is to produce others whom we will then exploit on s's behalf. Possibly one person's well-being could be increased by, for example, producing an entire slave population. But clearly any theory that *requires* this choice is false.

I note, finally, that plausible theories of fairness would not even begin to suggest that there is anything morally suspect about how s_3 has been treated in A. Fairness, indeed, suggests just the reverse. Increasing s_3's well-being requires a distribution of well-being that has already been declared to represent a wrong to s_4. Thus, consistent with personalism and fairness, we may assert:

(vi) s_3 is not wronged in A.

No one having been wronged in A, P^* thus implies that A is permissible.

In summing up, I use "$*$" and "!" as before to show that the indicated person has not, or has, respectively, been wronged at the indicated world. But I also need a way to indicate points where I am speculating about fairness. Thus, I write "n^*?" when I *think* that fairness will imply that the indicated person is *not* wronged at the indicated world and "$n!$?" when I *think* that fairness will imply that the indicated person *is* wronged at the indicated world. Then, the case of the second child is:

Case 5, Reproductive Trade-Offs, Annotated

	A	B	C
s_1	3*	3*	3*
s_2	3*	3*	3*
s_3	5*?	6*	4!
s_4	*	1!?	4*

Personalism's implication that B and C are both objectionable might be disputed. Thus, Broome suggests that we are compelled to the conclusion that C is better than B. Does C have some moral appeal that personalism just misses, some appeal that casts doubt on personalism's implication that C is morally objectionable?

It seems to me that we can agree that C indeed does have a certain appeal without rejecting the prior assessment that C wrongs s_3. According to what I have said, the parents wrong s_3 by choosing C. They ought not to have shifted well-being away from s_3 at a time when s_4 did not exist and need not ever have existed. This wrong to s_3 implies that C is morally objectionable. But suppose that the parents *do* produce s_4. At *that* point, since no one can change the past and undo what the parents have done, A is no longer accessible. Thus, at *that* point, accessible worlds consist strictly of B and C. Applying personalism and, when personalism leaves off, fairness, we plausibly obtain that at *that* point C is permissible and B, which wrongs s_4, is not. Thus, according to personalism, if the parents *do* choose to produce s_4, they have done something wrong. But to avoid *further* wrongdoing, they must distribute well-being between s_3 and s_4 in a fair way. They must, that is, choose C over B. And so in this sense C has a certain appeal over B, but an appeal that does not undermine the earlier assessment of C as objectionable.

This analysis suggests a more general way of accounting for the feeling that C is, in some sense, better than B without contradicting the assessment that both are objectionable. Thus, *if* it were the case that B and C exhausted the agents' accessible alternatives, personalism, taken together with fairness, *would* imply that someone has been wronged in B but not in C. At the same time, since B and C do not exhaust those alternatives, we do not obtain this implication. And so we can consistently maintain the prior assessment that both B and C are, as things stand and given the accessibility of A, objectionable.

P. D. James' novel, *The Children of Men*, explores the human reaction to the prospect of a future without children.[55] It is worth noting that the conclusions I have reached fall far short of suggesting that people should stop having children. My guess is that in parts of the world in which overpopulation is not a problem both parents and any first child are usually made better off, not worse off, by the addition of a second child. Perhaps only in cases in which resources are limited, or the first child has special needs, does a second child actually make things worse rather than better for anyone. In any event, even in cases in which a first child has an interest in a second child's *not* being produced, that interest will not automatically trump interests the *parents* might have in producing the second child.[56]

But what of the third child? The fourth child? It just depends—on how we define well-being and on facts about the parents, the already existing children, and other existing and future people. I doubt that we can make the assumption that more children always make things better for everyone.[57]

2.9.2 Infinite Populations

The second case presents a challenge for totalism. Compare two worlds, each containing an infinite number of people and each containing exactly the same people. Each member of one of the two worlds has twice as much well-being as that very same person has in the other world. Thus, where ellipses indicate an infinite number of people, and assignments of well-being within either of the two worlds do not vary from person to person, we have the following scenario:

Case 6, Infinite Populations

	A	B
...	1	2
s_m	1	2
s_n	1	2
...	1	2

This example comes from Vallentyne and Kagan, who write that "using standard mathematics" the total amount of well-being in each of the two worlds is "the same infinity, and so there seems to be no basis [on finitely additive value theories, including aggregative forms of totalism] for claiming that one is better than the other."[58] But clearly we want to say that *A* is objectionable in a way that *B* is not.[59]

How does personalism analyze this case? Since the well-being of each *B*-person is maximal, M* implies that no such person has been wronged; and P* thus implies that *B* is permissible. Since the well-being of each *A*-person is avoidably less than maximal, and since each *B*-person is also an *A*-person, D* implies that each person in *A* is wronged in *A*. P* implies, then, that *A* is impermissible. Personalism thus compares the two worlds in an intuitively plausible way.

It might be objected that a small adjustment in case 5 produces a problem case for personalism. Consider the case (also from Vallentyne and Kagan) in which the populations are infinite but there is "no meaningful basis for the transworld identification . . . or . . . there is such a meaningful basis but the worlds do not in fact have the same [people]."[60] Suppose that the two worlds have no one in common but that, as earlier, each *B*-person has twice as much well-being as each *A*-person. Then, the well-being of each person in each world is maximal. Given these facts, M* implies that no one has been wronged, and P* implies that no wrong has been done, in either world. Here we have an implication that some theorists may consider at an intuitive level problematic—or even "repugnant." I will return to this kind of case later, in the context of the "repugnant conclusion," in part 3.11.

2.10   Objections to Personalism

2.10.1   Are Suppositions Regarding When Someone Has Been Wronged Question Begging?

In developing personalism, I have relied on a number of suppositions regarding when a person has been wronged. Anyone who takes the view that determining whether a person has been wronged *first* requires a determination of whether agents have acted wrongly (*independently* of wronging any person) will consider these suppositions question begging. But I have meant to suggest here that personalism has us do things in the reverse order. We would first make the determination whether anyone has been wronged. Only then do we, by appeal to P*, determine whether agents have acted wrongly.

Indeed, to outlaw the independent determinations regarding whether someone has been wronged would be question begging in the other direction. Though the rough account of personal wronging that I have given in N*, M*, and D* is—like Broome's—"broad" and "structural," P* takes it for granted that there is a truth of the matter about personal wronging. But this means that we cannot even begin to evaluate P*—that is, to assess its implications—if we are not allowed some plausible suppositions about what that truth is.

2.10.2   Does Personalism Violate Pareto-Plus?

I earlier set aside, as inessential, the task of formulating some PAR* that would order worlds according to a person-affecting sense of the two-place relation "*X* is at least as good as *Y*." Such a PAR* would, in conjunction with Broome's P, in some cases tell us what we might permissibly do. Though setting aside the task as inessential, I did not deny that it could be coherently undertaken. Indeed, as a start on PAR*, I speculated that *X* is at least as good as *Y*, in the person-affecting sense, if no one is wronged in *X* and someone is wronged in *Y*.

Suppose that PAR* constitutes a part of personalism. And reconsider case 1, the case of Deprived. Since no one is wronged in *A* and Deprived is wronged in *C*, it follows from PAR* that in a person-affecting sense *A* is at least as good as *C*. A plausible extension of the principle would be that X is worse than Y if someone is wronged in X and no one is wronged in Y. From this extended principle it follows that C is worse than A.

A critic might note that the result that C is worse than A violates an important Pareto principle, sometimes referred to as "Pareto-plus."[61] According to this principle, X is at least as good as Y if some additional person s exists in X but not Y, s has a positive level of well-being in X, and X and Y are otherwise similar. The critic is correct on this point. Personalism does violate Pareto-plus. But I do not think that the fact that personalism rejects Pareto-plus constitutes a defect of personalism.

Pareto-plus is a fine totalist principle. A statement of totalism that does not conform to Pareto-plus may well be an inadequate statement of totalism. But there is no reason to think that Pareto-plus should be accepted as a constraint on *all* varieties of consequentialist theories. Averagism, for example, rejects the principle. Personalism does as well.

Dasgupta writes that the "principle is so appealing that many philosophers have felt no need to justify it."[62] Perhaps the reason the principle seems so appealing is that we find a second, restricted Pareto principle extremely plausible, according to which if X and Y contain *exactly the same people*, the fact that X is at least as good for each and every one of them as Y is implies that X is at least as good as Y.[63] Since we are firmly committed to the view that everyone in C, including Deprived, has at least as much well-being in C as in A, we might slip easily to the result that C is at least as good as A. How could an extra person who leads a happy life make things *worse*?

But a main tenet of personalism is that the relationship between "X is at least as good *for s* as Y" and "X is at least as good as Y" is complex. No principle within personalism licenses the inference from C's being at least as good *for each person in* C as A is to C's being at least as good as A. Rather, according to personalism, the ranking of worlds is under some PAR* roughly a matter of comparing worlds in respect of the personal wronging they contain. But, as we have seen, the fact that the level of a person's well-being is higher in one world than another does not itself imply that that person has not been in the one world wronged. Thus, according to personalism, though Deprived's well-being is greater in C than in A, C remains the morally lesser world, Deprived's having been wronged in C but not in A.

Is the result that C is the lesser world—despite there being more happy people in C than in A—a harsh result? An ascetic result? A grim result? No. A harsh result would be the implication that it is morally impermissible to bring Deprived into existence to begin with. And the personalist certainly does not countenance that inference. Rather, the implication is that, *if* we bring Deprived into existence, then—since we *can* do better for Deprived at no cost to anyone else—we ought do better for him. Thus, we have two morally permissible alternatives. But *C* is not one of them.

But would Deprived *prefer* to be brought into existence and wronged a little bit than never exist at all? Probably. But we can easily make sense of this preference without committing ourselves to the view that *C* is at least as good as *A*. Thus, Deprived's preference might really just be a recognition that his well-being is higher in *C* than in *A*. Likewise, our well-being in a world in which we exist is higher (at least, likely to be higher) than it is in a world in which we do not exist. Our preferences might be an indication of which world is better *for us*, but they do not by themselves determine, according to personalism, which is, morally, the better world. As we have observed, the relationship between "*X* is at least as good *for s* as *Y*" and "*X* is at least as good as *Y*" is complex; even if the former holds for *each s*, according to personalism the latter may still fail.

The criticism based on Pareto-plus assumes that part of the person-affecting project is to define a person-affecting, two-place sense of "*X* is at least as good as *Y*"—to serve up, that is, some PAR*. For this reason, one might think that an easy alternative way to avoid the specific criticism that we have just considered (and, I think, refuted) would be to abandon the task of defining a person-affecting sense of "*X* is at least as good as *Y*." But this approach does not entirely solve the problem. For the parallel criticism could be formulated in person-affecting terms—that is, in terms that avoid reference to any PAR* and, more generally, the task of defining a person-affecting "*X* is at least as good as *Y*." Thus, a critic might point out that Deprived is not, according to personalism, wronged in *A*. Moreover, *C* clearly is at least as good for Deprived as *A* is. From this the critic might infer that Deprived cannot have been wronged in *C*. For if we have not wronged Deprived by conferring on him *no* well-being, then how can we wrong him by conferring on him *some* well-being?

But this argument is not persuasive. When we think about it, the very idea that our having bestowed on someone some minimal amount of well-being (the "gift of life"?) instead of none at all *suffices* to show we have not wronged that person seems obviously false. Clearly, we wrong no one who never exists. But just as clearly bringing a person into existence, and conferring on that person just enough well-being to make his or her life one worth living, does not imply that we have not wronged that person. We bring a person into existence and take from her (say) what is fairly hers; or we starve her, somewhat; or we sell her into slavery. All these flawed lives may well be worth living, but in each case we have wronged the person whom we have brought into existence. The fact that she is not wronged if she does not exist, alongside the fact that our conduct does not make her life *so* terrible that it is *less* than one worth living, hardly excuses what we have done.

Certainly, rejecting Pareto-plus has its advantages. Dasgupta points out that "there would seem to be a problem with [Pareto-plus]: under fairly weak conditions the Pareto-plus Principle implies the Repugnant Conclusion. Parfit . . . calls this implication the Mere Addition Paradox."[64] Dasgupta goes on to argue that the repugnant conclusion, according to which it is morally permissible to create large numbers of people who enjoy "positive well-being" and have lives that are "good" is not truly "repugnant."[65] Thus, he does not reject Pareto-plus. Nonetheless, denying Pareto-plus provides another way of avoiding at least some versions of the repugnant conclusion. I will return to this point in the context of the nonidentity problem (chapter 3).

At the same time, I note that there is a certain role within personalism for a *modified* Pareto-plus principle. In particular, we should expect that any adequate theory of well-being would satisfy the basic "more is better" thrust of Pareto-plus. Indeed, in formulating N*, M*, and D* in terms of well-being, I have, in effect, already incorporated this modified principle into personalism. I have implicitly assumed, that is, that X is at least as good for s as Y is, if s has at least as much well-being in X as s has in Y. Without this background assumption, there would be little sense in the linkages I have established between personal wronging, on the one hand, and well-being on the other.

2.10.3 Does Personalism Violate the Independence Axiom?

A critic might suggest that personalism violates a principle known as the "independence of irrelevant alternatives," or simply the "independence axiom." Temkin describes the principle as follows:

> For any two situations A and B, to know how A compares to B all things considered, it is, at least in principle, sufficient to compare them directly in terms of each of the factors we care about. In such circumstances, knowing how A or B compare to other alternatives would be unnecessary, and indeed, completely irrelevant to knowing how A and B compare.[66]

The intuition here is that, where someone has already made the judgment that she (say) prefers tennis to swimming on a given afternoon, the information that she might go ballooning instead will not, assuming rationality, change the way she has ranked the options of tennis and swimming.[67]

The independence axiom can be understood as a constraint on any analysis of one world's being at least as good as another. On this understanding, if we think that world X is least as good as world Y given the inaccessibility of some world Z, then we should also think that X is just as good as Y given the accessibility of Z. But a basic tenet of personalism is that whether a person has been wronged in a given world depends critically on whether that person has a higher level of well-being in *some other accessible world*.

To see whether personalism in fact violates the independence axiom, reconsider Broome's problem case—the case of Deprived. By hypothesis, agents can bring about any one of A, B, and C, and the collection of A, B, and C exhausts the worlds that are accessible to the agents. As noted, according to personalism A and B are permissible but C is not. But we can now introduce a second case. This second case stipulates that A and C exhaust the collection of accessible worlds; B is excluded. With the elimination of B as an alternative, C maximizes Deprived's well-being. Personalism implies on these facts that *each* of A and C is permissible. To sum up:

Case	Alternatives	Evaluation in Respect of Personal Wronging
1	A, B, C	A and B are permissible; C is impermissible.
2	A, C	A and C are permissible.

Up to this point, none of the implications I have drawn from personalism conflict with the independence axiom as I have formulated it. These implications avoid conflict with the independence axiom for one very simple—and, one might think, technical—reason: the implications that I have drawn from personalism do not rank worlds in respect of the two-place "X is at least as good as Y" relation to which the axiom appeals. In other words, a violation of the axiom depends on a theory's ranking worlds in accordance with the two-place relationship to begin with. No ranking, no violation.

But a critic might insist that I not stand on this technical reply and, rather, again revive the project of defining a two-place, person-affecting sense of "X is at least as good as Y." We can see why such a revival might at least appear to put personalism in conflict with the independence axiom. I originally speculated that such a person-affecting principle, PAR*, would include that X is at least as good as Y if no one is wronged in X and someone is wronged in Y. And I extended this principle to provide that X is *worse* than Y if someone is wronged in X and no one is wronged in *Y*. Let us here again extend the principle, to provide that *X* and *Y* are equally good if no one is wronged in either *X* or *Y*. Then, with respect to case 1, in which *B* is an accessible alternative, personalism implies that *C* is *worse* than *A* (Deprived having been wronged in *C* but not in *A*). But if *B* is eliminated as an accessible alternative, as it is in case 2, we must also say that *C* is *not* worse than *A* (Deprived's well-being, in case 2, having been maximized in *C*). Thus:

Case	Alternatives	Personalist Ranking of Worlds
1	*A, B, C*	*C* is not at least as good as *A*.
2	*A, C*	*C* is at least as good as *A*.

Now we have generated a case in which worlds are ranked in respect of a two-place relation. Moreover, these rankings appear to conflict with the independence axiom. Clearly, the personalist ranking of *A* and *C* depends on whether *B* is accessible. Thus, if the independence axiom is understood to require that any ranking of worlds must be achieved independently of the accessibility of alternatives, this result violates the independence axiom.

But it is unclear how deep a criticism of personalism this is, in view of the fact that the personalist ranking of worlds that I have just sketched, such as it is, reduces eliminably to matters regarding whether or not those worlds include instances of personal wronging. Why *should* we anticipate, when we understand what the person-affecting ranking of worlds involves and that it involves something other than the total quantities of good contained in the respective worlds, that the ranking will not vary depending on the accessibility of various alternatives? The underlying judgment that whether Deprived is wronged in *C* depends on the accessibility of *B* is one that theorists might be skeptical of or disagree with. But it would be a mistake to think that the judgment is irrational. And it is obvious that the person-affecting ranking of worlds inherits the rationality of that underlying judgment, since it is simply another way of expressing that underlying judgment.

A critic might suggest that any adequate theory *must* provide at least a partial, irreducible, ineliminable ranking of worlds in accordance with a specified two-place relation. But before we conclude that this demand is one to which we should accede, we need an argument, and I know of none.[68] Just the reverse. The reason it might seem that consequentialist theories in general *must* rank worlds in accordance with some specified two-place relation is that consequentialist theories in general include criteria—like P—that link wrongdoing with agents' acting so as to bring about a world that is less than worlds agents might have brought about. But the person-affecting approach links wrongdoing with wronging people. So if we know under what circumstances agents wrong people *independently* of knowing how worlds compare in respect of a specified two-place relation, then we have no need to rank worlds in respect of such a relation to begin with.

A critic will do better suggesting that some important insight is to be gained from the independence axiom that personalism needs fully to incorporate—some insight that my "technical" reply does not fully comprehend. Such a critic might urge that there really is something irrational about changing one's firmly established preference ranking between two alternatives once one learns of the accessibility of some third alternative. With this point I am in complete agreement. But so is personalism. As noted, personalism takes as basic the three-place relation "*X* is at least as good *for s* as *Y*." And the three-place relation conforms perfectly to the independence axiom. Thus, if *X* is at least as good *for s* as *Y* is—that is, if *s* has at least as much well-being in *X* as *s* has in *Y*—this ranking of *X* and *Y* *with respect to s* will not vary depending on whether any *Z* is an accessible alternative. Personalism admittedly takes into account what alternatives are accessible at that point at which it makes a determination of whether *s* has been wronged. But no one thinks that totalism condones irrationality or violates the independence axiom just because totalism cannot make a determination of whether *X is wrong* without information regarding what alternatives are accessible. Likewise, no one should think that personalism condones irrationality or violates the independence axiom just because it cannot make a determination of whether *X wrongs s* without information regarding the well-being *s* has in each alternative to *X*.

Thus, the personalist may take the position that the version of the independence axiom appropriate to personalism is one that places a constraint on how the ranking of worlds *for people* can vary. One might note that the kinds of examples commonly used to motivate the axiom (at least, for philosophers; e.g., the tennis-swimming-ballooning example) more clearly illustrate the personalist version of the axiom (which appeals to the three-place relation) than the version of the axiom that I originally provided (which appeals to the two-place relation). Thus, such examples motivate us to think about a *person* preferring one collection of goods, *X*, to another, *Y*, and to opine that if any rational person really prefers *X* to *Y* his or her mind will not change depending on the availability of some third collection *Z*.

2.11   Pain and Sin

Personalism distinguishes between two concepts: wronging a person and conferring a certain amount of well-being on a person. This distinction is superficially like the lexical thesis that Parfit in *Reasons and Persons* attributes to Cardinal Newman. According to Parfit, Newman thought that "though both were bad, no amount of pain could be as bad as the least amount of sin."[69] "On such a view, there is not a single scale of value. Though there is no limit to the badness of pain, unlimited badness of this kind cannot be as bad as limited badness of another kind."[70] Thus, Parfit contemplates that "no amount of Mediocre lives could have as much value as one Blissful life."[71] Or, as Ryberg expresses the view, the smallest amount of one value "outranks any (even an infinite) amount of" another.[72]

According to Ryberg, this thesis is problematic.

> [C]an trumping be justified? In order to answer this it is not sufficient to compare the century of ecstasy and the drab eternity. Rather we should ask whether we would prefer even the smallest interval of ecstasy to the drab eternity. . . . Or perhaps a day of ecstasy to the drab eternity? Or, to put it differently, does even the smallest amount of Mozart's music outrank an infinite amount of muzak and potatoes? I do not think so.[73]

Ryberg's critique may be correct. But it does not apply to the distinction I have drawn between wronging a person and conferring a certain level of well-being on a person. Ryberg shows that it is implausible to suppose that one *type of well-being* will "trump" another *type of well-being* in every case—that the higher pleasures (Mozart) will always "trump" the lower pleasures (muzak). But that is not at all the distinction I have drawn. My two concepts—of wronging a person, on the one hand, and conferring a certain amount of well-being, on the other— play different roles in the analysis: the judgment that one (the former) is the case is the end result of the normative analysis, whereas the judgment that the other (the latter) is the case is just fodder for that analysis.

I will not claim to understand Newman's original thesis. But *if* we adopt a consequentialist version of sin as the gratuitous, avoidable diminution in someone's well-being *and* we expand pain to include, in general, any diminution in well-being, then we will have a view that sounds much closer to Newman's thesis as Parfit first describes it than to the lexical view that Parfit develops and Ryberg critiques.

Notes

1. Derek Parfit, *Reasons and Persons* (Oxford: Clarendon, 1984) (hereinafter, *RP*), 363.

2. Larry S. Temkin, "Intransitivity and the Mere Addition Paradox," *Philosophy and Public Affairs* 16, no. 2 (Spring 1987): 166.

3. Jan Narveson, "Moral Problems of Population," in *Ethics and Population,* ed. Michael D. Bayles (Cambridge, Mass.: Schenkman, 1976), 73. For a fuller and very clear statement of the person-affecting intuition—and one that illustrates why it is a difficult intuition to give up—see John Broome and Adam Morton, "The Value of a Person," *Proceedings of the Aristotelian Society,* supp. 68 (1994): 167–68.

4. Broome and Morton, "The Value of a Person," 167–68. As noted earlier, this judgment, it seems, assumes that the couple's producing the child is important to no one else (e.g., an older, or future younger, sibling).

5. Clark Wolf, "Social Choice and Normative Population Theory: A Person Affecting Solution to Parfit's Mere Addition Paradox," *Philosophical Studies* 81 (1996): 265.

6. See generally *RP,* 351–79. The puzzle cases include, most notably, the "depletion" case and the case of the "fourteen-year-old-girl"; *RP,* 358–61. Gregory Kavka has contributed to the series, among others, the cases of the "slave child" and the "pleasure pill."

7. *RP,* 378, emphasis added. Partha Dasgupta seems to accept Parfit's reasons for rejecting this principle. See "Savings and Fertility: Ethical Issues," *Philosophy and Public Affairs* 23, no. 2 (Spring 1994): 99–127, 117. Thus, he believes that "the addition of a person with a positive level of welfare [is] a good thing," though he describes a decision-making procedure whereby couples would differentially weight the utilities of existing family members and merely potential family members (116, 121–22). And thus he thinks that "Parfit's Mere Addition Paradox cannot be constructed out of the Pareto-plus Principle if the weight awarded to the well-being of actual people is sufficiently greater than that of potential people" (124). But "each generation is justified in awarding a higher weight to its own living standard when proposing the sizes of all future generations" (125).

8. John Broome, *Counting the Cost of Global Warming* (Cambridge: White Horse, 1992), 19–20.

9. Broome, *Counting,* 22–23.

10. Broome, *Counting,* 27.

11. Broome, *Counting,* 41.

12. Broome, *Counting,* 27. There is a caveat. He writes, "I do not insist on the complete truth of teleology. . . . But I do believe that teleology holds a large part of the truth. . . . I believe that the weighing up of goods and bads goes, at least, a long way towards determining what ought to be done. This is so only because I interpret the notion of good very broadly" (28).

13. Broome, *Counting,* 41–51.

14. Broome, *Counting,* 44.

15. Broome, *Counting,* 44.

16. See part 1.9.2 ("A Person-Affecting Reply to the Nonidentity Problem").

17. Broome, *Counting,* 26–27, 41. Broome sets aside, as I will, the problem of allocating blame or stating conditions under which a particular agent has done

something wrong. Nonetheless, P makes an implicit reference to agency, since accessibility is just accessibility for an agent or collection of agents. Thus, according to P, X is permissible if and only if there is no better world Y accessible to any agent or collection of agents. If X obtains and there is such a Y, the implication is that some agent, or some collection of agents, or perhaps *all* agents, have done something wrong in bringing about X. P also implicitly refers to a world from which other worlds are accessible for an agent or agents. Thus, the world where a meteorite hurtling toward Earth is with the push of a button converted into a feather is accessible from *some* world but not from, for example, the actual world. For our purposes throughout, we can take the world from which others we speak of are accessible to be the actual world. In formulating P and the principles that follow, I rely on Fred Feldman's analysis of the conditions under which a particular agent ought at a time to see to the occurrence of a particular state of affairs. See Feldman, *Doing the Best We Can: An Essay in Informal Deontic Logic* (Dordrecht: Reidel, 1986), 16–44.

18. Broome, *Counting*, 27.

19. Broome, *Counting*, 42.

20. Broome, *Counting*, 41, emphasis added.

21. Broome, *Counting*, 46.

22. Broome, *Counting*, 48, emphasis added.

23. Broome, *Counting*, 44.

24. Discussions of these various conceptions of well-being are cited in chap. 1, note 6.

25. Broome, *Counting*, 48.

26. Broome, *Counting*, 124.

27. Broome, *Counting*, 124.

28. Broome, *Counting*, 124. See also Broome and Morton, "The Value of a Person," 168. Broome expressly formulates a person-affecting sense of "X is better than Y" as a necessary and sufficient condition (*Counting*, 125; "The Value of a Person," 168). But, in view of the fact that we may not abandon our judgment that one alternative is at least as good as another in cases in which there are necessary trade-offs in levels of well-being, the necessary condition should be abandoned. This point was made to me by Roger Wertheimer.

29. Broome, *Counting*, 124.

30. Kenneth J. Arrow, *Social Choice and Individual Values*, 2d ed. (New Haven, Conn.: Yale University Press, 1973), 17. For purposes here and in what follows, it will not be a problem to think of the numerical assignments as encoding the supposition that a given person has more or less or the same level of well-being in one world as he or she has in another. But we should note that thinking of the numerical assignments along these lines may not, as a general matter, be satisfactory. Suppose, for example, that personalism is silent with respect to an issue of personal wronging, and we must turn to a theory of fairness. Then, our judgment that, say, s_1 has been wronged in A may be partly based on the fact that s_1 has just slightly less well-being in B than s_2 has but much less well-being in A than s_2 has. Were the numerical assignments to have only ordinal value, we would not be able to express this difference by reference to a system of numerical assignments.

31. Broome, *Counting*, 129–30 n.22 (citing Temkin, "Intransitivity," 138–87; Partha Dasgupta, "Population Size and the Quality of Life," *Proceedings of the Aristotelian Society* supp. 63 [1989]: 23–54; and Dasgupta, "Lives and Well-Being," *Social Choice and Welfare* 5 [1988]: 103–26). See also Broome, "The Value of a Person," *Proceedings of the Aristotelian Society* supp. 68 (1994): 167–85, 173–75.

32. Broome, *Counting*, 125.

33. Parfit attributes to Narveson the view that "making happy people . . . is . . . morally neutral" (*RP,* 394).

34. Temkin investigates, and rejects, a basis other than the one I sketch in what follows for the conclusion that the existence of the additional person in *C* makes *C* worse than *A*. This would be to argue that it is the *inequality* that *C* displays that makes *C* worse than *A*. "Intransitivity," 141–42. According to this approach, *C* would *not* have been worse than *A*, had Deprived's level of well-being in *C* been, say, 5 rather than 1. But in my view, since Deprived's level of well-being would still be lower in revised *C* than it *need* be—that is, than it is in *B*—the implication that revised *C* would be a permissible alternative is problematic. We turn to a discussion of "equalization" in part 2.7.5.

35. It seems that in rare cases individuals would have been better off never having existed at all. Notably, according to Broome's interpretation, the person-affecting intuition is bound to consider "wrongful life" issues as having nothing to do with moral law. But I will argue (in chap. 4) that the person-affecting intuition in fact provides a helpful way of looking at these issues.

36. I note my discomfort with the three preceding assertions. In the discussion of wrongful life, I will want to say of some people who in fact exist that it would have been better, from their own point of view, that they not have existed. With respect to claims of this kind, no problem with reference exists, for ex hypothesi the people of whom we speak exist. The principle I propose (N*, in what follows) implies that we would not have wronged any such people had we not brought them into existence. But the three assertions made in the text at this note suppose that we can refer to people, at least group-wise, who *never exist at all*. It is unclear to me that reference can be achieved under these conditions.

37. For further discussion, see R. M. Hare, "When Does Potentiality Count? A Comment on Lockwood," in *Contingent Future People*, ed. Fotion and Heller, 9–18, and Michael Lockwood, "Hare on Potentiality: A Rejoinder," in *Contingent Future People*, ed. Fotion and Heller, 19–26.

Of course, if someone exists, to avoid wronging that person agents must conduct themselves in certain ways with respect to that person, including, in some instances, maximizing or at least promoting that person's well-being. But often a way to increase someone's well-being is to bring that person into existence. Does it follow from these two points that agents are, after all, in danger of wronging someone by never bringing that person into existence to begin with? No. For if the person never exists, then agents would have been under no obligation with respect to that person's well-being. There would have been nothing wrong with that choice had agents made that choice. Thus, suppose that a person s exists in a world X and that agents are required to maximize s's well-being because they can do so at no cost to anyone else. It does not follow that agents are required to maximize s's well-being in a world Y in which s does not exist by, among other things, bringing s into existence in Y.

38. Indeed, as noted earlier, I am using the name "fairness" without loss of generality. Thus, although I think it plausible that, when personalism is itself silent, we should appeal to doctrines of fairness, I am in fact leaving this question open.

39. I note that the basic three-place relation described earlier unfurls conveniently to a basic four-place relation in the context of fairness: s has at least as much well-being in X as s' has in Y. But, since I do not attempt to provide a theory of fairness here, there is no need to bring this four-place relation into the discussion in what follows.

40. As Sen writes (*Inequality Reexamined* [Cambridge, Mass.: Harvard University Press, 1992], 134):

> To "complete" partial orderings *arbitrarily* for the sake of decisiveness, or convenience, or order, or some other worthy concern, may be a very misleading step to take. Even when the partial ranking is quite extensively incomplete, the case against "forcing" completeness may be quite strong. Babbling is not, in general, superior to being silent on matters that are genuinely unclear or undecided.

41. Discussions of the objection from justice are included in Broome, *Counting*, 41–44, and Parfit, "Overpopulation and the Quality of Life," in *Applied Ethics*, ed. Peter Singer (Oxford: Oxford University Press, 1986), 161–64. See also Richard B. Brandt, *Ethical Theory* (Englewood Cliffs, N.J.: Prentice Hall, 1959), 407–32, 480–96; and John Rawls, *A Theory of Justice* (Cambridge, Mass.: Harvard University Press, 1971), 22–33.

42. Theorists have proposed revisions of the usual formulations of totalism that seek to address the objection from justice. Broome, for instance, proposes that we can define overall goodness by including aggregate well-being as a good that can be "put together" with other goods, such as "equality" (*Counting*, 41). But since any collection of worlds is completely ordered in respect of aggregate well-being, it is unclear what room is left for equality. Rather, it seems that there will be a continuous and unresolved tension between aiming always for more well-being on the one hand and for more equality on the other. Feldman's reply to the objection from justice, which relies on a concept of value "adjusted for desert," avoids this tension. See his "Justice, Desert, and the Repugnant Conclusion," *Utilitas* 7, no. 2 (Nov. 1995): 197–201; and "Adjusting Utility for Justice: A Consequentialist Reply to the Objections from Justice," *Philosophy and Phenomenological Research* 55 (1995): 567. For further discussion of Feldman's view, see part 3.11.5.

43. For an overview of ways of evaluating inequality, see Sen, *Inequality Reexamined*, 88–101.

44. Sen, *Inequality Reexamined*, 7, 136–38 (on efficiency), and 138–43 (on the incentive argument).

45. See, generally, Sen, *Inequality Reexamined*, 138–43.

46. One might even worry that a principle of equalization is in fact inconsistent with a complete theory of fair distribution. See Ronald Dworkin, "What Is Equality? Part I: Equality of Welfare," *Philosophy and Public Affairs* 10, no. 3 (1981): 217–18.

47. Broome, *Counting*, 41.

48. Of course, if s's well-being is increased by bringing non-X people into existence whose level of well-being is itself maximal, then assuming the other conditions of D* are satisfied we might well conclude that the failure to increase s's well-being wrongs s.

49. For one such principle, see the preceding note.

50. Broome and Morton, "The Value of a Person," 175.

51. Broome and Morton, "The Value of a Person," 170

52. This case is, in substance, the case Broome sketches in Broome and Morton, "The Value of a Person," 170 ("Example 2").

53. Broome and Morton, "The Value of a Person," 171.

54. One might think that we could answer this question by making a second appeal to fairness. But we cannot, for two reasons. First, as we will see, personalism is not silent on the question of whether s_3 is wronged in C; and so the appeal to fairness would be unnecessary—and, based on the present scheme, which gives priority to personalism and invokes fairness only in those trade-off situations in which personalism is silent—illegitimate. Second, an appeal to fairness does not—in the absence of some further argument that eliminates A as a permissible alternative—in fact produce the result that s_3 is *not* wronged in C. Thus, the argument that fairness implies that s_3 is not wronged in C would have to include some such view as this: if s_3's lower level of well-being in C is *required* for a fair distribution of well-being, then it does not represent a wrong done to s_3. But the facts of the case—depending on how we ultimately understand fairness—might fail this condition. For, though well-being is unfairly distributed in B, it is plausible that well-being has been fairly distributed not just in C but *also in A*. Why might we think that well-being has been fairly distributed in A as well as C, given the greater distance in A between the well-being of s_1 and s_2 on the one hand and s_3 on the other? The idea is that s_1 and s_2, whose well-being has been maximized in A, have not, according to M*, been wronged in A. And we cannot—at least, we cannot consistent with the present scheme, which gives priority to personalism and invokes fairness only in those trade-off situations in which personalism is silent—revisit this judgment under the guise of fairness. Thus, we cannot—and, I think, do not want to—say now that s_1 and s_2 have been dealt with unfairly, and therefore wronged, in A. But if this is correct, then s_3's lower level of well-being in C is *not* required to satisfy the demands of fairness. A does that job as well as C does.

55. P. D. James, *The Children of Men* (London: Faber & Faber, 1992).

56. Things may be quite different in parts of the world that are overpopulated; perhaps having even a single child, in some parts of the world, or at some future time, will cause someone else to be hungry. But even here it may well be that the morally correct solution is *not* for people to stop having children in these regions but rather for resources to be diverted from regions that are better off.

57. Consider, for example, Doris Lessing's *The Fifth Child* (New York: Knopf, 1988). *That* child, according to personalism, we may want to avoid. Having said this, I hasten to add that once such a child exists he or she counts for moral purposes, and we are faulted if we do not distribute well-being to this child in a right way.

58. See Peter Vallentyne and Shelly Kagan, "Infinite Value and Finitely Additive Value Theory," *Journal of Philosophy* 44, no. 1 (Jan. 1997): 6.

59. Vallentyne and Kagan propose an intuitively plausible totalist device for evaluating worlds that implies that *Y* is indeed better than *X*. See "Infinite Value," 9–21.

60. Vallentyne and Kagan, "Infinite Value," 18.

61. Partha Dasgupta, *An Inquiry Into Well-Being and Destitution* (Oxford: Clarendon, 1993), 383. Here, Dasgupta refers to a slightly stronger principle, according to which extra people leading happy lives make one world *better* than another, otherwise similar world.

62. Dasgupta, *An Inquiry*, 383.

63. The difference between what we have called "Pareto-plus" and this second Pareto principle is that this second principle presumes that the worlds to be compared are "same person" worlds. Assuming we do not include as part of personalism such principles as retribution and equalization, personalism conflicts only with Pareto-plus and not with this second Pareto principle.

64. Dasgupta, *An Inquiry*, 383. See also Parfit, *RP*, 419–41. The mere addition paradox actually appeals to a slightly weaker principle than Pareto-plus, according to which extra people leading happy lives do not make one world *worse* than another, otherwise similar world (*RP*, 425–26).

65. Dasgupta, *An Inquiry*, 385.

66. Temkin, "Intransitivity," 159–61. See also Kenneth J. Arrow, *Social Choice and Individual Values*, 2d ed. (New Haven, Conn.: Yale University Press, 1973), 26–28.

67. This example is derived from an anecdote involving Sidney Morgenbesser that David Luban describes ("Social Choice Theory as Jurisprudence," 69 *Southern California Law Review* 521: 532–33 [1996], citing Keith Lehrer, "Metamental Ascent: Beyond Belief and Desire," *Proceedings of the American Philosophical Association* 63 [1989]: 19, 21–22).

[Morgenbesser] went into an Upper West Side restaurant and asked the waitress about the breakfast offerings.

Morgenbesser: I would like a roll or something, what have you got?
Waitress: I have a sweet roll or a bagel.
Morgenbesser: I'll have a sweet roll.
Waitress: I forgot. We also have onion rolls.
Morgenbesser: Oh, in that case I'll have a bagel instead.

68. Compare Tyler Cowen, "What Do We Learn from the Repugnant Conclusion?" *Ethics* 106 (July 1996): 760–61 (regarding the axiom of the "universal domain").

69. Parfit, *RP*, 413.

70. Parfit, *RP,* 414.

71. Parfit, *RP,* 414. For a more detailed discussion of the lexical, or "discontinuity," thesis, see Parfit, "Overpopulation and the Quality of Life," 145–64.

72. See Jesper Ryberg, "Parfit's Repugnant Conclusion," *The Philosophical Quarterly* 46, no. 183 (April 1996): 211.

73. Ryberg, "Parfit's Repugnant Conclusion," 211.

Chapter 3

The Nonidentity Problem

3.1 What Is the Nonidentity Problem?

3.1.1 Causing Pain and Saving Lives

Some of the things we do that might in other contexts seem clearly wrong in fact can be easily excused, or justified. Consider, for example, the imposition of "grievous bodily harm."[1] If the agent is a surgeon and the "grievous bodily harm" that is imposed is a matter of cutting into someone's chest in order to save her (say) life and if the life saved is one that is worth living, then what the surgeon has done is unobjectionable. Though he (say) has without a doubt caused the patient to suffer pain and other forms of ill-being, he has not harmed her in any sense that is "morally relevant."[2] This assessment seems correct even if the patient never had the chance to consent to the invasive procedure, having, perhaps, fallen unconscious while walking the dog. Thus, Parfit writes, "There is no objection to our harming someone when we know both that this person will have no regrets, and that our act will be clearly better for this person."[3]

In coming to the conclusion that the surgeon has not wronged the heart patient, we might be relying on something like the person-affecting principle M*:

M*: s is not wronged by agents in X *if*, for each world Y accessible to such agents, s has at least as much well-being in X as s has in Y.

Though the patient must undergo a painful recuperation, the surgeon may nonetheless have done the very best for her that he could have done. Others may fare better than she does; perhaps their hearts are healthier. But her well-being may in effect be capped by the condition of her heart. Suppose, then, that the surgeon has done the best for her that anyone could have done, given the condition of her heart and within the constraints of modern medical technology. The surgeon has thus done what he can do to maximize her well-being; there is no world accessible to him in which that very same person enjoys any greater amount of well-being. Given these suppositions, M* implies that the surgeon has not wronged the patient. Assuming that the patient is not otherwise wronged (say, later in life, by the surgeon or some other agent) and that no other existing or future person is wronged, according to P* no wrong has been done at all.

But suppose, on the other hand, that the surgeon has not really done quite the best for his patient that he might have. Suppose, for example, that he could have equally well treated her heart condition by prescribing a wonderful new drug—a drug that is nearly risk-free *and* highly effective. Perhaps he has not been keeping up with the medical literature and is unaware of the availability of this new drug. The surgeon might defend what he has done by claiming, accurately I think, that his performing the heart surgery saved the patient's life. The surgery was, after all, one link in a causal chain that concluded in her recovery. More well-being having been created for her than ill-being, the surgery creates consequences for her that are, on a net basis, positive. But an advocate for the patient might still think that she was wronged when the surgeon performed the heart surgery and imposed pain and other forms of ill-being that were not necessary to her recovery. This assessment of his conduct is consistent with M*, which does not excuse conduct in any case in which an individual's well-being has not been maximized. Moreover, we should recall D*:

D*: *s* is wronged by agents in *X if s* exists in *X* and there is some
world *Y* accessible to such agents such that:
(i)   *s* has more well-being in *Y* than *s* has in *X*;
(ii) for each person *s'* who ever exists in *X, either s'* has at least
as much well-being in *Y* as *s'* has in *X or s'* never exists in
Y; *and*
(iii) for each *s'* who ever exists in *Y, s'* exists at some time in *X*.

Depending on other facts, D* will imply that the surgeon *has* wronged the patient. Thus, suppose that prescribing the medication rather than performing the surgery could have been effected at no cost to anyone else. D* then implies that the surgeon's failure to do better for the patient than he has in fact done constitutes a wrong to her.

3.1.2 Causing Pain and Creating Lives

In the heart surgery case, an act is performed that is, on its face, *morally suspect*. Surgery is violent and causes pain and other forms of ill-being. But if the best that can be done has been done for the patient—if, for instance, there is no drug that obviates the need for surgery—M* implies that the surgery, morally suspect or not, does not in fact wrong the patient.

But now consider an act that does not *save* an existing person's life—the patient's—but rather *creates* a new person. Such an act is a link in a causal chain that concludes in the coming into existence of a new person. Suppose that the new person's life is, though worth living, flawed by this very act of creation. And suppose that no alternative, *better* means of bringing this person into existence was available. Suppose, in other words, that no other world was accessible to agents in which this very same new person enjoys any greater level of well-being. Based on these facts, M* implies that the performance of this act does not wrong this person. Assuming that this person is not otherwise wronged (say, later in life) and that no one else has been wronged, P* implies that nothing wrong has been done at all.

These implications may not themselves disturb anyone. So what, one might well ask, that personalism generates the result that agents have not wronged the happy, if not *perfectly* happy, people whom they have caused to exist and for whom they have done their best? So what that, in the absence of any wrong to any other person, personalism generates the result that agents have done nothing wrong at all?

But there is more to the nonidentity critique of the person-affecting intuition than this. To see the full thrust of the critique, it is necessary first to reflect on the phenomenon Kavka refers to as the "precariousness" of existence.[4]

3.1.3 The "Precariousness" of Existence

Some morally suspect acts—acts that cause pain and other forms of ill-being—have the effect of creating new lives, just as some such acts have the effect of saving old lives. But there is a distinction. The existence of the person *already* in existence is not, in general, sensitive to the little things in life. Once one exists, whether one's parent is away on business one week rather than the next does not normally threaten one with nonexistence. Even in the heart patient case, survival, though threatened, may well be independent of whether the surgery is performed in one hospital rather than another, by one surgeon rather than another, five minutes earlier or five minutes later.

In contrast, whether any given person's life is *created* is highly sensitive to the endless minutiae of history.[5] Consider with what ease our own coming into existence could have been forever derailed. Imagine how simply one parent might have chosen to attend one college rather than another or to take one job rather than another and then have missed altogether ever even meeting our other parent. And our parents being safely married hardly secures our own existence. Any little change in the sequence of events that in fact culminated in our own existence may well have tagged us forever as mere possibilia. For any little business trip or other difference in how things as a matter of fact unfolded might well have meant the insemination of one egg rather than another or the insemination by one sperm rather than another. But any substitution in the egg and sperm involved in our own conception might well have meant that *we* would never have come into existence at all.[6] Though our parents, once their existence and their partnership are fixed, perhaps would have produced between them *other* children had things been other than they in fact were, it is very unlikely that they would have produced *us*.

Who lives is thus a matter highly sensitive to such facts as when conception occurs, even how it occurs, and certainly between what parties it occurs. And these facts are themselves highly sensitive to the vast sea of history. Suppose that Hitler had died earlier in the course of World War II or that the Allies had taken a few years longer to win the war than they did. Then, half the readers of this book would never have been born at all. Their parents would never have met and married; and even had they met and married, they would not have had children precisely when they did. *Other* readers might have lived in their stead, and this distinct population might have then been scrutinizing some book or another. But they would very likely not have been scrutinizing this book by this author. Each of us, in effect, just missed nonexistence.

3.1.4   The Nonidentity Problem

Just how does the "precariousness" of existence challenge the person-affecting intuition? The phenomenon reveals that acts of an enormous variety bring people—more precisely, bring some people rather than some other people—into existence. Some of these acts are acts—like having sex at a certain time and place with one person rather than another—that are related in some obvious way to successful procreation. Acts in this category do not, we think, themselves normally *hurt* or *damage* those individuals they function to create. But other life-creating acts *do* seem hurtful or damaging to those very people whose lives they create. If personalism compels the conclusion that life-creating acts *never* wrong those whose lives they create so long as those lives are worth living, then personalism would seem to be seriously defective. For, as we will see, *some* of these acts *are* clearly wrong. And the result that some acts are "bad" though "bad for" no one flies in the face of the person-affecting intuition.[7] It is this challenge that Parfit labels the "nonidentity problem."[8]

But the nonidentity problem successfully challenges the person-affecting intuition *only if* it is clear that there *are* cases in which no one has been wronged even though a wrong has been done. Thus, we must examine the cases that Parfit claims prove this point. We will take them in two lots, a first group in part 3.2 and a second group in part 3.3.3. I will argue that with respect to none of these cases do we reach the critical judgment: that no one has been wronged though a wrong has been done.

According to Parfit, the nonidentity problem establishes the need for a theory that does not "take a person-affecting form."[9] Indeed, for Parfit, the nonidentity problem provides a basis for favoring totalism over any person-affecting approach. But totalism is, as we have seen and will see again, itself an imperfect view. Thus, whether the nonidentity problem presents a serious challenge to the person-affecting intuition may well be critical to how we ultimately compare totalism and personalism and which we in the end find more plausible.

But the nonidentity problem does not just target personalism and other forms of person-affecting consequentialism. Deontic and rights-based person-affecting approaches are equally targets, since they too connect wrongdoing and wronging people.[10] Most generally, anyone who accepts the nonidentity problem is thereby challenged to construct an otherwise plausible theory that explains how an act can be both "bad" *and* "bad for no one."[11] If bad for no one, then on what grounds bad at all? If wrong for no one, then on what grounds wrong at all? Of course, if the critical judgment—that no one has been wronged though a wrong has been done—is never reached, then there is no such challenge. We turn, then, to the cases that are intended to compel this judgment.

3.2   Three Nonidentity Cases

3.2.1   The "Depletion" Case

Parfit writes:

Suppose that we are choosing between two social or economic policies. And suppose that, on one of the two policies, the standard of living would be slightly higher over the next century. This effect implies another. It is not true that, whichever policy we choose, the same particular people will exist in the further future. Given the effects of two such policies on the details of our lives, it would increasingly over time be true that, on the different policies, people married different people. And, even in the same marriages, the children would increasingly over time be conceived at different times. As I have argued, children conceived more than a month earlier or later would in fact be different children. Since the choice between our two policies would affect the time of later conceptions, some of the people who are later born would owe their existence to our choice of one of the two policies. If we had chosen the other policy, these particular people would never have existed. And the proportion of those later born who owe their existence to our choice would, like ripples in a pool, steadily grow. We can plausibly assume that, after three centuries, there would be no one living in our community who would have been born whichever policy we chose.[12]

One of the policy choices that Parfit considers is a choice between depletion and conservation of important natural resources. Suppose that, if we choose depletion, "the quality of life over the next three centuries would be slightly higher than it would have been if we had chosen [c]onservation. But it would later, for many centuries, be much lower than it would have been if we had chosen [c]onservation."[13] Suppose that we choose depletion. Given the sensitivity of population identity to the vast sea of history (the "precariousness" of existence), the future people who live as a result of our having chosen depletion would not have lived at all had we chosen otherwise. And, though flawed by the scarcity of resources, their lives will be worth living. Parfit concludes that our choice "will not be worse for anyone who ever lives"; it is not, he writes, "against the interests of future people."[14] At the same time, he believes, we do have a "moral reason" *not* to choose depletion.[15] "Before we consider cases of this kind, we may accept the view that what is bad must be bad for someone. But the case of depletion shows, I believe, that we must reject this view."[16]

3.2.2   The "Slave Child" Case

The depletion case involves a choice that affects enormous numbers of people living in the distant future. In contrast, the "slave child" case that Kavka describes involves a choice of whether a single individual will be brought into a flawed existence within the agents' own lives. Kavka writes:

In a society in which slavery is legal, a couple that is planning to have no children is offered $50,000 by a slaveholder to produce a child to be a slave to him. They want the money to buy a yacht. Should they sign the agreement, accept the money, and produce the child[?] . . . On the assumption that life as a slave is better than never existing, their doing so would not harm the child. For if they turned down the slaveholder, they would either produce no children or—if they later changed their minds about becoming parents—produce *other* children.[17]

The couple on the yacht "could not have bestowed a better lot on *him* (or *her*). . . . But acting in this manner is outrageous. Surely it would be wrong for the couple to produce a slave child and to attempt to justify their action in this way."[18] Though the child has not been "harmed," according to Kavka, some wrong has clearly been done.

3.2.3   The "Pleasure Pill" Case

Kavka provides a final example. He envisions

a pill that, when taken just before sexual relations, has two effects. It heightens the pilltaker's sexual pleasure a tiny bit and insures that any child conceived would be mildly handicapped. As pausing to take the pill would change who is conceived, and as existence with a mild handicap is not bad on the whole, no one would be rendered worse off if a prospective parent not using contraceptive devices were to take the pill before sex.[19]

Kavka suggests—and surely we agree—that taking the pill in this context is wrong. At the same time, according to Kavka, no one is "rendered worse off" by the morally suspect act.

These three cases have common elements. Each begins with a morally suspect act—an act, that is, that produces pain and other forms of ill-being. In each case, the morally suspect act is causally linked to the subject's existence—that is, to a life that is, though flawed, worth living. And so it seems right to say that, despite the ill-being that has been created for the subject, the amount of well-being that has been created for the subject is on a net basis positive. Finally, in each case it seems correct to say that some wrong has been done. The question, then, is whether the person-affecting intuition compels the conclusion that the subject has not been wronged by the morally suspect, life-creating act.

3.3   A Person-Affecting Account of the Nonidentity Cases

3.3.1   An Appeal to "Doing the Best One Can"

The nonidentity problem appears to rely on something like the person-affecting principle M*:

M*: *s* is not wronged by agents in *X if*, for each world *Y* accessible to such agents, *s* has at least as much well-being in *X* as *s* has in *Y*.

For it seems natural to analogize the nonidentity cases to the first version of the heart surgery case in which the surgery is necessary to save the patient's life and no drug is available that obviates the need for surgery. Since the patient's life is worth living and that life could not have been saved had the surgeon not performed the surgery, M* implies that the surgeon has therefore not wronged the patient.

At various points in their texts, Parfit and Kavka suggest that something like M* is critical to generating the nonidentity problem. Thus, Parfit describes conduct that, he thinks, is not ultimately "bad for" anyone as "a *necessary part* of the cause of the existence of the people killed by the catastrophe."[20] And Kavka includes in the description of the slave child case that the couple on the yacht "*could* not have bestowed a better lot" on the child.[21] At other points, Parfit and Kavka suggest other ways of interpreting the nonidentity problem, and I will in due course consider these other interpretations. But I begin with M*.

According to M*, a given person is wronged *only if* agents have failed to do the very best that could have been done for that person—only if, that is, agents have failed to maximize that person's well-being. Where the best that can be done *has* been done, M* implies that the person has not been wronged. But I shall argue that if the nonidentity problem is understood to appeal to something like M*, then we cannot—contrary to what Parfit and Kavka anticipate—pull from the facts of the nonidentity cases the problematic inference that no one has been wronged.

To demonstrate this point, it will be useful to distinguish two types of cases. In cases of both types, a person *s* has an existence that is, though worth living, flawed in some way. I will call "type 2-alt" (for "two-alternative") those cases in which there is no accessible world that is *better* for *s* than *s*'s actual, flawed world; *s*'s actual level of well-being is, in other words, at least as great as *s*'s level of well-being in any other accessible world. At the same time, agents could have brought it about that *s* never existed to begin with. Thus, in type 2-alt cases, *s*'s options are limited to (1) a flawed existence and (2) no existence at all.

The following would be an example of a type 2-alt case. Here s_3 is the nonidentity victim, and I write, as earlier, "*n**" to show no wrong done to the indicated individual at the indicated world.

Case 7/Type 2-Alt Nonidentity Problem, Annotated

	A	C
s_1	5*	5*
s_2	5*	5*
s_3	*	1*

M* together with N* implies that no one has been wronged in either *A* or *C*. And P* implies that both alternatives are permissible.

I will call "type 3-alt" (for "three-alternative") those cases in which there is at least one accessible world that is better for *s* than *s*'s actual, flawed world. In type 3-alt cases, the subject's options thus are expanded, to (1) a flawed existence, (2) no existence at all, and (3) some *better* (i.e., relatively unflawed) existence. In this kind of case, the fact that a better existence is available for the subject means that M* does *not* justify the agents' imposing on the subject the lesser existence, for M* implies no wrong to the subject only when the subject's well-being has been maximized. Again writing "*n**" to show no wrong done, we have a case identical to the Deprived example from Chapter 2:

Case 1/Type 3-Alt Nonidentity Problem, Annotated

	A	B	C
s_1	5*	5*	5*
s_2	5*	5*	5*
s_3	*	6*	1

It is clear that M* implies the results that Parfit and Kavka anticipate only if the nonidentity cases are understood to be type 2-alt cases. For M* absolves the agent only when there is no third alternative in which the subject enjoys a relatively unflawed existence. But how plausible is the assumption that the nonidentity cases are type 2-alt cases?

We can suppose about the slave child case that the couple *could* not have entered into the agreement and then, once the child is born, have breached it or had it voided as illegal. The best version of the case is one in which it is a given that, once the agreement is signed, any child born to the couple is, irrevocably, a slave. But even given this supposition, how could it be that this child, in fact born a slave, *could* not have been brought into existence *without* the agreement's being entered into and thus *could* not have existed as a *non*slave? Humans, perhaps, cannot be born as nonhumans. Nor is there any accessible world in which people are not subject to the laws of, say, gravity. But being conceived pursuant to a commercial contract—and thus born a slave—is surely a mutable characteristic. It is like being conceived in Maine. The very same person in fact conceived in Maine could have been conceived in Ohio instead.

The same questions can be raised about the other nonidentity cases. How plausible is it that there is *no* accessible world in which *some* member of an impoverished future population in the depletion case enjoys ample resources? The ill-being in this case is presumably a function of the excessive size of the future generation. This means only that not *all* members of the future generation *could* have existed without resources being spread very thinly across the population. But it does not mean that *some* member could not have existed had resources not been spread so thinly. All that is needed, to avoid the implication from M* that depletion wrongs *no one*, is an accessible world in which at least one member of the depleted world enjoys greater resources and a correspondingly higher level of well-being. Since agents have many possible ways of implementing a conservationist policy, at least one of these ways is sure to produce an accessible world that meets this condition.

And how plausible is it that *no* accessible world exists in which the "mildly handicapped" child is born healthy in part because the child's parents refrain from taking the pleasure pill? The parents, Kavka says, "pause" to take the pill and so produce a particular child. But, regardless of what they *would* have done, *could* they not have, equally well, instead "paused" to contemplate the mysteries of human sexuality and then proceed to produce exactly the same child—*sans* handicap— they in fact produced?

As their authors describe them, these three nonidentity cases seem on reflection to be type 3-alt cases. But if the person-affecting principle the nonidentity problem appeals to is M*, then the nonidentity problem is invalid. For if the cases are type 3-alt, then the subjects' well-being has not been maximized and we cannot pull from the facts, by application of M*, the inference that the subject has not been wronged. Quite the contrary. Depending on the facts, D* implies that the subject *has* been wronged.

3.3.2   An Equivocation

A critic might think that I have misunderstood the nonidentity cases. Perhaps it is intended that the cases be *stipulated* to be type 2-alt cases.

So understood, the options open to the victims in each case are limited to (1) a flawed existence and (2) no existence at all. According to this interpretation, there is no accessible world in which the very same child has more well-being than that child in fact has as a slave. And according to this interpretation, the policies of conservation and depletion comprise exactly two discrete choices reflecting exactly two well-defined outcomes with populations that to a member do not overlap. But if this is the case, then by hypothesis there are *not* many possible ways of implementing a conservationist policy, and we cannot argue that surely one of those ways will give rise to a world in which at least one member of the depleted world enjoys greater resources and a correspondingly higher level of well-being.

If the nonidentity cases are stipulated to be type 2-alt cases, then M* implies the results avoided earlier and thus excuses, under P*, the kind of conduct that I earlier conceded was wrong. However, if the nonidentity cases are stipulated to be type 2-alt cases, then the nonidentity problem becomes vulnerable on another front. As type 2-alt cases, the nonidentity cases suppose that no matter how the child's parents conducted themselves they *could not* have brought the child in fact born a slave into existence as a nonslave. Consider, for example, a world in which the couple do not sign the agreement and then proceed to have *exactly* the same sex on *exactly* the same schedule as they do in the world in which the child is born a slave. *Exactly* the same ovum is then fertilized by *exactly* the same sperm. A nonslave child is ultimately born, who appears and behaves (at least initially) exactly like the slave child appears and behaves. But since the slave child case is stipulated to be a type 2-alt case, the nonslave child in the one world cannot be identical to the slave child in the other.

However implausible, this result is just a given if the nonidentity cases are taken to be type 2-alt cases. But then it should be obvious that, if the nonidentity cases are taken to be type 2-alt cases, these cases are *highly artificial* in a way their authors nowhere expressly recognize. Thus, the cases involve an equivocation of sorts. Imagining each case set in a world much like that which we know, we quickly make the judgment that some wrong has been done. But we are then expected to maintain that judgment even upon imaginatively shifting the case from a world much like that which we know to a world that is not really very like our own at all. The difference is with respect to accessibility. For accessible to any world at all like our own *is* some way of improving the lot of the slave child (just as there is some way of conceiving the child in fact conceived in Maine in Hong Kong). It seems to me that our initial judgment that some wrong has been done becomes at this juncture of the analysis unstable. *If* we can manage to reconceive the nonidentity cases as type 2-alt cases, it then becomes extremely murky whether any wrong has in fact been done.

In the end I believe that the nonidentity cases examined so far are best understood as type 3-alt cases and are probably intended by their authors to be understood in that way. The depletion case, the slave child case, and the pleasure pill case cannot in any natural way be conceived of as anything other than type 3-alt cases. And our intuitions remain firm only if the cases that we are relying on to generate these intuitions are as we grasp them to be and not obscure or ambiguous in some way that is arguably of moral significance.

3.3.3   More Nonidentity Cases: Parfit's "Two Medical Programs" Case

But the critic's case can be pushed harder. For it seems that cases involving morally suspect, life-creating acts can be described that, in contrast to the three cases we have already considered, are naturally understood as type 2-alt cases. Consider a woman who opts to become pregnant even though she knows that any child she produces will have a substantial risk of inheriting a genetically-based mild familial disorder, perhaps a mild digital deformity. Perhaps, indeed, the woman *knows* that any child conceived, say, this month will in fact suffer this deformity. Plausibly, this particular child could not exist and not be afflicted in the way described (the technology for "fixing" the genetic abnormality not being yet available). Does the woman do something wrong when she nonetheless *chooses* to have this child? Does she do something wrong by *not* waiting until next month to conceive? Does she do something wrong by *not* opting to use a donor egg rather than this one? If she is already pregnant, does she do something wrong by *not* taking the "morning-after pill" or otherwise having a very early abortion, and then in a month or two conceiving a perfectly healthy, but distinct, child? An assumption in each nonidentity case is that the woman's choice to have the child affects one way or the other and wrongs no other already existing or future person, including the woman herself. A second assumption is that the child's life is worth living. In the context of this type 2-alt case, if the woman has done something wrong I do not see it. The case strikes me as analogous in all significant respects to the heart case: though the patient suffers a certain amount of ill-being as a necessary consequence of the open-heart surgery, we do not think that performing the surgery wrongs her or that, under the assumption that she is not otherwise wronged and that no one else is wronged, any wrong has been done at all.

But suppose that the condition that afflicts the woman's child is

more serious than a mild digital deformity. The condition must be obviously not so serious that we have any question about whether the
child's life is worth living since, if the life is *less* than worth living, other
person-affecting grounds exist for declaring a wrong to the child done.
Perhaps the condition is a form of mild mental retardation. As in the
original case, the child cannot exist and not suffer the condition at
issue. And, as in the original case, it must not matter to anyone else
whether the afflicted child exists instead of a later-born healthier child.
The critic of the person-affecting intuition will urge that in this case it
is implausible to think that no wrong has been done; for here we have,
not a child who suffers in various ways from a mild digital deformity,
but a child who suffers in more extreme ways from a more serious
condition. But it remains unclear to me that the switch from a mild
digital deformity to a more serious condition makes any moral difference when it remains the case that the woman's choice represents the
best that could have been done for the child, the child's life is evidently
worth living, the child is not otherwise wronged (say, later in life), and
no one else is wronged at all (by, say, having to bear the burden of the
child's condition).

This case derives from Parfit's "two medical programs" case.[22] In
Parfit's example, we must choose between two options, which I will
refer to as "J" and "K."

J: Option J involves treating a thousand women who are pregnant for a rare condition. The treatment will prevent the babies
these women will ultimately give birth to from having a "certain handicap." But option J will also involve leaving other
women, who are not yet pregnant, untested for an untreatable
condition; and a thousand of these other women will ultimately get pregnant and, because of the condition, give birth
to babies who have precisely the same handicap.

K: Option K involves leaving the first thousand women—the
pregnant women—untreated, so that their babies (the very
same babies they have under Option J) are ultimately born
with the handicap. But it also involves testing the women left
untested by option J. A thousand of those women—the second
thousand—will be found to have the untreatable condition and
will be told to delay getting pregnant for two months. These
women then have a healthy but distinct set of babies than they
do under option J.[23]

Is it correct to appraise these cases differently? Parfit, adopting the
"no difference" view, suggests that it is not. He believes that the two

programs are morally equal given that the distinct lives are qualitatively equal and that no one else is affected either way. But the person-affecting approach implies that the two options are not morally equal.[24]

It seems to me that it is at least plausible that the two options should be appraised differently. If we choose option K, we see that things could have been made better for a thousand babies. In K, we hold a baby in our arms who, but for our choice not to treat, would have been born perfectly healthy. In J, we hold a baby in our arms for whom the best that can be done has been done. Given this difference, moral questions are plausibly raised about option K that are not raised about option J. Option J does the best for these babies, and for each other baby who exists, that could be done, but option K does not. And so it seems at least plausible to reject Parfit's "no difference" view. But the *reason* that there is a moral difference is not, as Parfit would have it, that the afflicted babies in option J "owe their existence to our decision."[25] It is rather that, if option K is chosen, agents could have done better for the afflicted babies who in fact exist than they have.

Parfit suggests that the appraisals of the two programs unfold in distinct ways on a person-affecting approach. And this is indeed true in the case of personalism. M* and N* imply that option J wrongs no one and so, under P*, is permissible. D* does not itself generate the result that the babies who do so well under option J are wronged under option K. But I have earlier advanced a person-affecting principle—a slightly modified D*—that does support this judgment.[26]

Not all theorists would agree with me about the moral difference between option J and option K. However, I believe that any residual moral unease one might feel about the person-affecting account I have given of the cases in which the subject *could* not have been made better off reflects a far different order of moral intuition than that firm conviction we all share regarding, say, the slave child and pleasure pill cases, which ooze moral turpitude.

Of course, the practical implications of what we say about the type 2-alt cases are significant, particularly given that the mysteries of the human genome are daily being revealed within, for example, the context of the Human Genome Project and the possibilities for screening for genetic abnormalities continuing to expand. As Brock and others have observed, what we say about Parfit's two medical programs case and other type 2-alt nonidentity cases will determine whether we think that the woman who resists genetic screening—who chooses to conceive and produce a child without first having that child certified genetically healthy—or perhaps who resists the use of a "morning-after pill" or other form of early abortion has committed a moral infraction.[27] It seems to me clear that in many instances choosing to have the afflicted child rather than the healthier child will burden others, including the woman herself; and this fact may provide a moral reason to choose the healthier child. But, if we focus strictly on cases in which no one else, including the woman, is made worse off by her choice to have the afflicted child rather than the healthy child (if we play that game), I see no ground for morally condemning the woman's choice.

In summary, M* makes a sharp distinction between type 2-alt and type 3-alt cases. Thus, personalism perceives a moral difference in the case in which we can, but do not, make a life better and the case in which a life is one that we cannot make better no matter what we do. If the nonidentity cases are conceived of as type 3-alt cases, M* has no application, and the worrisome result—that the subject has not been wronged—cannot be derived. If the nonidentity cases are understood as type 2-alt cases, M* then generates the expected result—that the subject has not been wronged. But understood as type 2-alt cases, it becomes significantly less clear that these cases involve any wrongdoing at all.

I have so far understood the nonidentity problem to appeal to the person-affecting principle M*. Before dismissing the problem altogether, we should consider the possibility that it is better construed as appealing to some person-affecting principle other than M*. Let us turn to this possibility now.

3.4   A Counterfactual Interpretation of the Nonidentity Problem

In each nonidentity case, it is stipulated that a morally suspect act a causes a person s to exist. In each case, it is plausible to describe this causal link between act and existence counterfactually. Had, contrary to fact, the morally suspect a not been performed, s "would" never have existed at all. Thus, Kavka writes that "pausing to take the pill *would* change who was conceived," and again, "if they turned down the slaveholder, they *would* either produce no children or . . . produce other children."[28] According to Parfit, "[i]f we had chosen the other policy, these particular people *would* never have existed."[29] Given, then, that s would never have existed had a not been performed (lawyers might say "but for" a) and that s's existence is one worth having, it is then inferred that a itself either makes things better, or at least not worse, for s. But if a makes things better, or at least not worse, for s than things would otherwise have been, it would seem that a is not "bad for," and does not wrong, s.

Construed in this way, the nonidentity problem relies on a counterfactual principle (CF) that implies no wrong done to an apparent victim if the act in question makes things better, or at least not worse, for that person than things would otherwise have been. Thus, where a world X includes an agent's performing an act a that causes s a certain amount of ill-being,

> **CF:** s is not wronged by a in X *if*, had a not been performed in X, some world Y would have obtained such that:
> (i) s never exists in Y, *and*
> (ii) s has at least as much well-being in X as s has in Y.[30]

In contrast to M*, the conditions of CF can be satisfied even when a case is understood to be a type 3-alt case. Thus, the principle will generate the anticipated results—that the slave child has not been wronged—without our having to engage in the mental convolutions necessary to suppose that somehow the slave child *cannot* exist as a nonslave. Rather, the supposition is made that, though the child *could* exist as a nonslave, the child *would not* in fact exist if the morally suspect act—the signing of the slave child agreement—were not performed.

But the nonidentity problem, if interpreted as appealing to CF, is not a problem for the person-affecting intuition as I have interpreted it. Nothing in personalism implies CF, and D* is inconsistent with CF. Moreover, CF is clearly false. Suppose a surgeon performs open heart surgery on a *kidney* patient whose *heart* is perfectly healthy. Suppose the surgeon defends his (say) act on the grounds that he needed to practice the open heart procedure and, had he not performed that procedure, he would have been irked and would consequently have removed his patient's name from the kidney transplant list, which would have, in turn, caused the patient to die. Though weak and in pain, the patient is still better off recuperating from open heart surgery than dying of kidney failure. Based on these facts, it is true that the patient would not have existed (i.e., would not have continued to exist) had the heart surgery not been performed. But we think nonetheless that what the surgeon has done clearly wrongs the patient. The surgeon ought to have, we think, both refrained from performing the heart surgery and managed to control his bad temper. Violating either of these obligations translates to a wrong done to the patient. It is irrelevant to the moral analysis of the case that, had the surgeon not violated the one obligation, he "would" have violated the other. CF, which implies otherwise, is therefore false.[31]

The case I have just described is a life-saving case. But applied to life-creating acts CF is no less problematic. Thus, suppose that a technician in a human fertility laboratory has responsibility for certain aspects of infertility therapies involving in vitro fertilization (IVF). These therapies include the usual retrieval of eggs from the ovaries of women, among others, whose fallopian tubes are malfunctioning, followed by the IVF procedure and the return of the eggs, now fertilized, to the women. Suppose further that in a particular case the procedure involves adding to the petri dish not the usual many, many sperm but rather a single sperm. (Perhaps it is a very special sperm.) The sperm and egg are perfectly healthy and fertilization would have proceeded normally had the technician simply done nothing at all. But suppose that the technician is not entirely pure of heart. Suppose that she has embarked on some private, unapproved research program. In accordance with this program, if she does not drop a certain experimental deforming solution into the dish, she will simply discard the contents of the dish. Suppose then that she drops the solution into the dish, fertilization proceeds, and the fertilized egg is transferred to the womb of the woman from whom the egg was originally retrieved. The baby is born afflicted with, say, a mild digital deformity. It is true that had the technician not dropped the solution into the dish, *this* baby *would* never have existed at all. But it is still quite clear that what the technician has done is not simply wrong but that it wrongs *this baby*. Again, CF is false.

Thus, the counterfactual interpretation of the nonidentity problem leads to a dead end. But it is premature to dismiss the nonidentity problem, for there is one final interpretation that we should consider. And I think that in some ways this third interpretation, based on probabilities, is the most plausible one of all.

3.5   A Probabilistic Interpretation of the Nonidentity Problem

We prefer, in general, agents with the power to affect our lives to make their choices with an eye to probabilities. The nonidentity problem can be construed as taking this view. According to this interpretation, the argument avoids both the stringent M* and the false CF. Instead, it relies on the idea that for any person the certainty of a flawed existence is generally better than an unflawed, but far from certain, existence. According to this view, agents, aiming (with restrictions) to do the best that they can for each existing and future person, have wronged no one if they strive for the former outcome rather than the latter.

Consider a simple example of the life-saving variety. Suppose that the probability of drug D_1 effecting a 90 percent cure for some illness that we have is 0.9. Suppose that the probability of drug D_2 effecting a 100 percent cure is 0.01. Suppose that with respect to each drug, if it is not effective to the extent stated, it fails altogether and we lose our lives. Suppose, that is, that no other levels of effectiveness are possible. Finally, suppose that the doctor prescribes D_1 and we are 90 percent cured. We may well think that these facts are sufficient to establish that we have not been wronged, despite the fact that we have been left with a 10 percent deficit. Indeed, we might think that we have not been wronged even though we do not know one way or the other whether the world in which we are 100 percent cured is inaccessible.[32] If this is what we think, then perhaps our theory is that regardless of whether the doctor has in fact avoidably decreased our well-being, he (say) has not wronged us since he made *at the critical moment* the correct choice. (In legal terms: though we may have been harmed by the doctor's act, since he has acted reasonably at the critical time he has breached no duty and so is not liable in negligence.) According to this view, the morally critical fact is not whether our well-being has been maximized by what the doctor has done, but rather whether what we might call our *expected* well-being has been maximized by what the doctor has done.

The nonidentity problem might likewise be understood to rely not on assessments of well-being but rather on assessments of *expected* well-being. Taking this approach, it does not matter that a better-for-*s* world is accessible if there is no accessible world in which *s*'s lifetime well-being is *expected* to be better.

This point may be put in the following way, assuming X in fact obtains:

ME*: *s* is not wronged by act *a* performed by agents at time *t* in X *if*, for each world Y accessible to such agents, the expected well-being at *t* of *s* in X, given the performance of *a*, is at least as great as the expected well-being at *t* of *s* in Y, given the performance of some different act *b* at *t* in Y.

The expected well-being at *t* of *s* in any world X, then, will be the lifetime well-being that *s* is calculated (by the usual summation of the probabilities of the various possible outcomes) as likely to have, given that agents act as they do in X at the time in question.[33]

The nonidentity problem can now be formulated in terms of ME*. Consider the slave child case. Let C be a world where a couple sign the slave child agreement; they produce, pursuant to the agreement, some child or another, say, Polly, born a slave. The question, then, is whether Polly has been wronged in C. To answer this question under ME*, it must be determined whether Polly's expected well-being in C at the time the couple sign the agreement is at least as great as Polly's expected well-being at the same time in other worlds, including those in which the couple do not sign the agreement.

Suppose that existence as a slave is pretty bad but not *worse*, from Polly's own point of view, than nothing; let us say that Polly's well-being in C is 5. Clearly, at the time the couple sign the agreement, the probability of Polly's coming into existence is less than 1. After all, the couple could sign the agreement and then breach it or step in front of a bus. But the success of the argument depends on the probability of Polly's coming into existence being relatively high at the time of the signing. For the idea behind this version of the nonidentity problem is just that the couple's signing the agreement benefits the child, Polly, by *increasing* the probability that she will enjoy an existence that is, though flawed, still a good thing from her point of view. Suppose (as Kavka does) that the couple, when they sign the agreement, intend to comply with its terms. Under these circumstances, it seems likely, though not certain, that they will succeed in making good on their promise. So suppose (though this supposition will ultimately warrant a further, much harder look) the likelihood of Polly coming into existence upon their signing the agreement is 0.9. The only other possible outcome, in the case in which the couple sign the agreement, for Polly is nonexistence. It seems correct to say that Polly's well-being in any outcome in which she does not exist is 0. The summation of the well-being Polly enjoys in each possible outcome multiplied by the probability that that outcome will obtain given the couple's signing of the agreement—Polly's expected well-being in C—is 4.5. Not bad!

The defect of this argument might already be painfully obvious. But before spelling it out, let us see how from this point the argument is supposed to proceed. For it is not quite done. To apply ME*, Polly's expected well-being given various alternative courses of action the agents might have undertaken must also be calculated. But it is easy to see that Polly's expected well-being given each of these alternative courses of action is *very* low. In some worlds—such as, say, *A*—if the couple does not enter into the slave child agreement, they will produce no child at all. In such worlds, the chances of Polly's existing are virtually nil. But even in worlds—such as, say, *B*—in which the couple act in such a way as to give Polly her best shot at existence, her expected well-being will still be, at the critical time, *very* low.[34] Thus, consider a world *B* where the couple decline, at the critical time, to sign the slave child agreement but go on to "try" to have the very child they would have had had they in fact signed the agreement and fulfilled its terms. Again, two outcomes are possible. One is that Polly exists as a non-slave. Suppose that such an existence is twice as good as existing as a slave, so that Polly's well-being in *B* is 10. The other outcome for Polly is nonexistence, in which case her well-being will be 0. But the probability that she will exist as a nonslave, given that the parents do not sign the agreement, is minute. There are too many contingencies—too many little things that can elevate some other individual out of the nearly endless army of possible children into existence in place of Polly. Suppose, then, that we vastly overstate the likelihood of Polly's existence as one in a million. There is no reason to bother with the calculation (and all those zeros!). It is perfectly clear that Polly's expected well-being in *B*, where the couple do not sign the agreement but otherwise "try" to produce the very child they would have had, will be far less than 4.5. For convenience, let us just say that Polly's expected well-being in *B* is 0.01 though it is in fact less than 0.01.

These suppositions can be summed up, with the numbers now representing levels of expected well-being rather than well-being in fact:

Case 8, Nonidentity and Expected Well-Being

	A	B	C
s_1	5	5	5
s_2	5	5	5
s_3		.01	4.5

And we are now in a position to apply ME*. The slave child's parents vastly increase Polly's expected well-being by signing the slave child agreement. Anything else—even the couple's *"trying,"* as in *B*, to produce the identical child as a nonslave—would have in all likelihood made things worse for her rather than better. Based on these facts, ME* implies that the couple, having in *C* maximized the child's *expected* well-being, have not there wronged the child. But clearly they have done something wrong. And so, concludes the nonidentity problem, the person-affecting intuition must be rejected.

But this version of the nonidentity problem is hopelessly defective. The locus of the defect is the supposition made earlier regarding the likelihood of Polly's existence in the case in which the couple sign the agreement—0.9. This supposition clearly is out of bounds. Perhaps the likelihood of the couple's producing *some* child or other once they sign the agreement is 0.9. The likelihood of their producing *Polly* is nowhere near 0.9.

This version of the nonidentity problem makes much of the precariousness of existence. It makes much of how improbable it is that *Polly* will exist given the nonperformance of some morally suspect act such as signing a slave child agreement. But for the Japanese bombing Pearl Harbor, triggering the United States' involvement in World War II, many of us probably would never have existed. However, proponents of the probabilistic version of the nonidentity problem put blinders on with respect to a second key point about probability: that it is also true that, even as the bombing raid was carried out, each of our then-future existences remained a highly improbable event. Likewise, *Polly's* existence remains, at the critical time, highly improbable even given the couple's signing of the agreement.

This last point bears emphasis. A theorist wanting to press the nonidentity problem might concede that Polly's existence is in fact not made *highly* probable by the couple's signing of the agreement—nothing like, say, 0.9—yet still insist that Polly's existence is made *more* probable than it would have been had the parents avoided the morally suspect act altogether. And it seems correct that this fact, if a fact, is all that would be needed to construct a successful version of the nonidentity problem. But it is not a fact. For whether Polly's existence is made more probable by the parents' signing than by their not signing depends on just how the parents go about not signing. Given the range of accessible worlds, they have a lot of alternatives. Thus, the couple (perhaps aiming, as they are imagined to have done in *B*, to produce, as a nonslave, the very child they would have produced had they signed the agreement) might pantomime the motions of signing the agreement without ever actually putting pen to paper and then proceed to conceive a child on a schedule as likely as any they might have used had they signed the agreement. This course of action would obviously not have guaranteed the existence of Polly. The point is, however, that it would have made Polly's existence just as likely as the couple's actually signing the agreement makes Polly's existence. Either way, the same vast sea of contingencies will come into play.

And so the stated assessment of probabilities must be revised. The probability of Polly's existence, given that the couple sign the agreement, is not 0.9 at all but some much lower number—some number indistinguishable from the probability of Polly's existence, given that the couple "tries," in the manner described, to produce the very child they would have produced had they signed the agreement. But the outcomes for the child are quite different: it is twice as wonderful to exist as nonslave than as a slave. Thus, the description of the case must be revised as follows:

Case 8, Nonidentity and Expected Well-Being, Revised

	A	B	C
s_1	5	5	5
s_2	5	5	5
s_3		.01	.005

Given this revised assessment of expected well-being, the conditions of ME* are not satisfied in *C*. Because Polly's expected well-being at the critical time in *C*, where she is produced as a slave, is *less* than her expected well-being at the same time in *B*, we never reach the problematic conclusion that Polly has not been wronged. Thus, even if ME* is included as part of the person-affecting intuition, this third nonidentity challenge fails as well.

One final point should be considered. A critic might question my assessment of Polly's likelihood of existence, given the couple's signing of the agreement, as *very* low. A part of the hypothetical is that *C* in fact obtain—that is, that the couple in fact sign the agreement and produce Polly, who is immediately and, we suppose, irrevocably handed into slavery. The project, then, is to determine whether, given that *C* in fact obtains and Polly exists as a slave, she has been wronged. But if Polly actually exists, then the critic might argue that the probability of her existing in *C* is neither 0.9 nor any much lower number but rather is 1. And this means that her expected well-being there is the full value of her existence as a slave—that is, 5.

This objection is flawed in two ways. First, applying the same mode of calculation the critic just used to determine that Polly's expected well-being in *C* is 5, we may infer that Polly's existence in *B* means that her expected well-being in *B* is 10. In view of *B* and Polly's joyous life therein, the conditions of ME* are again left unsatisfied. Second, and more critically, expected well-being—operating as a guide to the agent's choice—is to be calculated at the time at which the morally suspect act is either performed or not. Even in *C*, given all the information available to the agents at the time they make their choice, Polly's existence *then* remains highly improbable and ME* thus fails to vindicate the choice at issue.

3.6   Nonidentity Victims, Fairness, and Personal Wronging

In the type 3-alt nonidentity cases, personalism sets fairly stringent standards for letting the agent, from a moral point of view, "off the hook." We can, consistent with personalism, make the claim that the slave child has been wronged. We can make analogous claims about the subjects of the pleasure pill and depletion cases. In all these cases, agents could have acted so as to improve their victims' lots. Worlds in which the victims have more well-being, and more expected well-being, were available to agents at the critical times. The inferences from M* and ME* that no one has been wronged are in each case therefore blocked. Because personalism avoids the implication that the subject has not been wronged, there is no need to explain how it is that a wrong has been done though no one has been wronged. Thus, no basis exists for rejecting the core tenet of personalism, expressed in P*, according to which wronging people and wrongdoing are inextricably linked.

If personalism avoids the troubling implication that the victims have not been wronged, does it also support the implication that they *have* been wronged? Recall D*:

D*: *s* is wronged by agents in *X if s* exists in *X* and there is some world *Y* accessible to such agents such that:
(i)   *s* has more well-being in *Y* than *s* has in *X*;
(ii) for each person *s'* who ever exists in *X*, *either s'* has at least as much well-being in *Y* as *s'* has in *X or s'* never exists in *Y; and*
(iii) for each *s'* who ever exists in *Y*, *s'* exists at some time in *X*.

According to this principle, the slave child has been wronged if in some accessible world things are better for the child but worse for no one else, including the couple. Would an increase in the child's well-being require, given available resources, a decrease in the well-being of someone else? If not, D* implies that the child has been wronged. It should be noted that it is not a foregone conclusion that any increase in the child's well-being *does* require some decrease in the well-being of another. Whether the case involves a trade-off situation depends on a number of factors. If income has something to do with well-being and money is plentiful, the couple will have other means of getting their hands on $50,000 short of selling their child into slavery. But who says that income *is* well-being? I have not given much of an account of well-being at all. And if income is only indirectly linked to well-being, then the couple's receipt of $50,000 may not make any difference to their level of well-being.

Still, there is no guarantee that the slave child case does not involve a trade-off situation. Suppose that it does. Then, any increase in the child's well-being would require some decrease in the well-being of another. In this case, personalism hands the issue of whether the child has been wronged over to a theory of fairness. The question then becomes whether, given all the facts, it is *fair* to the child that her own well-being is avoidably low. Of course, the couple may simply opt not to have the child at all. Depending on how having the child and distributing well-being to her in a right way affects their own level of well-being, not having the child to begin with might be the morally correct choice.[35]

3.7   The Case of the Fourteen-Year-Old Girl and the Problem of Future Mistakes

There are residual nonidentity cases in which personalism exculpates conduct that many consider wrong. The most prominent of these is Parfit's example of the fourteen-year-old girl who chooses to have a child now rather than waiting until she is older and would be a better mother.[36] If the young girl waits to have a child until she is older and would be a better mother, she will not have the *same* child. Because of the precariousness of existence, any child the fourteen-year-old girl has now *can*not exist except as a child of a fourteen-year-old girl. Any theory that implies that the young girl does nothing bad when she has the child now rather than waiting and having some other, better off child later is, Parfit suggests, problematic.

Does personalism exculpate the young girl's choice to have a child now? M* implies that this choice does not wrong the child *if* the child's well-being has been maximized. Given the (vastly implausible) assumption that no one else (including the girl!) has been wronged by the girl's choice, P* implies, *if* the child's well-being has been maximized, that no wrong has been done. Thus, personalism exculpates the young girl's choice only under the assumption of maximization.

Suppose that the well-being of the young girl's child is maximized. Then, it is unclear that we will have any sense of moral discomfort about this case. For the child's well-being to have been maximized, it must be the case that *both* the young girl and *all other agents* who might affect the child's life one way or the other—the father, his parents, the young girl's parents, and the community at large—have done their best for the child. Perhaps the child, despite all these efforts, ends up with a less than perfectly marvelous life or even a less than average level of well-being. Are moral reservations about this type 2-alt case appropriate? It is not clear to me that they are.

Suppose, on the other hand, that the child's well-being has *not* been maximized. Suppose, further, that D* or perhaps considerations of fairness imply that this failure to maximize represents a genuine wrong to the child. In other words, some agent, either the young girl herself or someone else, ends up, when the child is, say, five years old, predictably, but quite avoidably, wronging the child. *Ought* the girl have chosen not to have the child, on the grounds that, if she has the child, the child will predictably, though quite avoidably, be wronged by someone or other in the future?

This question can be divided. First, *ought* the young girl to refrain from having the child so that *she* will not wrong the child in the future? The person-affecting response to this question seems straightforward and, intuitively, unproblematic. According to personalism, it is wrong to wrong people. The fourteen-year-old girl (indeed, anyone!) can avoid wronging her own child by never producing a child to begin with, and she can avoid wronging her own child by producing a child and then not wronging that child. Personalism thus does not imply that she unconditionally ought to refrain from having the child, given that she has the second option of having the child and refraining from wronging the child later. At the same time, personalism avoids the result that it is morally permissible for her to do something that is wrong.

Now we turn to the second question: *ought* the young girl to refrain from having the child so that *others* will not wrong that child in the future? Clearly, personalism implies that *these others* ought to avoid wronging the child at any time. These others avoid wronging the young girl's child in either of two circumstances: either she does not have a child, or she does have a child and they avoid wronging that child (by, e.g., treating the child fairly if the situation involves a trade-off). So far, so good. But the main issue is still unresolved: *ought* the girl to prevent *these others* from wronging her child by not having the child to begin with?

This last is an interesting issue. But I do not think it needs to be resolved here. However this issue is resolved personalism serves up plenty of blame. *Some agent* has wronged the child, according to personalism, and has, correspondingly, done something wrong. Someone remains, morally, on the hook for the wrong that has, by hypothesis, been done the child. To avoid the charge of an unconscionably loose moral standard—the charge that lies at the root of the fourteen-year-old girl objection—it seems that this result is all that is really required.[37]

3.8 A Totalist Solution to the Nonidentity Problem

Among the variations on the nonidentity cases outlined here, the most potent challengers to personalism seem to be those that suppose the subject's well-being to have been maximized, that is, the type 2-alt cases. M*, as noted, implies in each such case that the subject has not been wronged. P* then implies that, since the subject has not been wronged and since by hypothesis no one else has been wronged, nothing wrong has been done at all.

I argued earlier that the implication of no wrong done is not obviously false. Until the artificiality of the type 2-alt nonidentity cases is noticed, this implication might seem troubling. But once their artificiality is recognized, it seems to me that any residual moral discomfort that might be felt about these cases is far from sufficient to establish that personalism is false. Alternatively, we might turn our attention from these artificial cases to a case that is more naturally conceived of as a type 2-alt case—such as the case of the unavoidably afflicted child described in part 3.3.3. Here as well, I think, the person-affecting analysis, according to which that child has not been wronged and, given certain assumptions, that no wrong has been done at all, is not so problematic after all.

Still, we should consider alternative solutions to the nonidentity problem. For even if the nonidentity problem does not in itself reveal a problem with personalism, if there is some theory that is (1) inconsistent with personalism, (2) gives some *better* account of the nonidentity cases, and (3) is otherwise competitive with personalism, then we have a reason to opt for that theory instead. Thus, in what follows we consider two alternative approaches to solving the nonidentity problem: a totalist approach and a deontic approach.

3.8.1   "Same Number" and "Different Number" Nonidentity Problems

According to Parfit, the nonidentity cases involve agents who have wronged no one but still have done something wrong. Having rejected P*, Parfit takes up the challenge of explaining how it can be that a wrong has been done even though no one has been wronged—or, as he puts it, how it is that conduct that is "bad for" no one can still be "bad."

To begin to meet this challenge, Parfit proposes the principle Q:

> **Q:** "If in either of two outcomes the same number of people would ever live, it would be bad if those who live are worse off, or have a lower quality of life, than those who would have lived."[38]

On the assumption that the nonidentity cases are what Parfit calls "same number" cases, and independently of whether the cases are type 2-alt or type 3-alt cases, it is easy to see that Q implies that agents in each case have done something "bad" or at least that their choices have a "bad effect."[39] If a better alternative exists that contains the same number of people, even if these people are distinct people, it would be bad—wrong—according to Q to bring about the worse alternative. Thus, Q solves "same number" nonidentity problems by denying that the identity of the people who may have been made better off (that they are not, e.g., the same people as constitute the original, less well-off group) has moral significance.

But Q is restricted to "same number" cases. And the nonidentity cases can equally well, or, in the depletion case, better, be understood as "different number" cases. If conservation produces fewer people than depletion, or if we understand the pleasure pill and the slave child cases to involve couples who produce either a defective child or none at all, Q will not apply. Thus, even if we find Q plausible in itself, a more general theory—which Parfit calls "Theory X" and which he predicts will not take a "person-affecting form"—is needed to address "different number" nonidentity cases.[40] As it will turn out, we will need to come back to Q. But first we turn to the broader Theory X.

Parfit suggests totalism as an obvious initial candidate for such a Theory X. One of the versions of totalism I described earlier provides that agents ought to bring about the greatest total net aggregate amount of well-being that they can.[41] According to this version of totalism, acts that maximize well-being for each and every person who ever exists are still wrong if they produce a world that contains a lower total amount of net aggregate well-being than any other accessible world.

Totalism, which includes Q, analyzes "same number" nonidentity cases just as Q does. But totalism extends Q. Since totalism provides a pair-wise ranking of *any* collection of worlds, it ranks worlds that differ in respect of the number of people they contain.

3.8.2 A Problem for Totalism: The Choice Not to Reproduce

In some cases, totalism requires agents to produce a child when the better result seems to be moral neutrality. Consider, in particular, the type 2-alt "different number" nonidentity cases. In any type 2-alt case, the subject has either a flawed existence (though one worth having) or none at all. In a type 2-alt "different number" case, agents have the choice of bringing into existence this flawed subject or not bringing any new person into existence at all. On the assumption that whether the child exists matters to no one else, personalism is neutral on what the agents ought to do. In contrast, totalism implies that the agents *must* produce the new person and have done something wrong if they do not.[42]

Which is the better view? Depending on whether we think there is something to the notion that in certain circumstances procreative choices should be left to the individual, we might think cases of this sort illuminate an advantage that personalism has over totalism. Consistent with the demands of personalism, individuals may choose to have the child or not to have the child. In contrast, totalism *requires* that the individuals produce the child. More precisely: according to totalism, morality requires that the individual produce the child. The totalist demand is deeply problematic, though we should recognize, of course, that to claim that couples *ought* sometimes reproduce, or *ought* sometimes avoid reproduction, is not to imply that there *ought* be laws on the books to police their choices.[43] It is just hard to see why a couple must, as a matter of moral law, produce the flawed child (or, indeed, any child) rather than not. Perhaps one imagines that the couple are *obligated* to help the child achieve existence. But this does not seem right. It cannot be that we wrong people by leaving them out of existence.

It should be noted that the distinction just drawn between personalism and totalism holds even if the child has an existence that is not particularly flawed. Suppose that the child will have a life as happy and healthy as that of any other child. Parfit describes this "happy child" case as follows.

> A couple are trying to decide whether to have another child. They can assume that, if they do, they would love this child, and his life would be well worth living. Given the size of the world's population when this case occurs . . . this couple can assume that having another child would not, on balance, be worse for other people. . . . They believe that, if they have this child, this would be neither better nor worse for them.[44]

Totalism implies that they must have the child. In contrast, so long as the life is worth living and the flaw without remedy, personalism does not discriminate between the child whose life is more flawed and the child whose life is less flawed. Either way, personalism is neutral on whether the parents are required to produce the child. It seems to me that, even in the case of the happy child, personalism produces the more intuitively plausible results. While it is perfectly acceptable for the parents to have the child if they choose to do so, they have not done anything wrong if they choose *not* to do so, for whatever reason.

One last note. The implications of personalism that I have just described suppose, among other things, that producing the flawed child, or the happy child, matters to no one else. I will consider the case in which producing an additional child *does* matter, in fact *decreases* someone else's well-being, in part 3.10. But it is not premature to note here that, when producing an additional child *does* matter to someone else—when, particularly, producing an additional child is *good* for someone else, whether for a parent, an already existing child, or even the community at large—all that I have said about the neutrality of personalism and procreative freedom flies out the window. Suppose, for example, that a couple's only child has died, and suppose that the choice to have another child would be good for the mother and would not matter to anyone else, including, say, the father. In this context, personalism implies that the couple ought to choose to have another child. Or suppose that the choice would be very good for the mother, slightly bad for the father, and otherwise matter to no one. In this trade-off situation, a theory of fairness might step in. Depending on the facts, such a theory might imply that the couple ought, as a matter of fairness to the mother, have another child.

Another context in which personalism might restrict procreative freedom would be in the context of genocide. Procreation, in this context, might be good for a community of survivors. It might make things better for their children and their children's children and worse for no one. So long as the couple's choice to have another child is not bad for the couple, on these facts personalism would imply that the couple ought to choose to have a child.

Thus, personalism places limits on the ancient injunction to "go forth and multiply." But it does not abandon that injunction altogether. Perfectly consistent with personalism one can take the view that sometimes procreation is required by moral law. At the same time, we should bear in mind that the claim that couples *ought* sometimes to reproduce, or *ought* sometimes to avoid reproduction, does not imply that there *ought* be laws on the books to police their choices.

3.8.3   A Second Problem for Totalism: The Choice of the "Lesser" Child

I described, in part 3.8.1, how Q, a part of totalism, analyzes the type 2-alt "same number" nonidentity cases. Q implies that some wrong has been done in these cases. In contrast, personalism implies that, since no one has been wronged, no wrong has been done. Some theorists, for example, Parfit, think that the implications of Q in cases of this kind are more plausible than the person-affecting account of such cases.

But let us now reconsider the type 2-alt "same number" nonidentity cases in light of the issue of procreative freedom just raised. Thus, I noted, in part 3.8.2, that totalism sometimes implies, when it matters to no one, that we should have some child rather than none at all. Likewise, Q in some cases in which it matters to no one requires that we have the better, rather than the lesser, child.

Suppose that a couple is deciding whether to have a child whose existence will be unavoidably flawed in some significant way (thus, a type 2-alt case). The child's life is, we assume, worth living. Since the case is a "same number" case, the couple have the alternative, if they do not produce the defective child, of producing a *distinct* child—say, an "average" child—whose existence will be relatively unflawed. Thus, the couple's choice is between producing a child whose well-being is unavoidably capped (perhaps as a function of some genetic or chromosomal defect) or a *distinct* child who enjoys as much well-being as happy, healthy children often do. Given that no one else (including the couple) is affected either way, personalism is neutral on what the couple should do. Whether they opt to have the lesser or the better child, they have done nothing wrong. Q implies the contrary view. If the parents choose to have the lesser child, they have, while wronging no one, done something wrong.

Which result is more plausible? I favor person-affecting neutrality. Part of why I lean toward the person-affecting approach to this case is that I think this case (average versus lesser child) and the case in which the choice is between a "super" child and an average child should be assessed in the same way. Kavka describes a couple who contemplate having an average child. According to Kavka, if such parents

> choose to have a child, they are not obligated to take genetic-enhancement pills if this would insure the production of a (different but) "better" child—one that would be happier or contribute more to others' happiness.[45]

Q implies otherwise. As between an average child, whose well-being has been, more or less, maximized, and a super child, whose well-being will rise to higher than average levels as a function of his or her "enhanced" genetic design, totalism implies that the couple has done something wrong, though they wrong no one, if they choose to produce the average child rather than the super child.

In this pair of cases, the neutrality of personalism seems a point in its favor. Thus, Kavka writes that the couple "might justifiably prefer to reproduce naturally, without such interference."[46] We insist that the couple treat the baby they do have well, but our moral hackles, it seems, do not rise just because they choose to have the average child rather than the super child or, I think, just because they choose to have the lesser rather than the average child. Adapting a comment from Narveson: why do we think there is something wrong with producing a child whose life is "below average, but still good? [W]hy not complain if it were above average, but not perfect?"[47]

3.9　A Deontic Solution to the Nonidentity Problem

3.9.1　Restricted Lives and Acting "Wrongly Toward" Future People

A solution that Kavka discusses to the nonidentity problem suggests that it is "possible to act wrongly by wronging someone without harming him."[48] I have not yet needed a definition of "harm." Though I will need one soon—in chapter 4, to speak in the language of the law about wrongful life—none is, it seems, needed here. For Kavka's suggestion can be restated as follows: it is possible to "act wrongly by wronging someone" whose well-being we have nonetheless done our part to maximize. Thus, whereas the totalist solution to the nonidentity problem rejects P*, what I will call the "deontic" solution rejects M*. Though wronging persons and wrongdoing *simpliciter* may be inextricably linked, Kavka suggests that it may be a mistake to think that, just because a person's well-being has not been decreased, or has been increased or even maximized, he or she has not been wronged.

Kavka's account of what it is to "act wrongly toward" future people in cases in which we have not made "them worse off than they otherwise might have been" is based on the notion of a "restricted life."[49] A "restricted life," according to Kavka, is a life that is "significantly deficient in one or more of the major respects that generally make human lives valuable and worth living."[50] Thus, for example, "life as a slave is restricted," as are the "lives of persons significantly handicapped, either mentally or physically, from birth and of those struck . . . by illnesses."[51] Making use of this notion, Kavka suggests a principle according to which, "other things being equal, conditions of society or the world are intrinsically undesirable from a moral point of view to the extent that they involve people living restricted lives."[52] Accordingly, "there is something seriously wrong with people living restricted lives, which makes it incumbent upon others to stop this from happening if we can."[53] A questionable act, he writes, "can be condemned on the grounds that it foreseeably leads to (states of the world containing) restricted lives."[54] This is so, he thinks, even though "restricted lives typically will be worth living, on the whole, for those who live them."[55]

According to this view, the parents who sign the slave child agreement wrong—or, at least, "act wrongly toward"—the child they produce since in signing the agreement they thereby create a foreseeably restricted life. The same is true of the offspring of the pleasure pill, since persons who are "significantly handicapped" also lead restricted lives. Finally, in cases like depletion, the illnesses and indignities suffered as a result of a "very overcrowded world" would imply large numbers of restricted lives. In each case, the acts that create restricted lives are wrong, Kavka suggests, because they represent agents acting "wrongly toward" future people.

3.9.2   A Problem for the Deontic View: The Choice of the "Lesser" Child

According to Kavka, it is clear why the parents have no obligation to take "genetic-enhancement pills" and thereby to produce a super child when all they want is a regular old average child. Average people (presumably) do not have restricted lives and so producing them does not wrong them. Thus, Kavka's proposal has a certain advantage over Q.

At the same time, depending on the nature and extent of the flaw, the option to produce the unavoidable flawed child will be barred by Kavka's view just as it is in the "same number" cases by Q. Thus, if that child is, or will predictably be, "significantly handicapped, either mentally or physically," then producing the child, according to Kavka, wrongs the child.[56]

And so we must draw lines, according to Kavka, between *significant* mental and physical handicaps and *insignificant* mental and physical handicaps. But surely Down's syndrome often produces a significant mental handicap. According to personalism, so long as we have done the best we can for the child we produce, then we have not wronged that child, whether he or she has Down's syndrome or not. In contrast, as we have seen, Q implies that it is wrong to produce a Down's child when we might have, instead, produced some distinct child capable of achieving a higher level of well-being.

I have doubts that this implication from Q could be correct. But perhaps it is not clearly objectionable. Even so, the deontic view that Kavka describes goes one extremely implausible step further. According to his view, not only do we do something wrong when we produce the Down's child, we also wrong *the child*. According to the deontic view, this will be the case even when we have maximized the child's well-being. Though we may like the deontic implication in the slave child case, we are not, I think, so sympathetic to the analogous result in the Down's child case. In one case we want to say, with Kavka, that the child has been wronged; but in the other case we, I think, do not.

Personalism, of course, makes this very distinction. It implies no wrong done to the Down's child, who cannot exist and not suffer Down's syndrome, if we have done our best for that child. And it implies that some wrong has been done to the slave child, who could have existed as a nonslave and whose well-being therefore has not been maximized. Assuming no trade-offs, D* implies straight out that the slave child has been wronged; where there is some trade-off between parent and child, the issue will be whether it is unfair to the child to decrease her well-being (by selling her into slavery) in order to increase the couple's well-being.

Another more general problem with the deontic view should be mentioned. The view could be described as a form of person-affecting nonconsequentialism. It therefore is devoid of the basic consequentialist insight, according to which moral law does not hinge on categorical distinctions that are not themselves well understood in terms of producing goodness for people. I do not find, for example, the categories that Kavka sets up to be of any particularly obvious moral relevance. Indeed, I find them morally very iffy. Thus, according to the deontic view we must draw lines between "significant" and insignificant physical and mental handicaps. But surely the less offensive, less arbitrary approach is to draw a line between those instances in which we have done our best for people and those instances in which we have not.

3.10 Reproductive Trade-Offs: When Producing the Child Is Bad for Others

3.10.1 A Further Problem for Totalism

The nonidentity problem consistently appeals to cases in which the act of producing a child whose existence is in some way flawed does not affect the well-being of anyone else. For in cases in which the act *does* affect the well-being of some other person—cases that involve, that is, a *decrease* in the well-being of another—we always have the option of declaring the act to have wronged *that* person and thus the option of declaring, under P*, the act to be *wrong*. Those theorists who believe—mistakenly, I have argued—that the intuition implies that no wrong has been done in the type 3-alt cases believe that the nonidentity problem challenges the person-affecting intuition. Where on any independent grounds—including the grounds that someone else has been wronged—we avoid the conclusion that no wrong has been done, we avoid the challenge to the person-affecting approach. And so no case in which someone other than the child whose existence is flawed can be said to have been wronged gives rise to the nonidentity problem.

But cases in which the well-being of another is decreased by the choice to produce the child obviously do exist. It is easy to see how the parents' choice to produce a first child, or a second or third child, might decrease the well-being of one or both parents or of an earlier born child. In such a case, the parents could be said to have increased one person's well-being—the new child's well-being, by way of bringing that new child into existence—at a cost in terms of well-being to others. We can think of this case as involving a *kind* of trade-off (though, as we will see, the issues raised by this kind of case can be resolved within personalism proper and without any appeal to fairness). Thus, a child who suffers a significant mental or physical defect may burden other family members in serious ways and may sometimes, on a net basis, decrease their well-being. But children as happy and healthy as any child might hope to be can also burden families. If a new child would be added to a brood of many and if food is scarce and helping hands in short supply, or if a parent is older or ill, such a child could easily impose a net burden. Or perhaps a woman has simply had as many children as are good for her to have; perhaps one child, or two, or none at all, is the right number for her, and a second or third child would, on a net basis, decrease her level of well-being. I argued earlier that a weakness of totalism is that it *requires* parents to choose to have a child—moreover, to choose to have the *better* child—in cases in which the choice matters to no one else, including the parents (parts 3.8.2 and 3.8.3). On this basis, I favored the results of personalism, according to which, so long as the parents do their best for any children they opt to have, and assuming that their choice matters to no one else, moral law does not condemn whatever choice they make.

In the earlier discussion, the rallying call was procreative freedom. That call becomes decibels louder when procreation decreases the well-being of a parent, an already born child, or some other existing or future person. Indeed, it seems to me that a *disaster* for totalism is that it *requires* parents to produce a child in some cases in which doing so makes others worse off and no one better off. Thus, suppose that a woman believes, correctly, that producing a third child would be bad for her. And suppose that if she does choose to have a third child, she would be very, very good to the child and that the child would enjoy quantities of well-being that would more than counterbalance any cost to the woman. On these facts, totalism implies that the woman *ought* to have the child and that her choice not to do so is morally impermissible.

But these implications seem obviously false. If "having a child would be bad for the couple themselves, even to a small degree, that is a sufficient reason for them not to have one."[57] More generally, it seems that when the kind of trade-off that must be made is between the well-being of one who already exists and one who does not yet, and need not ever, exist, and assuming that what is done matters to no one else (including to no other future person), then there is *nothing* morally wrong with favoring the existing person and simply leaving the other out of existence to begin with.

The same kinds of issues arise in cases in which the trade-off involves someone other than a parent. Suppose that further procreation would be neutral for the parents but bad for their already existing children. If the parents would be good to any later born child, and if this child would be happy and enjoy significant well-being, then, depending on the extent to which already existing children are disadvantaged, totalism would imply that the parents *must* opt to have another child. Again, this implication seems obviously false. If parents, aiming to do their best for the children they *already* have, opt not to produce additional children, and if their choice matters to no one else, they have done nothing wrong. Often, of course, having an additional child is a great advantage to the already born, or at least not a disadvantage. And often having an additional child is, even if disadvantageous to already existing children, good for the parents. But the case at issue here has neither of these two features. Here, no one other than the child who does not yet, and need not ever, exist stands to gain, while flesh-and-blood children stand to lose.

3.10.2   A Person-Affecting Account of Reproductive Trade-Offs

Thus, cases in which producing new people is bad for others challenge totalism. Can personalism provide a more plausible account?

When the trade-off called for is between the well-being of an existing person and the well-being of a person who does not yet, and need not ever, exist, and the choices are limited to *increasing* the well-being of the existing person by not bringing the new person into existence and *decreasing* the well-being of the existing person by bringing the new person into existence, M* and N* exculpate the former choice. Thus, M* implies that no wrong has been done to the person whose well-being has been maximized, and N* implies that no wrong has been done to anyone who does not exist. P*, according to which agents wrong if and only if they wrong someone, thus declares the first choice permissible.

To evaluate the second choice—the choice to produce the additional child—we turn to D*:

D*: *s* is wronged by agents in *X* if *s* exists in *X* and there is some world *Y* accessible to such agents such that:

(i) *s* has more well-being in *Y* than *s* has in *X*;

(ii) for each person *s'* who ever exists in *X*, *either s'* has at least as much well-being in Y as s' has in X *or* s' never exists in Y; *and*

(iii) for each s' who ever exists in Y, s' exists at some time in X.

According to D*, failing to increase one person's well-being when we can do so by leaving some others out of existence and without decreasing the well-being of anyone else wrongs that person. Thus, take the case in which the well-being of the mother of the two children will decline if the couple choose to have a third child, and in which their not having the third child will not decrease the well-being of the father, the two already existing children, or anyone else. D* implies that the choice to produce the third child wrongs the mother.

Thus, *part* of the person-affecting intuition is that there is nothing wrong with refraining from producing additional people when doing so will make no one better off and some people worse off. This is true, according to personalism, however much well-being the child would enjoy were he or she to exist. But *another* part of the intuition is that there is something wrong with not making existing and future people happier when we can. Putting these two points together and assuming that what is done matters to no one else, we wrong someone if we can but do not increase that person's well-being by bringing fewer, rather than more, people into existence to begin with. D* reflects this conclusion.

Does the person-affecting result seem intuitively plausible? I think so. It seems that morality surely does not compel a woman to have any child, or another child, when doing so is bad for her and good for no one else.

3.11   The Repugnant Conclusion

3.11.1   The Case of Distinct Populations

I noted earlier that one might think (and Parfit, e.g., does think) that the principle Q provides a correct analysis of "same number" type 2-alt nonidentity cases—cases, that is, in which the choice to be made is between producing a person whose existence will be unavoidably flawed and producing another person whose existence will be relatively unflawed. Q directs that it is better to produce the unflawed person (part 3.8.1). In contrast, personalism remains neutral, implying that neither choice wrongs anyone and that neither choice is wrong (part 3.8.3).

In the context of this discussion, I also noted that some versions of totalism, which, unlike Q, cover "different number" nonidentity cases, do not make much progress over personalism. Regarding these cases, I said that personalism, as in the "same number" cases, remains neutral, while some versions of totalism *require* the production of the additional person. And this implication, I said, seems wrong (part 3.8.2).

By imagining a blown-up version of this latter case—the type 2-alt "different number" nonidentity case—we generate one version of what Parfit calls the "repugnant conclusion." Thus, Parfit compares a large population, A, each member of which enjoys a high level of well-being, with a much larger, completely distinct population, Z, whose lives are all just barely "worth living."[58] In total, the net aggregate amount of well-being in Z is greater than in A. Totalism considers Z the better alternative and thus condemns the choice of A.

According to Parfit, the conclusion that Z is better than A is "*intrinsically* repugnant."[59] Thus, as I have described it here, totalism, while solving, via Q, some versions of the nonidentity problem, is not ultimately a satisfactory candidate for "Theory X."

In contrast to totalism, personalism considers both A and Z permissible alternatives. Appealing, in other words, only to the "interests of all of the people who will ever live," the intuition implies that no wrong is done in A or in Z.[60] Since everyone's well-being in each world has been maximized, M* implies that no one has been wronged in either world and thus, under P*, that both worlds are permissible. I do not think that it could plausibly be argued that the personalist conclusion is *as* repugnant as the totalist conclusion, since personalism, unlike totalism, does not condemn the choice of A. But, as noted, the example that Parfit constructs for the purpose of demonstrating the repugnant conclusion is really just a large scale version of a case discussed earlier. The defense of personalism thus need not be repeated here.[61]

3.11.2 The Case of Overlapping Populations: The "Repugnant" Version of the Repugnant Conclusion[62]

I have, of course, assumed that the repugnant conclusion involves a comparison of two completely distinct populations. And thus I categorized the case as a type 2-alt case, understanding that, with respect to each person in Z, there are exactly two alternatives—(1) a flawed existence and (2) no existence at all.

But suppose that we change these facts. Suppose that the *reason* that people have such a difficult time in Z is that resources there are scarce. Z is, in other words, an overpopulated world. But this is a different kind of case altogether. For if the problem is overpopulation, then it seems that we should be able to improve the lot of at least some members of Z by not bringing into existence to begin with some other members of Z. But this means that the case is not a type 2-alt case but rather a type 3-alt case, a case in which a better world is accessible for at least one person in Z. And this in turn means that personalism avoids not only the conclusion that Z is obligatory but also the further conclusion that Z is permissible. For based on these facts there is some Z', smaller than Z, such that some Z-person s's well-being is *higher* in Z' than in Z; and if there is such a better-for-s Z', M* will not excuse the choice of Z.

Suppose further that every member of Z' belongs to Z (so that Z' is a pared-down version of Z), and suppose that every member of Z who exists in Z' enjoys at least as much well-being in Z' as in Z. Then, D* implies that s is *wronged* in Z; and P* then implies that Z is impermissible. In *dramatic* contrast, depending on the numbers, totalism produces, in this type 3-alt case, the same old repugnant conclusion that it produces in the type 2-alt case. Suppose, for example, that s_1 exists in Z and in Z', and that s_1 has 6 units of well-being in Z and 10 units of well-being in Z'. Suppose that s_1's higher level of well-being in Z' is achieved because s_2, who exists in Z and there enjoys (as did s_1) 6 units of well-being, does not exist in Z'. There are no other differences in the populations or distributions of well-being from Z to Z'; and Z and Z' exhaust the alternatives. Totalism, given these facts, *requires* Z and condemns Z'. Personalism, more plausibly, does just the reverse.

Thus, personalism makes a distinction between the type 2-alt repugnant case and the type 3-alt repugnant case, whereas totalism treats them as of a piece. Parfit suggests that, at an intuitive level, there is no distinction to be made. We might debate at length whether the person-affecting treatment of the type 2-alt case is compelling or whether it is significantly more plausible than the totalist treatment. But in the type 3-alt case, the person-affecting account is by far the more appealing one.

Let us look at a more concrete case. Suppose that we think twenty babies rather than ten being born overnight in the local hospital will stretch available resources and ultimately lead to various bad effects. And suppose that as a matter of fact twenty, rather than ten, babies are born. Then, to avoid the result, under M*, that no one has been wronged, the person-affecting theorist must show that a better alternative exists for some existing or future person. Suppose that none of the already existing community is disadvantaged by the twenty new babies. But suppose that some of the twenty babies themselves—all of them, by hypothesis, existing—*will* experience disadvantage. Then it is clear that some of the babies who are disadvantaged are such that things *could* have been made better for them. Some of them, in other words, *could* have existed without having suffered the adverse effects of overpopulation. Take, for instance, Jones' baby—Baby Jones. It *could* have happened that Baby Jones and *nine* other babies, rather than all twenty, were born overnight at the local hospital. Baby Jones then would have been better off.

Clearly, this alternative is accessible. Surely it is within the capacity of the fecund hypothetical community, acting jointly or severally, to bring about. This is not a case in which people are impregnated by spores that float through open windows and doors. Thus, the Jones family need only to have produced Baby Jones, while the Smith family, and some others, need only have refrained from producing Baby Smith, and some others. Of course, we can improve the lot of Baby Jones, by leaving out Baby Smith, or of Baby Smith, by leaving out Baby Jones. Either way, we have increased the level of well-being of *some* existing person by leaving others out of existence. It would be a mere sentimentality to protest that the thing is somehow not fair to whichever babies happen never to be brought into existence to begin with. As N* makes clear, we cannot wrong those who never have, do not now, and never will exist. On these facts, M* will not excuse bringing all twenty babies into existence.

We can make the case harder. Suppose that neither the already existing community nor any of the twenty new babies will suffer as a consequence of overpopulation. Suppose that the ones who will be hungry and miserable will exist generations from now. It matters not; the person-affecting analysis will not change. So long as *some* future, impoverished, hungry person *could* have had more well-being had our own generation numbered in the tens of billions rather than the twenties of billions—as long as that world is accessible—M* will not apply.

Does personalism imply the further result in this kind of case that choosing the larger population in fact wrongs someone and is therefore impermissible? The answer to this question depends on other facts. Thus, some cases of overpopulation may involve a trade-off. Suppose, for example, that not having a baby decreases the Smiths' well-being. Then, the conditions of D* will not be met, and personalism will be silent on the issue of whether bringing into existence all twenty babies, including Baby Smith, wrongs, say, Baby Jones. According to the scheme I have proposed, this trade-off situation would be handed over to a theory of fairness. In contrast, if there is no trade-off, then D* will imply that the choice of overpopulation wrongs each of the twenty babies.

The cases in which it is clear to me that there is a problem with the implication that the larger, less well-off population is permissible are those cases—like overpopulation—in which there is some way of making things better for some member or another of the larger, less well-off population. In contrast, with respect to any case in which there is no way of making things better for those who exist or will exist, it is not so clear to me that the implication of permissibility is problematic. Under what circumstances could the lot of at least one person in the vast and possibly miserable Z *not* be improved? Under what circumstances is there no better-for-some-s Z'? Perhaps Z is populated by people with a well-being-depressing chromosomal defect that cannot be remedied; but there is no overpopulation, and resources remain abundant. It is not at all clear to me that in such a Z, where everyone's well-being has been maximized, anyone has been wronged or that any wrong has been done.

3.11.3   The Difference between Personalism and Totalism

In their handling of the various sorts of cases we have discussed, personalism and totalism emerge as subtly but significantly distinct views. The alleged problem for personalism is that it countenances our bringing into existence "lesser" beings—individuals, that is, whose maximal well-being is fixed at some relatively low level. Thus, personalism but not totalism posits neutrality in the type 2-alt "same number" cases, a result that may seem questionable to some (though not to me). But compare the totalist treatment of the type 2-alt "different number" cases. As a function of its bias for procreation, totalism generates a clearly problematic account of cases of this sort—that we *must* reproduce—while personalism remains neutral. Even worse, depending on the numbers, totalism generates this result in cases in which reproduction markedly decreases the well-being of others, for example, a woman or an already existing child. Finally, the type 3-alt "different number" cases will hardly foster an allegiance to totalism. When the larger, less well-off population has some member in common with an alternative smaller, more well-off population, personalism is at least in a position to declare that common member wronged, while totalism again (depending on the numbers) *requires* the larger population. All told, personalism seems to provide the better approach to issues of reproductive choice.

3.11.4   Another Look at Infinite Populations

Problems similar to the repugnant conclusion arise when the totalist attempts to compare infinite populations. I have already noted that the infinite population cases challenge totalism, and I have noted the person-affecting analysis of those cases (part 2.9.2). All that remains to be said here is that, whether we suppose an infinite type 2-alt case or an infinite type 3-alt case, standard forms of totalism will imply that neither infinite population is better than the other since total well-being is infinite for each. In contrast, personalism distinguishes between the two types of cases, permitting the world where people enjoy a lower level of well-being only in the type 2-alt case. Thus, the distinction that personalism makes between these two types of infinite population cases follows the distinction that personalism makes between the two types of repugnant conclusion cases. As I have suggested, I find the distinction that personalism draws with respect to the two types of repugnant conclusion cases plausible, and I likewise find plausible the distinction that personalism draws with respect to the two types of infinite population cases.

3.11.5   Feldman's Concept of Adjusted Utility

The formulation of totalism I have focused on up until this point ranks worlds by aggregating a single, unadjusted good, well-being, within those worlds. But not all totalist theories have this feature. Thus, for example, I earlier described what is sometimes called Parfit's "perfectionism."[63] This view denies that all values necessarily "lay on the same scale."[64] Parfit proposes that this two-valued formulation might both solve the nonidentity problem and avoid the repugnant conclusion. But, as Ryberg suggests, a perfectionism that effectively addresses the repugnant conclusion in its many variations requires an implausibly rarified notion of the kind of value that counts for moral purposes.[65]

Feldman describes a form of totalism that relies on less troubling distinctions between kinds of value. Thus, Feldman suggests a view according to which the value "for the world" of a person receiving a certain amount of the good can be adjusted depending on the extent to which the amount *received* corresponds to the amount of good *deserved*.[66] For instance, if an individual receives a very small quantity of whatever it is that makes life worth living and deserves a great deal more, "[i]t is then bad for the world."[67] In this case, the value for the world of the person's receiving much less than he or she deserves is *negative*, despite the fact that the value for the person is marginally positive.

Applying this view to the repugnant conclusion, we will derive, according to Feldman, a quite distinct set of implications than those earlier attributed to totalism. The world *Z*, where many people have lives just barely worth living, turns out to be worse than *A*, where fewer people have lives well worth living. This is because the people of *Z* deserve much more well-being than they in fact have, and the people of A have at least the amount of well-being that they deserve. Thus, the value of Z is actually negative. "In short, Z is a horrible world."[68] A is not, and "[o]ur axiological intuitions are preserved."[69] Feldman concludes that "not all forms of totalism imply the Repugnant Conclusion."[70]

The implications we draw from Feldman's totalist theory will depend on how we understand the concept of desert, which functions as a primitive for Feldman.[71] If we set too low a standard for desert, we do not avoid the repugnant conclusion. Consider, for instance, the conclusion that an enormous population Z, each member of which has the level of well-being he or she deserves but no more, is better than some pared-down population A, each member of which has the level of well-being he or she deserves *plus* a nice heap more. If we think that the objects of our moral concern *deserve* very little, this conclusion might well strike us as, if not repugnant, then still troubling—particularly, as I have argued, in the case in which the populations of A and Z are not completely distinct. For this reason, we might set a higher standard for desert. Suppose, then, we think that people deserve a plentiful amount of the good things that life has to offer. On this view of desert, the stipulation that each member of Z has exactly the amount he or she deserves ensures that we will not be particularly troubled by the conclusion that Z is better than A. But then Feldman's theory encounters a milder version of the problem Ryberg describes in connection with Parfit's perfectionism. Imagine a person whose life is well worth living but includes less than a plentiful quantity of the good things that life has to offer. Suppose, indeed, that her (say) well-being has been maximized. And suppose that agents might have avoided producing this person without decreasing the adjusted well-being of others. Feldman's totalism implies that the world where the person does not exist is better than the world where she does exist.

Perhaps I have created a false dilemma. Perhaps the level of well-being that we *deserve* is neither a bare cut above that which makes life worth living nor the amount that would be generated by plentiful quantities of the good things that life has to offer. Perhaps the level of well-being that we deserve is some third amount. A natural theory of what this amount might be links the concepts of desert and equality. According to this theory, the amount of well-being that people deserve is just their equal share. But this natural understanding will not work for purposes of addressing the repugnant conclusion since, by hypothesis, all Z-people, like all A-people, share equally in well-being. Feldman suggests other "likely sources of desert," including the straightforward idea that "[i]n virtue of *being a person*, [one who is innocent] deserves a certain amount of happiness."[72] This seems uncontroversial. But it does not tell us very much about desert. That we must search further for an adequate concept of desert is not really a criticism of Feldman's view. It may well be the case that plausible forms of totalism can effectively address the repugnant conclusion. But we cannot be sure that this is so until we understand desert.

Notes

1. Derek Parfit, *Reasons and Persons* (Oxford: Clarendon, 1984) (hereinafter, *RP*), 374.
2. Parfit writes, "[W]e should revise the ordinary use of the word 'harm.' If what we are doing will not be worse for some other person, or will even be better for this person, we are not, in a morally relevant sense, harming this person" (*RP*, 374).
3. Parfit, *RP*, 374.
4. Gregory Kavka, "The Paradox of Future Individuals," *Philosophy and Public Affairs* 11, no. 2 (1981): 93.
5. Kavka describes the "precariousness" of existence in "The Paradox of Future Individuals," 93. See also Parfit, *RP*, 351–61.
6. Parfit actually limits this principle to conceptions that occur a month or more apart. According to Parfit, "[i]f any particular person had not been conceived within a month of the time when he was in fact conceived, he would in fact never have existed" (Parfit, *RP*, 372). Presumably the additional clarity derives from the fact that the spread of a month implies not just a different sperm but also a different egg. It is clear that riveting issues of identity arise at this point. *Would* a distinct but genetically identical sperm—or *nearly* genetically identical sperm—necessarily imply a distinct person? I say more about these issues in chap. 1, note 62, and chap. 5, note 37.
7. Parfit, *RP*, 359.
8. See generally Parfit, *RP*, 351–79.
9. Parfit, *RP*, 378.
10. Parfit, *RP*, 364–67.
11. Parfit, *RP*, 363.
12. Parfit, *RP*, 361.
13. Parfit, *RP*, 362.
14. Parfit, *RP*, 363.
15. Parfit, *RP*, 363.
16. Parfit, *RP*, 363. In the parallel "risky policy" case, Parfit supposes not some mere diminution in the well-being of future people as a result of a present day choice but rather an out-and-out catastrophe—burying nuclear waste in earthquake-prone areas and thereby causing thousands of future people to die at an early age of an incurable disease. Clearly, he thinks, and perhaps more clearly than in the case of depletion, such a choice has a "bad effect" though it is not "bad for, or worse for, any of the people who later live" (373).

17. Kavka, "The Paradox of Future Individuals," 100. One only has to recall the character of "schoolteacher" in Tony Morrison's *Beloved* to become extremely uncomfortable with the assumption that the child who is born or made a slave will not have a level of well-being that is in fact negative (New York: Knopf, 1987). I make the assumption, for purposes of looking at the problem, understanding that it may in any given case be false. If the assumption is false, then the case presents no challenge at all to a person-affecting approach.

18. Kavka, "The Paradox of Future Individuals," 101.

19. Kavka, "The Paradox of Future Individuals," 98.

20. Parfit, *RP,* 374, emphasis added.

21. Kavka, "The Paradox of Future Individuals," 101.

22. See Parfit's discussion of the "two medical programs" case (*RP,* 366–71).

23. Parfit, *RP,* 367.

24. Parfit, *RP,* 367–71. See also Dan W. Brock, "The Non-Identity Problem and Genetic Harms—The Case of Wrongful Handicaps," *Bioethics* 9, no. 3/4 (1995), 269–75. Brock, like Parfit, argues that the fact that in one program a child is born whose life might have been made better and that in the other program a child is born whose life could not have been made better makes no moral difference. In Brock's view, the applicable moral principle for these kinds of cases—which he calls cases of "wrongful handicap"—provides that "[i]t is morally good to act in a way that results in less suffering and less limited opportunity in the world" (273). Thus, according to Brock, the woman who is informed by her doctor that she should wait two months to get pregnant or else risk giving birth to a child who is "mildly retarded" acts in a "morally good way by . . . waiting to conceive a normal child" (270, 273). I see the suffering and the limited opportunity this child might experience; but I do not see this *wrong to no one* that Brock thinks the woman has done. Perish the thought, but one wonders whether this woman's choice is being taken from her on bogus moral grounds and whether cases of "wrongful handicap" are really in any genuine sense *wrongful* at all. If the real concern is the additional burden that raising a mentally retarded child rather than a "normal" child imposes on others, including, perhaps, the father or the community, then why not *say* that and analyze the case as a trade-off?

I note that Parfit's "no difference" view commands wide adherence. Indeed, even theorists who accept, to one degree or another, the person-affecting intuition nonetheless introduce into their theories at defined junctures other types of principles necessary to affirm Parfit's "no difference" view. See, e.g., Clark Wolf, "Social Choice and Normative Population Theory: A Person Affecting Solution to Parfit's Mere Addition Paradox," *Philosophical Studies* 81 (1996): 263–82, especially 276–78; Jan Narveson, "Future People and Us," in *Obligations to Future Generations*, R. I. Sikora and Brian Barry, eds. (Philadelphia: Temple University Press), 1978: 49–56; and Ingmar Persson, "Genetic Therapy, Identity and Person-Regarding Reasons," *Bioethics* 9, no. 1 (1995): 16–31. Persson, for instance, suggests that we have a *stronger* "person-regarding reason" for bringing into existence one person than we have for bringing into existence a distinct person "if the benefit to [the former] is the bigger one" ("Genetic

Therapy," 29). But the "person-regarding" approach Persson suggests is not, of course, the approach reflected in personalism, according to which identity matters.

25. Parfit, *RP*, 368.

26. As noted earlier, if s's well-being is increased by bringing non-X people into existence whose level of well-being is itself maximal, then assuming the other conditions of D* are satisfied we might well conclude that the failure to increase s's well-being wrongs s (chap. 2, note 48).

27. Brock, "The Non-Identity Problem and Genetic Harms," 269–75.

28. Kavka, "The Paradox of Future Individuals," 100, emphasis added.

29. Parfit, *RP*, 361, emphasis added.

30. Clause (ii) of (CF) compares the amount of well-being s has in X with the amount of well-being s has in a world in which s does not exist. Without this condition, it could happen that s's life in X is less than one worth living, in which case it would seem that the agent's causing s to exist in X would wrong s.

31. Matthew Hanser likewise gives an account of the nonidentity cases in which what things "would have been" like for the subject is not critical ("Harming Future People," *Philosophy & Public Affairs* 19, no. 1 (Winter 1990): 47–70, 57). Rather, Hanser considers what kinds of effects agents can be held "responsible" for, arguing that agents may be responsible for the foreseeable harms of a morally questionable act but that agents do not get credit for any offsetting "accidental" effect of their act. "[A]gents of actions only accidentally affecting the identities of future people cannot plausibly be taken to act in order to ensure one group of people's coming into existence rather than another's" (61). His purposive, motivational account of the nonidentity cases is, of course, quite distinct from the kind of account I am suggesting here.

32. It is not obvious to me that this way of thinking is correct. It may be that what we should say about this example is just that we do not know whether we have been wronged. We do not know whether we have been wronged because, under these conditions of uncertainty, we do not know whether the world in which D_2 effects a 100 percent cure is accessible.

33. The basic notion behind ME* could be formulated differently. See Ronald N. Giere, *Understanding Scientific Reasoning* (Harcourt Brace, 1997), 119–289. See also Henry E. Kyburg, Jr., *Probability and Inductive Logic* (London: Macmillan, 1970).

34. Kavka notes this point, writing ("The Paradox of Future Individuals," 100, n.15):

> It is enormously improbable that the couple, if they turned down the slaveholder, could succeed in producing the same child they would have produced had they accepted, even if they tried. For it is unlikely that they could arrange conditions of conception similar enough to "what would have been" to ensure that the very same sperm would fertilize the same egg.

Though the child *might* exist as a nonslave, agents are unlikely, according to Kavka, to be able to bring about the child's existence as a nonslave "even if they tried."

35. The person-affecting analysis of this case thus parallels the treatment given to case 5, involving reproductive trade-offs, in part 2.9.1. The difference is just that here it is the parents' level of well-being that varies, depending on whether they treat the child well, rather than an older sibling's.

36. Parfit, *RP,* 357–61.

37. Once we suppose that the real worry is that the child will be wronged not by being brought into existence but rather later in life—at, say, age five or so—by someone or another, this case is probably better understood to raise the problem of future mistakes rather than as a challenge to personalism. For a good discussion of this problem, see Angela Curran, "Utilitarianism and Future Mistakes: Another Look," *Philosophical Studies* 78 (1995): 71–85.

38. Parfit, *RP,* 360.

39. Parfit, *RP,* 360.

40. Parfit, *RP,* 378.

41. Assuming we understand "well-being" and "whatever makes life worth living" as synonymous, this statement of totalism is roughly equivalent to Parfit's "Impersonal Total Principle" (*RP,* 387). The latter contains a restriction—that other things are equal—which does not come into play for our purposes here.

42. The kind of case that we have just described—the type 2-alt "different number" nonidentity case—is really just a small-scale version of what Parfit calls the "repugnant conclusion." It is, in fact, the repugnant conclusion that leads Parfit to question whether totalism could possibly be a satisfactory candidate for Theory X. The best candidate for Theory X ought to solve *both* the nonidentity problem *and,* he suggests, the repugnant conclusion (*RP,* 387–90). We will return to the repugnant conclusion in part 3.11.

43. Mill is very persuasive on the distinction between how we ought to conduct ourselves and to what extent the state ought to take steps to make us conduct ourselves one way rather than another. See Mill, *On Liberty* (New York: Appleton-Century-Crofts, 1947), 76 and, generally, chap. 4.

44. Parfit, *RP,* 381. This case introduces Parfit's discussion of the "repugnant conclusion." But it seems to me in some ways a better test case than the repugnant conclusion, in that it avoids certain questions about what is possible that are necessarily invoked by the repugnant conclusion.

45. Kavka, "The Paradox of Future Individuals," 99. I omit here the phrase with which Kavka concludes this sentence ("or contribute more to others' happiness"), since it is not clear to me that the couple has no obligation to produce the distinct but happier child when doing so makes others better off.

46. Kavka, "The Paradox of Future Individuals," 99–100.

47. Narveson, "Moral Problems of Population," in *Ethics and Population,* ed. Michael D. Bayles (Cambridge, Mass.: Schenkman, 1976), 78.

48. Kavka, "The Paradox of Future Individuals," 97.

49. Kavka, "The Paradox of Future Individuals," 97, 105.

50. Kavka, "The Paradox of Future Individuals," 105.

51. Kavka, "The Paradox of Future Individuals," 105.

52. Kavka, "The Paradox of Future Individuals," 105.

53. Kavka, "The Paradox of Future Individuals," 106.

54. Kavka, "The Paradox of Future Individuals," 105–6.

55. Kavka, "The Paradox of Future Individuals," 105 n.23.

56. Kavka, "The Paradox of Future Individuals," 105.

57. Broome and Morton, "The Value of a Person," *Proceedings of the Aristotelian Society* supp. 68 (1994), 167–68. This judgment, it seems, assumes that the couple's producing the child is important to no one else (e.g., an older, or future younger, sibling).

58. Parfit, *RP,* 387–90.

59. Parfit, *RP,* 390.

60. Parfit, *RP,* 384 (discussing his "Down Escalator Case").

61. Some theorists (but not Parfit) have suggested that person-affecting views in some general way avoid the repugnant conclusion. See Wolf, "Social Choice and Normative Population Theory," 273–78. But as mentioned earlier Wolf's interpretation of the person-affecting intuition is distinct from personalism (note 25).

62. Partha Dasgupta uses this expression. See *An Inquiry Into Well-Being and Destitution* (Oxford: Clarendon Press, 1993): 383.

63. See part 2.11 ("Pain and Sin").

64. Parfit, "Overpopulation and the Quality of Life," in *Applied Ethics*, ed. Peter Singer (Oxford University Press, 1986), 160–64.

65. See part 2.11 ("Pain and Sin").

66. Feldman, "Justice, Desert, and the Repugnant Conclusion," *Utilitas* 7, no. 2 (Nov. 1995): 194–201.

67. Feldman, "Justice, Desert, and the Repugnant Conclusion," 198.

68. Feldman, "Justice, Desert, and the Repugnant Conclusion," 202.

69. Feldman, "Justice, Desert, and the Repugnant Conclusion," 202.

70. Feldman, "Justice, Desert, and the Repugnant Conclusion," 206.

71. Feldman, "Justice, Desert, and the Repugnant Conclusion," 196.

72. Feldman, "Justice, Desert, and the Repugnant Conclusion," 196–97, nn.15, 17.

Chapter 4

Wrongful Life

4.1 The Value of Life

Until this point, we have supposed that the subjects of the various hypotheticals have lives that are *worth living*. We have supposed that their lives are good for them, on a net basis, rather than something they are better off without. We have supposed that their level of well-being is in the positive range. Thus, for example, in the slave child case we supposed that being a slave was bad—but not so bad as to make the child's life *less* than worth living. Partly on the basis of this supposition, the proponent of the nonidentity problem claims (mistakenly, I argued in chapter 3) that the slave child is not wronged by having been brought into existence as a slave. But even the proponent of the nonidentity problem leaves open the possibility that a person has been wronged in a case in which that person's existence is so full of pain and other forms of ill-being that he or she would have been better off never having existed at all.

While the actual frequency of lives *less* than worth living will depend on what we take well-being to be, such cases would seem to be rare. The flaws in our own lives are mostly not so severe as to push the level of our well-being down into the negative range. But there does not seem to be any foundation for the view that existence is *always* a good thing from the point of view of the one who exists, no matter what the facts or what the flaw. The supposition that the child's life as a slave is better for the child than never having existed at all may be, depending on how we understand well-being, a plausible one (though better still for the child to exist as a nonslave). But surely cases much worse than the case of the slave child can be imagined. The possibility of cases sometimes arising in which nonexistence is the better state is at the heart of the infant-plaintiff's claim of *wrongful life*, according to which the defendant, by negligently bringing the plaintiff into existence to begin with, *wrongs* the plaintiff.

Critics argue that the claim of wrongful life should not be recognized by courts as a legitimate cause of action in negligence. The element of the wrongful life claim that has received the most attention is *harm*. For a jury or judge acting as finder of fact to determine that the defendant's negligence harms the wrongful life plaintiff, it seems that the jury must determine that the plaintiff has been made *worse off* by the defendant's negligence. And to determine that the plaintiff has been made worse off, it seems that the jury must compare how things were, or would have been, for the plaintiff and how things in fact are, as a consequence of the defendant's conduct, for the plaintiff. But in the wrongful life context, had the defendant not been negligent, the plaintiff would never have existed at all! According to critics, in these circumstances there is no reasonable basis for determining whether the plaintiff has been made worse off or better off by the defendant's negligence. Perhaps the plaintiff has not been *made* either worse off or better off by having been brought into existence. For how can things have been like anything at all from the point of view of the one who does not exist? And if things are not like anything at all from the point of view of the one who does not exist, how can they have been *made worse*? Thus, critics conclude that the jury, having no reasonable basis for comparing how things were, or would have been, for the plaintiff, with how things in fact are for the plaintiff, likewise has no reasonable basis for a finding of harm.

But I will argue that a reasonable basis exists for making the necessary comparison between existence and nonexistence. Such a comparison involves, I will argue, a comparison between the value, from the plaintiff's point of view, of existence and the value of nonexistence, again, from the plaintiff's point of view. As it happens, I believe that the latter is the much easier valuation to give.

To complete the account of harm, however, it is not enough to show that there is a reasonable basis for comparing existence and nonexistence. A complete account must also provide a principled means of identifying the two states that are to be compared against one another. *Which* state must be worse for the plaintiff than *which* other state for the plaintiff to have been harmed? As part of the initial test of harm in part 4.4.1, the two states that are to be compared are identified counterfactually. According to this initial test, to determine harm the comparison must be made between what things *would have been* like for the plaintiff and what things *are* like for the plaintiff. I make use of this test in parts 4.4.2–4.4.4 to illustrate how the necessary comparison between existence and nonexistence may reasonably be made.

Ultimately, however, we will see that the counterfactual test requires modification (part 4.4.4). Thus, Feinberg argues that any adequate test of harm must address the problem of the *baseline*. I outline such a test, which I call a *modal* test, in part 4.6.

It is significant that the *legal* account of wrongful life that I will ultimately provide is supported by the person-affecting account of wrongful life—that is, by the *moral* account. It means that personalism provides a reason to think that the law of negligence should be understood to embrace the claim of wrongful life. Moreover, the person-affecting account of wrongful life gives us, I believe, the tools that we need to address the problem of the baseline. Thus, along the way we will examine the person-affecting account of wrongful life (part 4.5).

A practical complication arises in cases in which the infant-plaintiff has been very, very well cared for and his or her life as a factual matter made worth living by the herculean efforts of the infant's parents and others. I address this practical issue—the problem of *deflected ill-being*—in part 4.7.

Some critics of wrongful life argue that the very notion that nonexistence in some cases would have been better for a person than existence is both inconsistent and semantically defective. Though I agree that we need to steer clear of these dangerous shoals, I think the shipping lane is in fact pretty broad. I address these issues in part 4.8.

Of course, personalism is not the only moral theory that could be put forward as a principled basis for settling issues that arise out of wrongful life. Still, personalism is not a bad candidate to turn to when the law of negligence is on its own terms indeterminate or when questions of the direction of the law's progression arise. I have, in earlier chapters, addressed some major objections to the person-affecting approach. Moreover, claims of wrongful life are typically brought as claims in negligence, and person-affecting consequentialism and the law of negligence share certain common ground. Indeed, the first topic of this chapter will be to point out this common ground (part 4.2). As a second matter, some of the real-life contexts in which claims of wrongful life have been made will be described (part 4.3).

4.2 Personalism and the Law of Negligence: Common Ground

4.2.1 The Requirement of Personal Wronging

A community's desire to outlaw what totalism or averagism would identify as wrongdoing that wrongs no one could give legislative bodies a rationale to put certain statutory schemes into place. But the claim that a wrong has been done, stripped of the claim that *someone* has been wronged, will never by itself provide the foundation for any common law tort claim. Personalism likewise, by way of P*, provides that a wrong is done if and only if someone is wronged. Personalism and the law of negligence thus have in common that both excuse conduct in the absence of a flesh-and-blood wronged person.

4.2.2   The Requirement of a Discernible Effect

Second, personalism, with its roots in utilitarianism, and negligence law are closely related in respect of the *kind* of effect on or consequence for people they consider significant. Thus, for purposes of establishing a claim in negligence, the harm that is claimed must be of a kind that a typical finder of fact—whether judge or jury—can readily understand as a loss. It is often of the tangible, palpable variety. Examples include physical or emotional pain and suffering and the loss of life, limb, liberty, property, or reputation.[1] Thus, no special instructions to the jury in, for example, natural or human rights theories, or the Kantian distinction between treating people as ends rather than as means alone, is necessary.

Does the law of negligence recognize only adverse effects? Clearly not. In determining harm, the distinction will be made between the case in which a leg is amputated to prevent the spread of cancer and the case in which a leg is severed in an automobile accident. The *negative* in the cancer case and the automobile accident may be equivalent. But the *positive* in each case will be different. In one case the life is saved, and the other case it is not. Because the positive will be netted against the negative in each case, the legal conclusion regarding harm will be quite different.

It is plausible to construe personalism similarly to focus not on the utterly mysterious but rather on the comprehensible—possibly even the quantifiable and (by supposition) the comparable. Happiness, pleasure, income, resources, autonomy, and capability are all good candidates for well-being, and unhappiness, pain, indebtedness, dependence, and incapacity all good candidates for ill-being. And, like the law of negligence, personalism incorporates a netting rule. Well-being must be in some way netted against ill-being as part of determining the overall lifetime well-being of any person.

4.2.3   The Rejection of Aggregative Efficiency as Primary Value

A third common feature between personalism and negligence theory is that both reject the totalist assumption that the value of any given alternative can be assessed by aggregating, or summing up, the value of the alternative for each person who there exists. On the moral side, comparisons of aggregate well-being do not, according to personalism, determine whether some wrong has been done. On the legal side, considerations of aggregative efficiency do not by themselves determine whether a duty exists or liability will attach. Thus, within a democratic system the people might prefer the law of negligence to reflect, and thoughtful judges may understand the law of negligence to include, values other than aggregative efficiency. Of course, claims in negligence must allege not just that some flesh-and-blood plaintiff has suffered harm of a particular sort but also that the defendant has *breached* a *duty of care* he or she had to save the plaintiff from the sort of harm that the plaintiff suffers. The specific duties we are taken to have, for purposes of the law of negligence (e.g., not to construct dangerous but "attractive" conditions, like unfenced swimming pools, even on our own private property; if we are ophthalmologists, routinely to test for glaucoma even in the absence of any complaint from the patient), may have little to do with aggregative efficiency. They are, rather, duties that have been settled on us over time through a capacious and evolving common law tradition.

Even though the duty element in negligence is not in fact limited by aggregative, or group, considerations, one might think that it *should* be limited in this way.[2] One might think, in other words, that judges and legislators *should* appeal to considerations of aggregative efficiency in determining how the law of negligence is to be interpreted, how it shall progress, and when to settle new duties on people or relieve them of old ones. Aggregative efficiency is, of course, a concept that totalism digests with ease. According to the totalist, if things can be arranged so that more total good can be produced at no more cost and if there exists no still better way of arranging things, then things *ought*, morally, to be arranged in this way.

Many economists avoid endorsing aggregative efficiency as having any sort of primacy over other values.[3] But some economists are less reticent.[4] And the idea can pop up anywhere. Thus, regarding recent U.S. immigration policy, one popular weekly publication included an article flatly stating that

> [t]he fact that immigration hurts the poor and benefits the rich doesn't necessarily make it a bad thing. To decide whether this is a worthwhile trade-off, we need to know how significant the net benefits from immigration are.[5]

This is a rather startling, if off hand, endorsement of aggregative efficiency as a primary social value.

The very availability of personalism as an alternative theory belies the notion that morality, or even rationality, *requires* that we understand the law of negligence in terms of *aggregative* efficiency. It is not that personalism does not value efficiency. It does value efficiency—but a *nonaggregative* form of efficiency. Thus, where agents have maximized well-being for a given person, M* implies that that person has not been wronged; and when agents can, at no cost to others, but do not increase an existing or future person's well-being, D* implies that that person *has* been wronged.[6] Moreover, consistent with personalism, we might sometimes use an aggregative calculation as a rule of thumb for evaluating the extent to which competing arrangements have value *for each person* (thus a "rising tide lifts all boats," etc.). At the same time, however, personalism requires that we move, at defined points, away from aggregative considerations. Personalism thus expressly avoids leaving trade-off, or distributional, issues between rich and poor to some totalist accident of the bottom line. Rather, it hands such issues off to some independent theory, for example, of fairness. Such a theory would presumably imply that the right thing to do is to leave the bread on the table of the poor family rather than move it to the table of the rich. In contrast, absolutely no guarantee exists that allowing the poor to have their bread will be an option endorsed, *or even permitted*, if the issue is left entirely to considerations of aggregative efficiency.[7]

Often, of course, there is a coincidence between what we consider to be sound negligence theory and totalism. Thus, we do not think that the pediatrician has a duty to order a spinal tap to rule out meningitis for *each* child who comes into the office with a headache. Ordering a spinal tap for *each* such patient is not "reasonably," we might say, required of pediatricians. We are really saying that the cost, both in dollars and to the children tested, would be enormous; and we want to use our resources elsewhere. On this basis, the pediatrician is considered not to have breached any duty even in the unusual case in which a child dies of meningitis after coming to the pediatrician with a headache. But this case hardly proves that sound negligence theory shares its theoretical underpinnings with totalism or other aggregative approaches rather than with personalism, since there is no reason to think that personalism would generate any distinct result in this case.

Moreover, in other instances sound negligence theory seems to put aside considerations of aggregative efficiency. Thus, the law of negligence expects the pediatrician to conduct business as a reasonable and prudent member of the profession. So, *even if provably inefficient from an aggregative perspective*, if members of the profession normally order a spinal tap when a child has high fever, a bad headache, and a stiff neck, the isolated pediatrician who fails to do so will violate a duty of care, which violation may ultimately cause the child's death or disability. A court that attaches liability in this kind of case has not departed from the straight and narrow of the common law and equally has not violated any principle of rationality or, in my view, morality. This seems so even if it is inefficient, on an aggregative basis, to hold the pediatrician to this particular standard of care. Here, the law of negligence reflects a value that is distributional in nature: it refuses to trade off some enormous portion of one child's well-being for the benefit of a few cents in the pockets of many.

Personalism itself might come to this very same conclusion by either of two routes. Depending on what well-being is, the meningitis case might not involve a trade-off at all. Thus, the few cents saved—even multiplied by the number of children ultimately tested—by each member of the community by not testing might not qualify as a plus in terms of well-being to the individuals who constitute the community. Suppose, however, that the meningitis case does involve a trade-off. In this case, personalism proper is silent, and the issue must be considered in light of a theory of fairness. But such a theory may likewise imply that the trade-off in favor of the child is permissible or, indeed, required.

Personalism and negligence theory thus share substantial common ground. Because of this common ground, personalism is a viable source of ideas for lawyers and judges as they work to sort out the new issues in negligence that continually arise as a function of new technologies and changing and increasingly complex societal norms and practices. Personalism offers, for example, one way of understanding and delimiting the tort of wrongful life. I turn to wrongful life now.

4.3 What Is an Action for Wrongful Life?

4.3.1 The Theory of Wrongful Life

Wrongful life represents a relatively new claim in negligence. Until very recently, doctors have not had the ability to identify the circumstances that increase a couple's risk of producing congenitally defective children or to prevent the conception or birth of these children. Babies just came, and the event was usually considered a happy, or even blessed, one. But even if it was not, there was nothing that anyone, including the doctor, could have done to prevent it. Thus, the doctor was not blamed or held responsible for the new life regardless of how adverse the circumstances of that new life.[8]

But things have changed. Doctors now have much more knowledge than they did in the past about the relationship between, on the one hand, parental age and lifestyle and, on the other, the risks of producing a defective child. Even more critically, the Human Genome Project is now well under way, and the possibilities for preconceptual screening for particular hereditary diseases continuously expanding. Moreover, techniques, including sonogram and amniocentesis, are now available by which doctors can gain significant additional information regarding specific fetuses. And, finally, doctors can now legally provide the means to prevent both conception and birth. When the risk that the child will be born with some significant defect is high, clear communication from the doctor to the potential parent and sound birth control will often do the trick of preventing conception to begin with. In other cases, abortion may be called for.

As doctors have come to be able to detect ever more risks, and do more to prevent those risks from eventuating, we have come to expect more of them. A doctor has, we therefore think, duties of inquiry and disclosure as well as a duty of care in providing birth control and performing abortions. When the doctor breaches his or her duty, the question arises whether the doctor should be held accountable for the suffering of the child who owes his or her very existence to the doctor's breach.

Like all claims in negligence, wrongful life claims assert that the child-plaintiff has suffered harm as a consequence of the defendant's breach of duty. The twist of wrongful life is that the harm that is claimed to arise out of the defendant's negligence is not the underlying defect that causes the child's life to be flawed in some way beyond the norm but rather the child's *life itself*. For the underlying defect in the wrongful life case is typically a chromosomal or genetic defect. It is typically a fact of nature that the afflicted child *could* not have been saved from, given the state of current medical technology, by the most careful and skilled medical team.[9] All the defendant could have done, then, was to take steps to keep that particular child from existing at all. And the wrongful life claim asserts that the doctor had a legal duty to do just that.

It is the harm issue and the related damages question, not the duty, breach, or causation issue, that have become so controversial in the wrongful life cases. Thus, critics ask how life itself can constitute a harm to the person who lives.

Before we turn to issues of theory, it is useful to consider some of the actual cases in which the claim of wrongful life has been made. The disorders on which claims of wrongful life have been based are extremely varied. And one issue will be how serious the disorder must be to ground a claim of wrongful life.

4.3.2   Examples of Wrongful Life Claims

Wrongful life cases involve situations in which a doctor or other medical personnel have negligently failed to take steps to prevent the existence of a child who suffers from genetic or chromosomal defects. Sometimes the negligence involves a failure to screen couples for or counsel would-be parents with respect to their risks of producing a defective child. In other cases, the negligence consists in the substandard performance of some medical procedure, treatment, or technique, such as amniocentesis or abortion.

Risks have in fact eventuated. And at least in some cases the circumstances are troubling enough—the child, that is, suffers enough—that we are forced, I believe, to take the claim of wrongful life seriously however highly we regard the wonder of life itself. Thus, in one instance parents had already given birth to two children suffering from neurofibromatosis, a disease resulting from a hereditary defect that causes developmental changes of the nervous system, skin, muscles, and bones.[10] The changes can be extremely disfiguring and discomfiting, and there is no known treatment or cure. The couple wanted to avoid a third pregnancy.[11] But the negligently performed vasectomy was ineffective, and later there was a failed abortion. The third baby was born with the disease.[12] In another case, the parents of a Down's syndrome infant alleged that the doctor failed to inform them that the incidence of Down's syndrome increases as women age and that he additionally failed to advise them of the possibility of amniocentesis.[13] In California, expectant parents, aware that they may be carriers of Tay-Sachs disease, sought screening for the recessive gene.[14] Tay-Sachs is a progressive, degenerative disease of the nervous system. The disease primarily affects the Eastern European Jewish population and is fatal. It is characterized by mental underdevelopment, convulsions, vision loss, and muscle softness.[15] The laboratory that did the screening incorrectly reported that neither husband nor wife was a carrier, and the couple's baby was indeed born with Tay-Sachs.[16] In another case, a couple previously had one child with polycystic kidney disease, who died five hours after birth. They were advised that the disease was not hereditary and that the chances of having a second child with the disease were practically nil. But the second child did have the disease and survived for only two and a half years.[17] A Texas couple had one child with Duchenne muscular dystrophy. When they learned of a second pregnancy, the doctor assured them that the wife was not a genetic carrier of the disease. The second child was born with the disease. The couple argued that, had they received accurate information, they would have chosen abortion.[18]

When *parents* sue the doctor for negligence in these kinds of cases, their claim is that the emotional and financial burden of raising a defective infant constitutes a legal harm. The parents' action, referred to as an action for *wrongful birth*, is well established.[19] In contrast, the defective *child's* claim, referred to as a claim for *wrongful life*, has typically *not* been recognized as a legitimate claim in most states.[20] Thus, complaints alleging wrongful life typically will be dismissed for "failure to state a claim." No jury will be permitted to hear evidence regarding the defendant's negligence or the circumstances of the child-plaintiff's life, and the case will be over with before it even begins.

Does it matter *to the child* that the child is not compensated, so long as the defendant is liable for money damages to the *parents*? A damage award paid to the parents is intended to compensate the parents for their emotional pain and suffering as well as for extraordinary out-of-pocket expenses they will incur as a function of caring for a child with special needs.[21] Such expenses may include substantial medical bills and, if the child lives long enough, special schooling and child care arrangements. No one doubts that many parents suffer emotionally and financially when their children are revealed to have serious chromosomal or genetic disorders. But if the parent suffers, so must the child. It is, after all, the *child* who lives the defect—who feels the pain, who cannot balance this pain by taking the usual child's pleasure in life, who is restricted to a very small, perhaps very lonely, world and to endless discomforts and indignities. Why should medical personnel be immune from liability for the child's harm? Why should they not pay for the entire cost of their negligence? Why should the child be placed at risk of a damage award inadequate to compensate the child fully—including to pay for loving nursing care, lavish pain therapy, and pleasant surroundings?

Moreover, even a large damage award paid to the parents will benefit the child only to the extent and in the respects that the parents choose. Thus, suppose the parents are richly compensated for their pain and suffering and their extraordinary medical expenses. Presumably the parents will be required by the terms of the compensation package to continue to care for the child. They cannot both receive the damage award and place the child for adoption. Beyond this minimum, however, it is unclear that they must do more for the child than what is necessary to avoid charges of abuse, neglect, or unfitness. Thus, like any other parent, they will be permitted to take solace as they please, in theory leaving themselves as well as the child indigent once the money has been spent. The device of a trust for the benefit of the child offers a better approach.[22] Such a trust could be administered by co-trustees consisting of one or both parents as well as one or more independent fiduciaries acting for the benefit of the child.

One last reason that it matters whether the child's claim is recognized alongside the parents' is that the child's claim has a longer life than the parents'. Statutes of limitations for medical malpractice vary from state to state. But normally they range from two to three years after the point at which damage has occurred or, more liberally, from two to three years after the point at which the damage has been or should have been discovered by the exercise of reasonable diligence.[23] However, even in states that have adopted the more generous statute many wrongful birth claims may be barred as untimely. But this result is unfair to the child. Why should the *child* be held responsible—and left uncompensated—for the *parents'* perceived untimeliness? A different rule applies in cases in which the plaintiff is a minor. In such cases, the statute of limitations typically does not begin to run until the child has reached the age of majority. Thus, a significant time period exists during which the parents' claim will be barred but the child's claim permitted.[24]

4.4   When Does Life Itself Constitute a *Harm*?

4.4.1   Obstacles to Establishing Harm

I earlier noted the critics' question of how *life itself* can possibly constitute a harm—how existence itself can possibly make the plaintiff *worse off* than nonexistence. At the same time, wrongful life plaintiffs clearly suffer pain and other forms of ill-being. Moreover, it is apparent that, however long the child lives, he or she is likely to be made to some degree better off by a well-endowed trust—one that goes beyond the financial contribution the parents can reasonably be required to make. Loving nursing care, lavish pain therapy, safe and pleasant surroundings, and, in some cases, special education or training over the course of an entire life represent enormous expenses. Why, then, would anyone doubt the wrongful life plaintiff's capacity to establish legal harm or wonder whether an award of money damages for the benefit of such a child is appropriate?

One might propose that imposing pain on someone *suffices* to harm that person and thus that, since it is easy enough in the wrongful life context to establish whether the plaintiff suffers pain, it is easy enough to establish whether the plaintiff has been harmed. But there is a problem with this naive "pain as sufficient for harm" view. Pain and other forms of ill-being as a general matter do not always indicate harm.

Each time a child gets a vaccination she (say) may experience *pain*. But we do not think she has thereby been *harmed*. Thus, even if we take the view that pain is the kind (or one kind) of effect that *can* harm, it seems clear that pain is not sufficient for harm.

Alternatively, one might propose that harm is a matter of imposing on someone a *net* negative effect. According to this view, giving the vaccination does not harm the child since the value to the child of being protected against getting a dread disease netted against the pain the child feels is *positive*. So, no harm done. But this account of harm will not do either, at least for purposes of negligence theory. Suppose the doctor carelessly injects an outmoded vaccine that protects the child against the dread disease but also—unlike the new, improved vaccine—causes the child to be violently ill for two days. Or suppose that a surgeon negligently performs open heart surgery, imposing trauma and other forms of ill-being on the patient. Suppose that the patient's life is saved but that a certain medication would have been as effective as surgery in treating the patient's cardiac disorder. In both instances, the net effect of the act at issue is positive. But clearly the subject has been, both in a legal and in any ordinary sense, harmed.

A third test of harm requires the plaintiff to show that the defendant's conduct has made things *worse for* the plaintiff than things *would otherwise have been*—that is, than things would have been in the absence of the conduct at issue. The insight of this test—the *counterfactual test*—is that harm is an essentially comparative matter. We compare how things are for the plaintiff with how things would have been, and say that the plaintiff has been harmed if the former is worse than the latter. Assuming the defendant would have used the new, improved vaccine had he not carelessly reached for the outmoded vaccine, the child is made worse off than she would otherwise have been and is therefore harmed. At the same time, the child is made better off when given the correct vaccine and is therefore, though perhaps *hurt*, not harmed.

According to the counterfactual test, the states that are to be compared are how things *would have been* for the plaintiff in the absence of the defendant's negligence and how things *in fact* are for the plaintiff. As we will see, the problem of the baseline implies that this counterfactual test is in fact problematic. Nonetheless, the counterfactual test provides a useful initial account of harm. Though the test will ultimately require revision, harm will remain an essentially comparative matter.

But understanding harm as an essentially comparative matter—whether we accept the counterfactual test or, as I propose, opt for another—generates a major difficulty for wrongful life. In the ordinary negligence context, a comparative account of harm operates in a straightforward fashion. In the ordinary context, the counterfactual test requires that a comparison be made that we think can be made reasonably—between how things in fact are for the plaintiff and how they would have been. But, in the context of wrongful life, we seem to be required to compare how things in fact are for the plaintiff and *nonexistence*.

I thus see no way to sidestep—for either moral or for legal purposes, and whether we accept the counterfactual test of harm or opt for some other—the comparison between existence and nonexistence in the wrongful life context. But many critics of wrongful life have found this a daunting task. The court in *Becker v. Schwartz* put the point this way:

> Whether it is better never to have been born at all than to have been born with even gross deficiencies is a mystery more properly to be left to the philosophers and the theologians. Surely the law can assert no competence to resolve the issue, particularly in view of the very nearly uniform high value which the law and mankind has placed on human life, rather than its absence.[25]

Justice Weintraub, dissenting in *Gleitman v. Cosgrove*, shifts the focus to a distinct worry:

> Ultimately, the plaintiff's complaint is that he would be better off not to have been born. Man, who knows nothing of death or nothingness, cannot possibly know whether this is true.[26]

Two views are expressed in these passages: that we attach a "high value" even to a flawed existence—a point that raises what Steinbock calls the "sanctity of life" argument[27]—and that the value of nonexistence is an unknown. *Either* of these views would, if true, provide a good reason to reject the claim of wrongful life. The former view implies that existence, always having a high value, is never worse than nonexistence. And the latter view implies that the two states that must be compared to find harm can never be reasonably compared since we do not have a clue what the value of nonexistence is.

But I want to reject both of these views. Thus, I will argue that there is no reason to think that each and every existence, no matter how flawed, is always better than nonexistence from the point of view of the one who exists. Moreover, it seems to me that the epistemic limitations under which we suffer do not in fact render us unable to know the value of nonexistence. I will conclude that we can make the comparison that we need to make to test for harm in the wrongful life context, and thus that the need to make this comparison does not provide any court with a reason to refuse to recognize wrongful life claims as failing to state entirely proper causes of action in negligence.[28]

4.4.2   The Value of Nonexistence

Can we really say nothing about the value of the "utter void of non-existence" for the one who does not exist?[29]

I want to put this question aside for a moment before directly responding to it. It is important to note that, in giving an account of the wrongful life claim, I am not even beginning to address rationales for euthanasia.[30] Thus, the wrongful life claim that it would have been better for the plaintiff had the plaintiff never existed to begin with does not imply that it would be better now to end the plaintiff's life or for the plaintiff now to die or be "allowed" to die.[31] For all kinds of reasons, ending the life of an already existing person may be a very bad thing even in a case in which a wrongful life claim may appropriately be made. Thus, perhaps the worst is over for the child and, relationships in place, the best is yet to come.[32] Perhaps, however burdensome his or her life, the child now has a kind of life instinct and, in effect, consciously or not, clings to life in a way that we must respect. Perhaps ending the child's life will have profound ill effects on the parents, who love and need *this* child and will not be placated by the message that they can always set about producing some other, healthier baby. Finally, perhaps there are over-arching reasons to avoid altogether the business of urging that exceptions be made to the usual proscription against ending the life of any person.

But the claim that the infant-plaintiff *should never have come into existence to begin with* is not in tension with any of these four points. Thus, to say that it would have been better for the child, from the child's own point of view, never to have existed at all does not imply that *now* the better thing for the child is to end the child's life or for the child to die. In person-affecting terms: leaving the child out of existence from the beginning cannot wrong the child, but ending his or her life once that child exists may very well wrong the child.[33]

Thus, I set aside the question of the value of ending a life to the one whose life is to be ended. And I focus, instead, on the question raised by wrongful life: from the point of view of the plaintiff, what is the value of nonexistence, not in the sense of now dying, but in the sense of *never having existed at all*?

Whether we think in terms of *moral* value—that is, well-being—or *legal* value, it seems that we can meaningfully assess the value of non-existence for the plaintiff. On the moral side I have supposed that it makes sense to think of worlds as ordered relative to each person who in fact exists at any time in respect of how good such worlds are for that person. I have supposed, in other words, that it makes sense to compare worlds in terms of how much well-being they accord to a particular individual. And whatever it is that makes one world better or worse than another for a given person seems to be the kind of thing that can be reduced for that person in some third world to nothing at all. In some cases in which the reason well-being is, relative to a person, nothing at all, that person can be imagined to exist in a neutral, neither happy nor sad state. But in other cases a person's well-being might be nothing at all because he or she does not exist. Thus, it fits nicely with the system of numerical assignments that I have used throughout this work to say that the well-being an existing person has in any world in which that person does not exist is "zero."[34]

But the term *well-being* as I have used it until this point expresses an exclusively *moral* concept. And an aim of this chapter is to provide an account of the wrongful life plaintiff's claim of *legal* harm. But we can, usually allowing the context to do the work of disambiguating for us, understand "well-being" to express a *legal* concept as well. Thus, the law of negligence protects against certain adverse, or negative, effects. It protects against certain sorts of losses, including physical and emotional pain and suffering, the loss of life, limb, liberty, property, reputation, and incapacity generally. But the law of negligence does not embrace only negative values. It also promotes certain *positive* values. Thus, the law of negligence is capable of making the distinction between the case in which a leg is amputated to save a person's life and the case in which the leg is severed in an automobile accident.

On the moral side, the plaintiff in any world in which he or she does not exist experiences neither pleasure nor pain, neither happiness nor unhappiness; has no education and suffers no misinformation; has no autonomy and suffers no constraint; has no income and no expenses; is neither capable nor incapacitated. Whatever our concept of *moral* well-being, the assignment of a zero level of well-being in any world in which a given person does not exist is plausible. And on the legal side the same inference can be made. The wrongful life plaintiff—who in fact exists—suffers no physical or emotional pain and no loss of life, limb, or property, or capacity of any kind and enjoys no mitigating gain or benefit in any world in which he or she never exists to begin with. Again, whatever *legal* well-being is, the assignment of a zero value is plausible. More generally still, whether the analysis is legal or moral, nonexistence neither furthers nor hinders any of the plaintiff's interests and has no value or disvalue of any form for the plaintiff. And so the plaintiff's well-being in any world in which the plaintiff does not exist, whether for legal or moral purposes, does not really seem an unknown. Rather, zero seems to hit the mark precisely.

It goes without saying that it is not true as a matter of logic or independently of any semantics for the natural language that one might propose that the value of nonexistence for any person is zero. Rather, the point here is that the numerical scheme that I have used to express the various suppositions that I have made throughout this work regarding the relative values of pairs of worlds for specific individuals provides us with a way to meaningfully express the value for any existing person of any world in which that person never exists. Indeed, in a way, understanding nonexistence as having a zero value has a preexisting intuitive appeal that particular positive and negative assignments lack. Thus, we do not have a sense, independent of any specific analysis, of whether a given person in a given situation has a level of well-being of "2" or, say, "4" (though we may have a sense of whether a given person has half as much well-being in one situation as in another). But when we turn to nonexistence, it seems that we are more or less stuck with zero.

Someone who considers nonexistence itself, in the sense of never having existed at all, to be for the one who never exists a very bad state rather than, as I have, a neutral state sets an extremely high standard for the wrongful life claim. To succeed, the plaintiff must show that the value of his or her existence is less than the value of a very bad state. But if we consider never having existed at all as having a neutral, or zero, value, we do not set quite such a high standard. For then the plaintiff need only show that the value of her existence is less than zero. Cohen considers such an approach to "expand" the standard for wrongful life to include cases in which the child suffers, not a "devastating illness," but rather simply a "serious disease."[35]

4.4.3   The Value of a Flawed Existence

Figuring out that the value of nonexistence for the plaintiff is none at all, or zero, does not settle the question of *harm*. Harm is a comparative matter and requires the plaintiff to have been made *worse off*. Should it turn out to be the case that existence by some necessity always is better than nonexistence for the one who exists—always, that is, has some positive value or level of well-being for the one who exists—then it will turn out to be the case that imposing existence never *harms* the plaintiff.

Is it the case, then, that, no matter what pain an infant suffers and how little pleasure she (say) is able to take from her own existence, that existence is *always* necessarily better for her than nonexistence?

Is it true that, on a net basis, her level of well-being will always be positive?

To settle this question, it seems enough to note that whether one world is better for a given person than another world depends both on facts about well-being and on facts about ill-being. Thus, the final tally of well-being for any particular person at any world must take ill-being into account, possibly in some very complicated way.[36]

But as soon as it is agreed that the final tally of well-being must be made on a net basis, it seems that it must also be acknowledged that for some people in some circumstances the balance may tilt toward ill-being. There is nothing to prevent this from happening. There is no metaphysical support that braces up the ill-being side of the scale so that it cannot in some instances outweigh the well-being side.

The view that each life necessarily has positive net value for the person who lives is not, I think, merely implausible. It is also harsh in refusing to recognize the depths of human suffering and, accordingly, in disallowing any basis for the amelioration of that suffering. In the view of the blind optimist, no matter what the facts, things are really never *that bad* for the infant-plaintiffs who claim wrongful life. But unfounded optimism is out of place in any system of justice.

4.4.4 The Comparison to Nonexistence, Three Examples, and One Problem

It thus seems plausible that, from the plaintiff's point of view, whatever the facts and circumstances of the plaintiff's life, the value of never having existed at all can be assessed at zero (part 4.4.2). Moreover, it seems plausible that in some instances the value of existence itself, given all the facts and circumstances of the plaintiff's life, is in the negative range (part 4.4.3). We noted earlier that, according to the counterfactual test of harm, for the jury to determine that the defendant's negligent breach of duty has harmed the plaintiff, the jury must determine that the plaintiff has been made worse off than the plaintiff would otherwise have been. We can now propose that the plaintiff has been made worse off by having been brought into existence just when what I will call the plaintiff's *factual* level of well-being is less than the zero level or, equivalently, just when the plaintiff's factual level of well-being is in the negative range. According to this account of how the comparison with nonexistence is to be made, if the plaintiff's level of well-being is, on a net basis, negative, bringing the plaintiff into existence harms the plaintiff; otherwise it does not.[37]

Let us consider three different cases, starting with an ordinary medical malpractice case.

Case 9: As a result of the obstetrician-defendant's negligence in the delivery room, the infant-plaintiff becomes disabled in a way that causes him (say) to suffer. His life is, despite its flaws, worth living, and his factual level of well-being remains positive.

According to the counterfactual test, to determine whether the plaintiff has been harmed we look to see whether the plaintiff has been made worse off by the defendant's negligence than the plaintiff would otherwise have been. In other words, we compare the plaintiff's factual level of well-being—how things in fact are for the plaintiff—with how things would have been for the plaintiff had the defendant not been negligent. Here the plaintiff exists in both of the two states to be evaluated and compared. The comparison requires imagination but is not otherwise tricky. The former state being worse for the plaintiff than the latter, we conclude that the plaintiff has indeed been made worse off and thus has been harmed.

We turn now to a case in which the defendant's negligence gives rise, not to the plaintiff's condition, but to the plaintiff's very existence.

Case 10: As a result of the defendant's negligence in advising a couple as to their risk of producing a child with a given chromosomal or genetic defect, the plaintiff is conceived and born, suffering precisely the defect regarding which the defendant failed to advise. As a result of this defect, the plaintiff suffers. But the plaintiff's suffering is not so enormous that she (say) does not enjoy and take pleasure in life. Thus, as in case 9, the life is, despite its flaws, worth living, and the plaintiff's level of well-being remains positive.

Again, to determine harm, we ask whether the plaintiff has been made *worse off* by the defendant's negligence. To answer this question, we compare as before the plaintiff's factual level of well-being with how things would have been for the plaintiff in the absence of the defendant's negligence. It is a given that the plaintiff's factual level of well-being is positive. Had the defendant not been negligent, the plaintiff would never have existed at all. According to the account that I propose, the plaintiff's level of well-being would then have been zero. Comparing the plaintiff's factual, positive level to the zero level, we conclude that the plaintiff has not been made worse off and thus has not been harmed.

Finally, we turn to case 11.

Case 11: As a result of the defendant's negligence in advising a couple as to their risk of producing a child with a given chromosomal or genetic defect, the plaintiff is conceived and born, suffering precisely the defect the defendant failed to disclose. As a result of this defect, the plaintiff suffers enormously. Pain and disability so fill the plaintiff's life that she (say) is able to eke out only the smallest degree of pleasure. Her life is less than one worth living and her level of well-being is negative.

Comparing the plaintiff's level of well-being in each of the two states—again, the plaintiff's factual level of well-being, which is negative (a given), with the zero level—we determine that the plaintiff has been made worse off by the defendant's negligence and thus has been harmed.

The account just given suggests a way to make the comparison between states in which one exists and states in which one does not exist. However, to give a complete account of wrongful life, it is not enough to show that comparisons to nonexistence may reasonably be made. We must also define an adequate test of *harm*, for it is this latter test that picks out *which* two states are to be valued and compared. As noted earlier, the counterfactual test of harm itself is not adequate to this task. We might say, following Feinberg, that the counterfactual test does not adequately address the problem of the *baseline*.[38]

Consider case 9, a routine case of medical malpractice. We assessed harm by comparing the plaintiff's factual level of well-being with that level of well-being the plaintiff *would have had* had the defendant not been negligent. But it seems that this counterfactual test of harm will not in general be quite accurate. For applying this test to *peculiar* sets of facts and circumstances can produce unexpected, and apparently incorrect, answers. Thus, it is always possible that for one reason or another a given plaintiff's disability on a net basis will make the plaintiff *better off* than he or she would have been in the absence of the defendant's negligence in a case in which we think that the plaintiff has in fact been *harmed*.

In most contexts courts will—correctly, it seems—seek to avoid this complication. The law of negligence can be seen to condone, at least implicitly, a form of *assumption* that functions to screen out certain complex realities from the jury's assessment of the claim of harm. In effect, though courts recite their interest in "what would have been," the legal focus will not always precisely be on *what would have been*. Suppose that the defendant argues correctly that, but for her (say) carelessness in the delivery room, the baby *would* have gone home with his (say) parents twenty-four hours or so after birth and *would* then have suffered in even worse ways in the hands of his own abusive parents. Instead, because of the defendant's carelessness, the baby spends several months in the neonatal intensive care unit rather than at home with his parents. In consequence, the defendant, far from harming the baby, has rescued him!

However truthful and well-documented this line of argument is, no court should be interested in it and may cite doctrines of relevance or prejudice to avoid it. But the court's refusal to allow this line of argument is not a function of the fact that the court somehow *knows* this sequence of events would not have occurred. After all, the court might not have this knowledge, and the sequence of events might perfectly well have occurred. The court's lack of interest in this line of argument is, rather, a function of its making a certain assumption. Always, to assess harm, the court must have the jury compare the plaintiff's factual situation with *some* other state—what Feinberg calls the "baseline."[39] The assumption that the court puts into place, then, is as to what this baseline is. Thus, for example in the careless obstetrician–abusive parent scenario a court might take the plaintiff's baseline to be a more or less averagely healthy life. In the case described the *assumption* of what would have been—the baseline—does not match the reality of *what would have been*.

In this particular case, at an intuitive level the assumption as to baseline seems entirely appropriate. We do not think that the defendant *should* be released from liability on the basis of, for example, what the parents *would* have done to the child had the defendant acted with due care. At the same time, to take the baseline in typical medical malpractice cases, like case 9, to be a more or less averagely healthy life is ad hoc until some principled basis on which to do so is defined. We must, in other words, supply a test of harm that improves on the counterfactual test. I believe that the person-affecting account of wrongful life—the *moral* account—will be useful in filling this gap. Thus, once I have sketched the person-affecting account in part 4.5, I will then return, in part 4.6, to the problem of the baseline.

4.5   A Person-Affecting Account of Wrongful Life

The legal account of wrongful life requires a comparison between nonexistence and existence. But so does personalism. For moral purposes personalism will take into account, among other things, whether the plaintiff's well-being as a matter of fact has been *maximized*. To leave open the possibility of existence as a wrong, personalism must therefore recognize nonexistence as an accessible state for the plaintiff and be able to compare the plaintiff's level of well-being at any world in which the plaintiff does not exist with the plaintiff's factual level of well-being.

In addressing wrongful life, the most critical of the person-affecting principles are M* and D*. M*, which applies just in those instances in which the subject's well-being has been maximized, exculpates conduct:

M*: s is not wronged by agents in X *if*, for each world Y accessible to such agents, s has at least as much well-being in X as s has in Y.

In the wrongful life context, M* exculpates the defendant's negligence in those cases in which no world better for the plaintiff was accessible to the defendant. But among the worlds accessible to the defendant are worlds in which the plaintiff never exists to begin with. In those worlds, the plaintiff's level of well-being is zero. If, as a matter of fact, the plaintiff's well-being is in the negative range, then the conditions of M* will not be satisfied, and M* will not exculpate the conduct. But suppose that the plaintiff's level of well-being is positive. And suppose that the case is a typical wrongful life case, so that the various flaws in the plaintiff's life are *unavoidable*: they are given rise to by underlying chromosomal or genetic defects and are "facts of nature" that we presently lack the capacity to repair. Neither the defendant nor any other agent has the wherewithal to have brought *this* infant-plaintiff into anything but a flawed existence. On these suppositions, agents, including the defendant, *have* maximized the plaintiff's well-being. M* then implies that the plaintiff has not been wronged. This is so even if the plaintiff's existence is, though still worth living, in fact significantly flawed.

In contrast to M*, D* is inculpatory. In certain circumstances, D* implies that agents have wronged a person when they have *not* maximized that person's well-being. Thus:

D*: s is wronged by agents in X *if* s exists in X and there is some world Y accessible to such agents such that:
  (i) s has more well-being in Y than s has in X;
  (ii) for each person s' who ever exists in X, *either* s' has at least as much well-being in Y as s' has in X *or* s' never exists in Y; *and*
  (iii) for each s' who ever exists in Y, s' exists at some time in X.

Among those accessible worlds one must consider to determine whether the subject, according to D*, has been wronged are those worlds in which the subject does not exist. If any such world is better for the subject and worse for no one else, then the subject is wronged by having been brought into existence. Suppose that the plaintiff's factual level of well-being is in the negative range. Then, a world in which the plaintiff does not exist would have been better for the plaintiff. And, assuming the plaintiff's not existing would not have made anyone else worse off, D* implies that the plaintiff has been wronged. Perhaps it seems likely, in the wrongful life context, that leaving the plaintiff out of existence to begin with could have been accomplished at a cost to no one. Still, we should note that in cases in which leaving the plaintiff out of existence does involve a cost to someone, personalism would hand the issue over to a theory of fairness.

Finally, note that, given N*, the analysis avoids any sort of "damned if we do, damned if we don't" critique. Thus:

N*: s is not wronged by agents in X *if* s never exists in X.

The defendant may, under D*, wrong the plaintiff by bringing him or her into existence, but N* implies that the defendant wrongs no one who never exists at all.

We are now in a position to provide a person-affecting account of each of the three cases described earlier. Taking case 9 first, let $s_1, \ldots, s_n$ represent other existing and future people, including the parents, and let d represent the defendant and p the child-plaintiff. Let A represent what has in fact occurred. The question then is whether what has in fact occurred—A—constitutes a wrong to p. A thus includes the obstetrician-defendant's carelessness in the delivery room and the effect that the defendant's carelessness has on the child. Let B represent an alternative in which the defendant is not careless and the baby emerges from the delivery room in good health. Suppose also that the defendant's conduct does not, in fact, benefit anyone else. Finally, suppose a set of numbers that reflects the relative value, in terms of well-being, of A and B as described for each subject. Then, our facts are these:

Case 9, Routine Medical Negligence, Annotated

	A	B
s_1	5*	5*
...	5*	5*
s_n	5*	5*
d	5*	5*
p	3!	5*

Using "*n**" and "*n!*" as before to record the implications of personalism, we can note that since the plaintiff's well-being has been maximized in *B* M* implies that he is not there wronged. But D* implies that he is wronged in *A*, since the defendant's acting with greater care—that is, bringing about *B*—would not have imposed a cost on anyone else. (On another set of suppositions, of course, fairness may play an essential role.)

Now consider case 10. In this case, the claim is that the defendant's negligence leads not to the child's suffering but to her very existence. In contrast to case 9, *this* very child *could not* have been born healthy, whatever care the defendant had taken in the delivery room or otherwise. No world is accessible, in other words, in which this child both exists and enjoys a higher level of well-being. Of course, worlds in which the child never exists at all are accessible to the defendant. But in this case the child's level of well-being is positive, and so it is not the case that the child would have been better off never existing to begin with.

Again, let *A* represent what in fact occurs, including the defendant's careless conduct, the end result of which is the child's existence. Let *B* represent an alternative in which the defendant is not careless and the child does not exist. Finally, suppose a set of numbers that reflects the relative value, in terms of well-being, of *A* and *B* for each subject. Then:

Case 10, Wrongful Life, No Harm, Annotated

	A	B
s_1	5*	5*
...	5*	5*
s_n	5*	5*
d	5*	5*
p	3*	*

The plaintiff's well-being has been maximized in *A*, and M* implies that she has not been wronged in *A*. This is so despite the fact that her level of well-being is well below average. Nor, according to N*, is the plaintiff wronged in *B*. It thus would have been perfectly permissible for the defendant to have acted more carefully and have not brought the plaintiff into existence to begin with.

Finally, we turn to case 11. As in case 10, in case 11 the child's claim is that the defendant's negligence has led, not to the defect, but to the child's very existence. Again this existence is itself flawed, and the child suffers accordingly. And again there is no issue of delivery room carelessness. The defect is one that cannot be avoided if the child is to exist at all. Thus, as in case 10, there is no accessible world in which *this* very child exists and has a higher level of well-being. The difference between case 10 and case 11 is the extent to which the child suffers. In case 11, the child's suffering is so great as to render life *less* than worth living. Never having existed to begin with is thus, from the child's own point of view, her better state. Thus:

Case 11, Wrongful Life, Harm, Annotated

	A	B
s_1	5*	5*
. . .	5*	5*
s_n	5*	5*
d	5*	5*
p	$-5!$	*

On these facts, D* implies that the child has been wronged in A, and M* and N* imply that no one else, including the child, is wronged anywhere else.

4.6   The Problem of the Baseline and the Modal Test of Harm

In the person-affecting account of wrongful life just given, we did not need to make any reference to harm. But the legal account, sketched in part 4.4, makes frequent reference to harm. Always, to assess harm, the court must have the jury compare the plaintiff's factual situation with *some* other state. Feinberg calls this other state the "baseline."[40] Earlier, this baseline state was identified counterfactually. The plaintiff's factual situation was thus compared to what the plaintiff's state *would have been* in the absence of the defendant's negligence. But we noted that this counterfactual test of harm was not quite right. In this part, we examine how the counterfactual test needs to be modified.

As Feinberg puts the point, harm requires the plaintiff's interests to have been "adversely affected" by the defendant's conduct; if there has been, from the plaintiff's own point of view, no "setback," then the plaintiff has not been harmed.[41] Thus, according to Feinberg, any test of harm requires a "starting point or 'baseline' from which the direction of advance or retreat is charted and measured."[42]

But if we need a baseline, then we also need a principled way of determining, for each individual whom we suspect to have been harmed, what the baseline for that individual is. Otherwise, we do not know which of the plaintiff's many, many alternative possible states—

including, of course, nonexistence—is pertinent to the assessment of whether the plaintiff has been made worse off.

What, then, is the test for the baseline? For purposes of assessing harm in case 9, I supposed that the case was a routine medical malpractice case and took the plaintiff's baseline to be a more or less averagely healthy life. But by what principle is *this* the baseline? And—more to the point—on what basis is it assumed that *nonexistence* is the baseline for cases 10 and 11, the two wrongful life scenarios? Without answers to these questions, the legal account of wrongful life given earlier remains incomplete.

As Feinberg suggests, in the routine case it seems natural to take the baseline to be the subject's level of well-being immediately prior to the point at which the suspect act has its effect. Suppose that a patient walks into a psychiatrist's office and the ceiling caves in as a result of the landlord's negligently having failed to correct a plumbing problem one floor up a week earlier. The patient is knocked unconscious to the floor. In such a case, harm is, it seems natural to surmise, established and measured by comparing how well off the patient was when he walked into the office (unhappy but unbruised) with how well off the patient is now that the ceiling has landed on his head (unhappy and bruised).

But, as Feinberg argues, defining the baseline by reference to a time line will not work. For there clearly are instances of harm in which there is no "worsening" over time of a subject's prior state. A person can be harmed, in other words, even in cases in which that person's condition has not been made to decline from one moment to the next. Imagine a patient who, as a consequence of some easily treated disorder, is in terrible pain. The doctor negligently prescribes the wrong medication, and the pain, though perhaps reduced, persists. In this case, the patient's condition does not *worsen* as a consequence of the doctor's negligent act. If the baseline is the patient's state just prior to the point at which the defendant's negligence has its effect, then the patient has not been *harmed* by the defendant's negligence. But this result, Feinberg notes, is false.[43]

Such cases impel us in the direction of a counterfactual test. According to the counterfactual test, the baseline becomes the plaintiff's "interest" as it *"would be"* had the defendant not been negligent.[44] But as noted earlier, although courts recite their interest in "what would have been," their focus is not always precisely on *what would have been*.[45] Thus, a court will not and should not be interested in the line of defense described earlier, according to which the plaintiff would have been even worse off, at the hands of his own abusive parents, had the defendant not been negligent.

Feinberg attributes this defect in the counterfactual test to the phenomenon of "causal overdetermination," which arises when two independent events are each causally *sufficient* to impose the adverse effect on the victim.[46] Consider Feinberg's case of the "two schoolyard bullies" who both aim to beat up another child.[47] One succeeds. Had the one who succeeded not inflicted the beating, the second bully "would have" stepped in to do the job. Thus, the hurt and bleeding child is not worse off than he or she "would have been" had the first bully refrained from engaging in the beating.

Feinberg poses a second problem case as well. A man on his way to the airport is severely injured as a result of a taxi driver's negligent collision. Because the passenger is in the hospital with, say, a broken leg, he is not on the plane, which develops engine trouble and crashes.[48] In both cases, if the baseline is identified in terms of what "would have been" in the absence of the questionable conduct, the result is that the subject has not been harmed. But in both cases this seems incorrect.

Feinberg suggests a way of revising the counterfactual test that narrows the baseline to what is *usual* or *expected* or *normal*. According to this revised test, the plaintiff's baseline is what things would have been like for the plaintiff in the absence of the defendant's negligence *"in the normal course of events insofar as they were reasonably foreseeable in the circumstances."*[49] Applying this "doubly counterfactual" test to the taxi driver case, we find that the passenger's baseline is one of those averagely healthy ones. It is what the driver *would* have reasonably foreseen things to have been like for the passenger, assuming a normal course of events, in the absence of the driver's negligence. In the normal course of events insofar as they were reasonably foreseeable to the driver, the plane would not have crashed. In his injured, hospitalized state, the patient is thus worse off than he is in the baseline and so has been harmed. Thus, according to Feinberg, the "subsequent plane crash does not get [the taxi driver] off the hook."[50]

This seems correct. But in other cases the revised test does not work as well. Consider, again, Feinberg's schoolyard bullies case. The second bully's stepping in to do the job when the first bully does not *is* both normal and reasonably foreseeable in the circumstances described. But if the child's being beat up is normal and foreseeable whether the first bully does the deed or not, the baseline for the child becomes the state of having been beat up. Thus, on the revised counterfactual test as well we derive the false result that the child has not been harmed. More generally: that a diminution in well-being is both normal and foreseeable, in addition to being what "would have been" had the questionable act not been performed, does not imply no harm done.

Thus, we remain in need of a principled means of identifying the baseline for purposes of assessing harm in the negligence context. The temporal test and both the counterfactual tests suffer essentially the same defect: the potential for hazards entirely independent of the defendant's negligence can mean that there is no difference, from the plaintiff's point of view, whether the defendant is negligent or not. We need some device by which such hazards can be screened out as irrelevant to the analysis in appropriate instances.

On the moral side, no need to provide a test for harm exists. At the same time, we can discern a "baseline" of sorts that has been relied on in each of the various person-affecting analyses that have been given. It is the subject's *maximal* state. If there is no accessible world in which the subject's well-being is higher, then the subject has not been wronged; but if there is such an accessible world, we must, in effect, justify the departure from it (by appealing to, e.g., considerations of fairness) or else be held accountable.

By analogy to the moral analysis, I suggest, as the plaintiff's baseline for purposes of determining legal harm, the plaintiff's *maximal* level of well-being. Then, to determine the baseline, instead of asking, "Other things being equal, but in the absence of the defendant's negligence, what level of well-being *will*, or *would*, the plaintiff possess?" the question would be, "What level of well-being *could* the plaintiff possess, in the absence of the defendant's negligence?" or more simply, "What, at the outset, is the plaintiff's *maximal* level of well-being?" According to this view, then, the plaintiff has been *harmed* in those cases in which the plaintiff has been made worse off than the plaintiff is in his or her maximal state.[51]

As a general matter, the harm element in the negligence action functions to rule in, assuming the presence of the remaining elements of duty, breach, and causation, or to rule out, whether or not those other elements are present, claims in negligence. Harm is, in other words, part of the definition of negligence. The problem with the temporal and the counterfactual tests of harm is that they rule out too many cases in which we think that the defendant is at fault and should be held responsible for the consequences of his or her conduct. They allow a standard that is in specific cases too low.

An alternative test, which I will call the *modal* test, takes into account all those possible worlds accessible to agents—all those worlds that agents, acting jointly or severally, have the capacity or ability to bring about—and considers what those worlds are like for the plaintiff. Does the modal test go too far in the other direction, ruling in too many cases in which we think that the defendant is *not* at fault?

It might be objected, that is, that identifying the plaintiff's maximal state as the baseline for determining harm sets too high a standard, leading, in inappropriate cases, to findings of liability. But consider how easily the parallel objection on the moral side can be answered. It would just be noted that the fact that a person's level of well-being is *lower* than it is in some other accessible world does not at all by itself imply that that person has been *wronged*. Likewise, it is black-letter law that the harm element alone is not sufficient to establish the defendant's liability in negligence. If the harm element is expected to bear too much analytical weight within the negligence analysis—if included under the heading of "harm" are issues better settled under the headings of "duty" and "breach"—then it will be very difficult to formulate an intuitively satisfactory test of harm that does not bias the negligence analysis in a way that is unfair to the plaintiff.

A way out of this dilemma is not to expect so much from the harm analysis. Thus, designating as the plaintiff's baseline the plaintiff's maximal state makes it is easier to establish harm than one might have thought, but from this fact it does not follow that it easier than it should be to reach a conclusion of negligence.[52]

Consider, again, the example of the psychiatric patient who is a victim of a collapsed ceiling and who ends the session not merely unhappy but also bruised. And suppose that the patient's unhappiness is itself *nothing* that the psychiatrist can "fix" in one session. The patient's unhappiness over the next hour is thus a fact beyond agency control, like a volcano's erupting; there is no accessible world in which the patient's mental condition has been returned to normal or made healthy by the end of the hour. On the other hand, there is some accessible world in which the patient does not emerge from the session both unhappy *and* bruised. After all, the landlord (presumably) had the capacity to repair the leak that caused the ceiling to collapse the week before. The level of well-being the patient enjoys in a world in which the landlord manages a prompt repair of the leak but the patient remains unhappy represents the patient's *maximal* level of well-being. Taking the plaintiff's baseline as his maximal state, we find that at the end of the session with the psychiatrist the patient is *worse off* than he is in the baseline state and thus, on the account I propose, has been harmed.

Is the *psychiatrist* therefore liable in negligence for the harm that has befallen the patient? The maximal account of harm creates no analytic need to hold the psychiatrist liable. The psychiatrist may be let off the hook, not on the grounds that the harm element is missing (it is not), but rather on the grounds that the psychiatrist has breached no *duty* that he has toward the patient. Thus, the psychiatrist has no duty to fix leaks or through prescience or mere luck to decide to hold the session in the coffee shop rather than the office. By like analysis, the landlord is responsible. Thus, the extent of harm to the plaintiff will be the same, whoever is liable. And the distinctions we make regarding liability will be on other grounds.

Consider how the modal test can be put to use in Feinberg's cases—the schoolyard bullies case and the taxi driver case. In the schoolyard bullies case, we may take the baseline to be the child's well-being in a world in which he is beat up by neither of the two bullies. Then, comparing the child's factual plight with his baseline, we obtain the expected results—that the child has been made worse off and thus has been harmed. Do we get the further, problematic, conclusion that the first bully and the second bully are *equally* liable for the harm that has been imposed? No. The first bully has done the deed, breached the duty, and caused the beating. He will be liable. But on the assumption that the second bully does not equally, by way of, say, omission or conspiracy, cause the beating, he will not be liable since breach and causation are missing in his case.

In the plane crash case, again we take the passenger's baseline to be that state in which he is involved in neither a car nor a plane crash. Has he, then, been harmed? Since he finds himself worse off than he is in the baseline, he has been harmed. It is, again, a problem for the proposed baseline if the airline turns out to be liable for the harm that has been caused. But on grounds other than harm the necessary distinction between the taxi driver and the airline can easily be made. Thus, only the driver, not the airline, violates a duty by failing to get the passenger safely to the airport, and only the driver's conduct, not the airline's, causes the passenger to suffer a broken leg.

In working through cases 9–11 earlier, I identified the baseline by appealing to a counterfactual test of harm. And this test seemingly gave the right answers, but only because we relied on certain assumptions about the cases themselves—that, for example, the cases were routine and involved no peculiar facts and the parents were not psychopaths. The modal test, in contrast, seems to give intuitively correct answers to the harm question whether or not the cases are perfectly routine.

Suppose that case 9 is not, after all, a routine medical malpractice case. Suppose that but for the defendant's negligence the infant-plaintiff would have gone home with his parents soon after birth and would then have suffered in even worse ways than he has in fact suffered. According to the modal account of harm, this peculiar fact is automatically screened from the analysis. It is irrelevant that the plaintiff's condition would have been even worse in the absence of the defendant's negligence. The baby's factual level of well-being being less than his maximal level, that is, his baseline, the baby has suffered harm. At the same time, liability for this harm does not attach to the baby's own parents since they neither breached any duty they had toward the baby (having never had the chance to breach any duty) nor acted so as to cause the baby harm. Rather, liability, rightly, attaches solely to the defendant who, by hypothesis, breached her duty toward the infant and whose breach of duty caused the baby to suffer the condition that diverted the baby from home to the NICU to begin with.

Consider, then, case 10. In this case, the doctor negligently brings the plaintiff into an existence that is, though flawed, worth living. Applying the counterfactual test, I earlier took the plaintiff's baseline to be nonexistence. In contrast, according to the modal test, the plaintiff's baseline is the state in which the plaintiff both exists and has a good (though unavoidably less than averagely good) life. This means that the plaintiff's level of well-being in the baseline just is the plaintiff's factual level of well-being. One state therefore clearly not being worse than the other, the plaintiff has not been harmed. Thus in this case, though the analysis changes when the modal test shifts the baseline from nonexistence to the plaintiff's maximal state, we nonetheless reach exactly the conclusion we reached earlier.

In case 11, the counterfactual test and the modal test identify exactly the same baseline—nonexistence. Thus there is no need to modify the earlier account of case 11 here.

A main point to note is that the legal analysis of cases 9–11 in this part is entirely supported by the implications of the moral account set out in part 4.5. Personalism thus provides a reason to think that the law of negligence should be understood to embrace the claim of wrongful life.

4.7   The Problem of Deflected Ill-Being

According to both the counterfactual test of harm and the modal test, the level of well-being the plaintiff in fact has (the plaintiff's factual level of well-being) is to be compared against some other (the baseline) to determine harm.

But consider that when a baby is born in circumstances that suggest wrongful life the baby's mother and father, perhaps the baby's grandparents, perhaps an extended family, and maybe the community, including the medical community, may pull together to do what they can for that baby. Pulling together, they give a lot to the baby. In terms of money, energy, thought, worry, planning, time, attention, and sheer hard labor, perhaps they give much more than the law requires them to give. This is so even taking into account the fact that the law will likely require the parents to do more for a baby with a serious medical condition and extraordinary needs than for the perfectly healthy baby.

And, with luck and depending on the nature of the disorder, their herculean efforts may pay off. Clearly, good medical care, loving nursing, lavish pain therapy, safe and pleasant surroundings, physical therapy, and, in some cases, special education and training are likely to make a big difference in the baby's life and the level of well-being the baby can be expected to have over a lifetime. If it makes enough of a difference, then the baby's lifetime level of well-being may net out to some *positive* level. But, according to the modal test of harm, if the baby's level of well-being is positive, then the baby's having been brought into existence does not harm the baby.

But this seems not to be the right result. The baby's parents and others save the baby from experiencing potentially vast levels of ill-being partly by deflecting ill-being from the baby to themselves. The court in *Schroeder v. Perkel* wrote that

> foreseeability of injury to members of a family other than one immediately injured by the wrongdoing of another must be viewed in light of the legal relationships among family members. A family is woven of the fibers of life; if one strand is damaged, the whole structure may suffer. The filaments of family life, although individually spun, create a web of interconnected legal interests. This Court has recognized that a wrongdoer who causes a direct injury to one member of the family may indirectly damage another.[53]

To allow the defendant to establish "no harm done" by pointing to the modest level of well-being that the plaintiff as a matter of fact enjoys—a level of well-being that has been lovingly, conscientiously inflated—would be unfair to those who have shouldered the defendant's responsibility. Entirely independent of the pain and suffering that the parents might allege in the context of a wrongful birth action, the defendant's negligence has given rise to ill-being, perhaps enormous quantities of ill-being, whether this ill-being is left with the baby or taken up by the parents.

We also find interconnected legal interests outside the family setting. Consider the mountain guide who carelessly loses a member of his (say) party. Suppose that the lost member is then rescued by some third person. But the rescue requires the shifting of resources from the rescuer to the lost climber. If the rescuer herself, say, then succumbs to the elements, it is improper to let the mountain guide "off the hook" either morally or legally. We would not accept, in this context, the mountain guide's "no harm done" argument.

Ill-being may be thought of as having been deflected in this case from the lost climber to the rescuer. Likewise, in some cases of wrongful life we might understand ill-being to have been deflected from the infant-plaintiff to the parents and others. In such cases, the defendant should remain liable even if the baby's level of well-being is positive, depending on the extent of ill-being that has been handed off from the baby to the baby's entirely foreseeable "rescuers." But the theory under which the defendant would be liable should remain a theory of wrongful life. It should thus be available to the plaintiff even if, for one reason or another, the defendant is not liable to the parents under a theory of wrongful birth.

The problem of deflected ill-being does not indicate a difficulty with the modal test of harm. Rather, it reveals a problem with any rigid adherence to the inference from the finding that *the baby* has not been harmed to the conclusion that *no harm has been done*. Harm has still been done, even if it has been humanely deflected from the baby to the parents or others. Thus, the modal test of harm does not require revision. Rather, in assessing harm, the jury must be allowed to take into account the baby's level of well-being—which, with luck and lots of hard work, will be modestly positive—*and* the parents' level of well-being, which may have been substantially depressed. The defendant will not be liable for the entire difference between the parents' factual level of well-being and their maximal level of well-being. Rather, the defendant will be liable only for the portion of that ill-being that the defendant had the duty to prevent under the theory of wrongful life. In particular, the defendant will be liable only for that amount of deflected ill-being that has been shifted from the baby to the parents (and perhaps not all of that, if the parents are themselves under a legal duty to shift a certain amount of ill-being from the baby to themselves in any case).

The analysis thus has become a bit more complicated. But the complication is not one that can be avoided. We do not want to provide the parents or others with an incentive not to do their best for a baby who suffers. Thus, we do not want to insist that recovery in the wrongful life context be made to require that the baby's life in fact be less than one worth living, or that the baby in fact be in an "an excruciatingly painful" state to establish harm.[54] Equally, we do not want the defendant to escape liability just because the parents have succeeded in their attempt to make life better, perhaps even worth living, for their child.

Allowing the jury to take into account not just the plaintiff's level of well-being but also the extent to which ill-being has been deflected from the plaintiff to others clearly broadens the potential for recovery in wrongful life cases and helps to avoid the charge that the "distinctive feature [of the analysis] is to limit wrongful life actions to birth impairments that are utterly debilitating."[55]

At the same time, if, even taking into account deflected ill-being, the plaintiff's level of well-being remains positive—if, in other words, the defect that is asserted is mild—then the harm element is missing from the case and the defendant should not be held liable. Some courts would permit a finding of harm even in a case in which the disorder is mild.[56] But this result is not always particularly well-reasoned. Indeed, according to one court, "[l]aw is more than an exercise in logic, and logical analysis, although essential to a system of ordered justice, should not become an instrument of injustice."[57] But I have grave doubts that justice requires or even can tolerate inconsistency in any meaningful sense.

Though I believe that bringing someone into existence who could not otherwise exist and who suffers a mild chromosomal or genetic defect would not constitute a harm to that person, nothing about the view I describe suggests that damages claimed in connection with wrongful life should be limited in any special way. Thus, the successful wrongful life plaintiff would be entitled to claim all damages, commensurate with the extent of the harm imposed (including deflected harm), that any ordinary victim of negligence is entitled to claim, including damages for medical expenses and pain and suffering and punitive damages.[58] Of course, the finder of fact will not be able to calculate this amount precisely. But that this is so is not a legitimate reason to establish a special damages rule for the wrongful life context. A lack of precision is common in calculations of compensatory damages, whatever the nature of the legal claim.[59]

4.8   Logical Objections to Wrongful Life

4.8.1   A Problem of Consistency?

Critics of wrongful life sometimes suggest that the very idea that the plaintiff might have been better off in a world in which the plaintiff does not exist is logically inconsistent. Feinberg describes this objection as follows. "Since it is necessary to *be* if one is to *be better off*, it is a logical contradiction to say that someone could be better off though not in existence.''[60] Heyd may be making the same point when he writes that:

> We find it hard enough to assess the harm involved in death, yet we know at least that even if death means complete annihilation (nonexistence), it occurs *to* someone. We can decide that the extent of harm done to a person by taking his or her life is proportional to the expected net good that could have accrued in the rest of the natural lifespan. All this is of no help in the case of "birth in defect." Had the plaintiff . . . not been conceived . . . would *this* boy have been *better off*?[61]

And:

> If the child wants to sue the doctor for tort he must present the court with a real alternative in which he would allegedly have been *better off*. This alternative is . . . nonexistence. But in that case . . . even if [life and nonlife were commensurate] the child could only prefer his own death (by suicide or euthanasia) to his miserable life, but not "his" nonconception.[62]

Although more poetically, the court in *Gleitman v. Cosgrove* may be expressing the same concern in the following passage.

> By asserting that he should not have been born, the infant plaintiff makes it logically impossible for a court to measure his alleged damages because of the impossibility of making the comparison required by compensatory remedies.[63]

Feinberg's formulation of the problem is the clearest. The plaintiff claims that he or she would have been *better off* never existing at all. But to be better off is to be—that is, to exist. And the plaintiff cannot consistently claim that he or she would have been better off existing in a world in which he or she never exists.

But there seems to be no basis—no basis we are compelled to accept, in any event—for the view that worlds that make one "better off" are necessarily worlds in which one exists. Indeed, our understanding of the human condition militates in the other direction: we *do* think that an existence can be so miserable—so bad for the one who exists—that it may have been better for this person never to have come into existence to begin with. Having made this judgment, it is unfathomable that there is no way to express it consistently in the natural language or some barely formalized revision of that language. Having made this judgment, the question should *not* be, "Is there some way of expressing this judgment such that it is rendered inconsistent?" but *rather*, "Is there some way of expressing it to render it consistent?"

When we say that someone who suffers dreadfully would have been better off never existing to begin with, we are pointing out that nonexistence offers that person neither pleasure nor pain; neither happiness nor unhappiness; neither benefits nor burdens; would have neither benefited nor burdened that person; would have neither hindered nor promoted that person's interests; and would have, more generally, accorded to that person neither any well-being nor any ill-being whatsoever. And we are claiming that a world in which all this is true is a world that is better for that person than the world under scrutiny. Expressed otherwise: we are saying that a world in which that person's level of well-being is *zero* is better for that person than a world in which that person's level of well-being is *negative*. A critic might try to reformulate the objection, pressing the point now that to say that the person's level of well-being is *zero* implies that the person *exists*. In some cases in which a person's level of well-being is zero that person might exist yet be neither happy nor sad. But there is no reason to think that this is necessarily the case; and it is just a mistake to think that it is so as a matter of *logic*. Is the implication of existence an implication or a presupposition that we *must* accept? One *might* adopt an interpretation of the bits of natural language at issue that render them inconsistent, but why should we, when other interpretations are available that consistently express the original judgment?[64]

4.8.2   A Problem with Reference?

The passages quoted from Heyd suggest a second point in addition to the inconsistency point that Feinberg describes.[65] The second point is a point about reference. The idea would be, roughly, that an assertion like "Bill Clinton has a zero level of well-being in any world in which he does not exist" is incoherent. Here the critique is *not* that the assertion itself inconsistently implies that Bill Clinton both exists and does not exist in some world. Rather, the critique is that the proper name "Bill Clinton" cannot *have* a referent within any world in which Bill Clinton does not exist and thus that the assertion that is critical to the analysis that I have given is, in fact, no more capable of truth or falsity than such incomplete utterances as ". . . is a pomegranate" or ". . . is meaner than. . . ."

But this critique misses its mark. Since Bill Clinton does exist and has been duly and properly anointed "Bill Clinton," there is no issue about the referent of "Bill Clinton." When we talk about what things would have been like had Bill Clinton never existed at all—as we surely can meaningfully do—we maintain, for the proper name, the referent that we have already established.

Likewise, should anyone have proposed to bring a wrongful life claim on behalf of a person *who never existed at all*, a point about reference would be in order. On many plausible theories of how proper names establish reference, we cannot name those who never exist. But such is not the case with wrongful life claimants. Reference to wrongful life plaintiffs clearly *can* be achieved. Thus, suppose that George is some now existing, flesh-and-blood wrongful life plaintiff. Part of the claim made on his behalf is something like this: "George would have been better off never existing to begin with" or, equivalently, "George's level of well-being in any world in which George never existed at all would have been higher than it in fact is." Have we managed to generate a problem with reference? No. "George" in this sentence refers to George, the flesh-and-blood George, the child a videotape of whom is now being viewed in a court of law. If George's parents can feed him, care for him, love him, and diaper him, then the claim on his behalf can certainly manage to *refer* to him. The factual link between name and object does not come undone, and the counterfactual assertion made incoherent, just because we ask what things would be like had the object named never existed at all.[66]

Notes

1. The harm that results from a tort must be "capable of being compensated in an action at law for damages." See William L. Prosser and Page Keeton, *Law of Torts*, 5th ed. (Minneapolis: West, 1984), §1.1, at 4.

2. See also Prosser and Keeton, *Law of Torts*, §5.30, at 143 (discussing the duty element in terms of the need to protect against "unreasonable risk"). For a summary discussion of some basic concepts of efficiency, see George P. Fletcher, *Basic Concepts of Legal Thought* (Oxford: Oxford University Press, 1996), 155–71.

3. Thus, Amartya Sen shoulders the task of investigating equality as well as efficiency. See Sen, *Inequality Reexamined* (Cambridge, Mass.: Harvard University Press, 1992), 7–8, 129–52. The attention within economics to the tension between the value of efficiency and competing values is ongoing. See Nicholas Mercuro and Steven G. Medema, *Economics and the Law: From Posner to Post-Modernism* (Princeton, N.J.: Princeton University Press, 1997), 21–24, 187–89. Not all moral totalists content themselves strictly with efficiency. Thus, Feldman suggests a totalist theory of "justicized utility" according to which utility has relevance in determining the total good only to the extent that it is deserved, whereas the relevance of any disutility, to the extent undeserved, is correspondingly magnified. See part 3.5.11 ("Feldman's Concept of Adjusted Utility"). However, both Feldman and, to my knowledge, most economists remain committed to the notion of efficiency as an aggregative, or group, value.

4. Mercuro and Medema put the point as follows (*Economics and the Law*,

189, citing Richard Posner, "Strict Liability: A Comment," *Journal of Legal Studies* 1 [Jan. 1973]: 221):

> [T]here are those contributors to Law and Economics who simply argue that society ought to go forward with those (and only those) legal changes that are determined to be efficient. To those in law who argue that efficiency should not be the primary social value, the burden is placed on them to demonstrate why a standard (based in justice or fairness) that imposes avoidable costs should nonetheless be adopted.

See also Posner, *Economic Analysis of the Law*, 4th ed. (Boston: Little, Brown, 1992), chap. 6 ("Tort Law").

5. John Cassidy, "The Melting-Pot Myth," *The New Yorker*, 14 July 1997, 42.

6. See part 2.7.6 ("Summing Up Personalism").

7. See part 2.7.4 ("Theory of 'Fair Distribution' ").

8. The cases that will be considered in what follows involve instances in which the defendant is a doctor or some other health care professional or entity. But people outside the health care profession can also carelessly cause existence. For example, an early case that invoked the claim of wrongful life named the *father* of the illegitimate child-plaintiff as defendant! See *Zepeda v. Zepeda*, 41 Ill. App. 2d 240, 190 N.E.2d 849 (1963).

9. In some cases in which the defect does not arise as a "fact of nature" a wrongful life claim might still make sense, though it would not be a claim against the agent responsible for the defect (or at least not against the agent insofar as the agent is responsible for the defect). Thus, suppose that the chromosomal or genetic defect or other disorder that causes the child to suffer is one that *some* agent or another—say, a contractor disposing improperly of toxic waste or a pharmaceutical company manufacturing thalidomide for the purpose of treating leprosy or symptoms of HIV—*could* have avoided imposing. A wrongful life claim might in certain circumstances still be brought against a doctor *as a distinct agent* who has been requested to give advice regarding the risk imposed by the toxic substance or to provide birth control or an abortion to avoid that risk's eventuating. In this dual-agent context, the harm cited in the wrongful life claim would be not the defect but, as in the usual single-agent context, the life itself. Thus, the wrongful life claim may remain cogent even though the defect has not arisen as an unavoidable "fact of nature." We just say that the plaintiff might have two claims—against the agent whose breach is responsible for the defect *and* against the agent whose breach is responsible for the plaintiff's life. Only the latter of these two claims would be a claim for wrongful life.

10. *Speck v. Finegold*, 497 Pa. 77, 81–82 & n.2, 439 A.2d 110, 112 & n.2 (1981).

11. *Speck v. Finegold*, 497 Pa. at 81–82, 439 A.2d at 113.

12. *Speck v. Finegold*, 497 Pa. at 82, 439 A.2d at 113.

13. *Berman v. Allan*, 80 N.J. 421, 423–24, 404 A.2d 8, 10 (1979).

14. *Curlender v. Bio-Science Laboratories*, 106 Cal. App. 3d 811, 815–16, 165 Cal. Rptr. 477, 480 (1980).

15. *Curlender v. Bio-Science Laboratories*, 106 Cal. App. 3d at 816 n.4, 165 Cal. Rptr. at 480 n.4.

16. *Curlender v. Bio-Science Laboratories*, 106 Cal. App. 3d at 816–17, 165 Cal. Rptr. at 480–81.

17. *Park v. Chessin*, 60 A.D.2d 80, 83, 400 N.Y.S.2d 110, 110–11 (N.Y. App. Div. 1977).

18. *Nelson v. Krusen*, 678 S.W.2d 918, 919–20 (Tex. 1984).

19. *Schroeder v. Perkel*, 87 N.J. 53, 70, 432 A.2d 834, 853 (1981); *Berman v. Allan*, 80 N.J. at 432, 404 A.2d at 17; *Speck v. Finegold*, 497 Pa. at 88, 439 A.2d at 116; *Harbeson v. Parke-Davis*, 98 Wash. 2d 460, 467, 656 P.2d 483, 488 (1983).

20. In a handful of cases, courts have recognized causes of action for wrongful life. See *Turpin v. Sortini*, 31 Cal. 3d 220, 239, 643 P.2d 954, 966, 182 Cal. Rptr. 337, 349 (1982); *Curlender v. Bio-Science Laboratories*, 106 Cal. App. 3d at 830, 165 Cal. Rptr. at 489; *Procanik v. Cillo*, 97 N.J. 339, 352, 478 A.2d 755, 762 (1984); *Harbeson v. Parke-Davis*, 98 Wash. 2d at 479, 656 P.2d at 495. But even courts that recognize causes of action for wrongful life typically limit the extent of the plaintiff's damage claim. New Jersey, for example, permits the wrongful life plaintiff to recover special damages for extraordinary medical expenses but not damages for pain and suffering or for the plaintiff's "impaired childhood." *Procanik v. Cillo*, 97 N.J. at 352–53, 478 A.2d at 762–63.

21. See *Schroeder v. Perkel*, 87 N.J. at 75–76, 432 A.2d at 845–46, and *Berman v. Allan*, 80 N.J. at 433, 404 A.2d at 18.

22. See *Procanik v. Cillo*, 97 N.J. at 358, 478 A.2d at 765 (Handler, J., dissenting in part).

23. Prosser and Keeton, *Law of Torts*, §5.30, at 144.

24. The parents' action was barred by the statute of limitations in, for example, *Procanik v. Cillo*, 97 N.J. at 345, 478 A.2d at 758. Joel Feinberg catalogues additional reasons why the wrongful life action is not simply a redundancy in view of the availability of the wrongful birth action. See "Wrongful Life and the Counterfactual Element in Harming," *Social Philosophy & Policy* 4, no. 1 (1988): 156–58.

25. *Becker v. Schwartz*, 46 N.Y.2d 401, 412, 413 N.Y.S.2d 895, 900, 386 N.E.2d 807, 812 (1978).

26. *Gleitman v. Cosgrove*, 49 N.J. 22, 63, 227 A.2d 689, 711 (1967) (Weintraub, J., dissenting in part).

27. Bonnie Steinbock, "The Logical Case for 'Wrongful Life,' " *Hastings Center Report* 16, no. 2 (April 1986): 17 (discussing *Berman v. Allan*, 80 N.J. 421, 404 A.2d 8). See also *Gleitman v. Cosgrove*, 49 N.J. at 31, 227 A.2d at 693 (referring to the "preciousness" of life).

28. Others also find some way of comparing existence and nonexistence and thus conclude that wrongful life claims should be recognized. See, e.g., Feinberg, "Wrongful Life," 145–78. Some theorists avoid the issue of comparing existence and nonexistence but still reach the conclusion that wrongful life claims should be recognized. For a recent summary of the state of the legal literature on the subject, see F. Allan Hanson, "Suits for Wrongful Life, Counterfactuals, and the Nonexistence Problem," *Southern California Interdisciplinary Law Journal* 5 (1996): 7–12.

29. See *Gleitman v. Cosgrove*, 49 N.J. at 31, 227 A.2d at 692.

30. Cynthia Cohen persuasively distinguishes between the values of "pre-conception nonexistence" on the one hand and death on the other ("The Morality of Knowingly Conceiving Children with Serious Conditions: An Expanded 'Wrongful Life' Standard," in *Contingent Future Persons*, ed. Nick Fotion and Jan C. Heller [Dordrecht: Kluwer Academic, 1997]). She writes that "we find that we ascribe different degrees of value to preconception nonexistence and to death. We view death as terrible, but consider preconception nonexistence to be neither good nor bad" (34). According to Cohen, death

> is terrible, in part, because it prevents us from having future goods that we would have had if we had remained alive. . . . The awfulness of death is also grounded in the fact that it robs us of those goods that we already have. . . . Preconception nonexistence, on the other hand, does not involve the loss of life's goods, nor does it deprive us of goods that we already possess (34).

See also Christopher J. Grainger, "Wrongful Life: A Wrong Without a Remedy," *Tort Law Review* 2 (Nov. 1994): 164–74, especially 167–69 (criticizing courts' failure to distinguish between whether a child should never have been born and whether a child should now die and taking the latter edict, but not the former, as in tension with a legitimate "sanctity of life" principle). For a discussion of a "wrongful living" cause of action, see *Anderson v. St. Francis-St. George Hospital*, 77 Ohio St. 3d 82, 83–89, 671 N.E.2d 225 (1996). See also Tricia Jonas Hackleman, "Violation of an Individual's Right to Die: The Need for a Wrongful Living Cause of Action," *University of Cincinnati Law Review* 64 (1996): 1355.

31. Compare John Harris, *Wonderwoman and Superman: The Ethics of Human Biotechnology* (New York: Oxford University Press, 1993), 96–97, and Feinberg, "Wrongful Life," 165–66.

32. But it does not follow, from the fact that it is not now in the interests of the plaintiff to die, that the plaintiff's life is, overall, a good thing from the plaintiff's point of view. Like the victim of a serious burning, a bright future, post-trauma and post-healing, does not necessarily (though it may) make the period of trauma and healing "worth it."

33. Jefferson McMahan notes that it is a point in favor of person-affecting principles generally that they are able to make this distinction though totalism, e.g., cannot. Thus, according to McMahan ("Wrongful Life: Paradoxes in the Morality of Causing People to Exist," in *Rational Commitment and Social Justice: Essays for Gregory Kavka*, ed. Jules Coleman and Christopher Morris [Cambridge: Cambridge University Press, forthcoming]), an "acceptable" theory

> must imply that failing to save a person whose life would be worth living is, other things being equal, not just worse but significantly worse than failing to cause a person to exist. And this implication must not just be a contingent feature of the way the mathematics works out. . . . Person-affecting considerations seem indispensable.

Robert Elliot describes this intuition from the opposite perspective ("Contingency, Community and Intergenerational Justice," *Contingent Future Persons*, ed. Fotion and Heller, 164):

[C]onsider a case where we might choose between curing someone of a continuing, painful affliction and bringing someone into existence. The choice is 'revenue neutral' in terms of maximizing total well-being, each option resulting in the same net increase in total well-being. There is reason though to choose the former option.

Compare R. M. Hare ("When Does Potentiality Count?" in *Essays in Bioethics* [Oxford: Clarendon Press, 1993]: 90), according to whom merely possible people have an interest in coming into existence; when we deny them this option, we have done something that is "defeasibly wrong." Taking a healthy, happy child who in fact exists, I might agree with Hare that never having existed at all would have been *worse for* that child. But I would also say that never having brought the child into existence at all could not have *wronged* that child—a point implied by N*.

34. My assessment of the value of nonexistence is based on a student comment on the issue of whether damages can rationally be calculated in the wrongful life context ("A Cause of Action for Wrongful Life: A Suggested Analysis," *Minnesota Law Review* 55 [1970]): 64–68).

The question then is whether the necessary computations can be made. Can values be placed on the state of nonexistence and the state of existence with defects in order to approximate a compensatory amount? [Some courts have made statements that seem to] imply that some negative value has been assigned to the state of nonexistence . . . [but in] an extreme case it would seem that one could make the following valuation:
Life without defects = a plus value (+)
Nonexistence = 0
Life with defects = a minus value (−).

Ingmar Persson comes to a similar conclusion ("Genetic Therapy," *Bioethics* 9, no. 1 (1995): 27–30). See also Cohen, "The Morality of Knowingly Conceiving Children with Serious Conditions," 32–35.

Robert Elliot, discussing Persson's idea that nonexistence can be assigned a "zero-value," writes that "[i]t does not make sense to suggest that [a person, Simon's,] non-existence can be evaluated from Simon's point of view, except in those states of affairs in which Simon exists" ("Contingency, Community and Intergenerational Justice," 162–66, 163). But Elliot's critique of Persson—who is writing about the nonidentity problem—seems not to apply to the account of wrongful life that I propose. According to Elliot, Persson, in giving an account of how it is that bringing someone into existence may benefit that person, requires it to be true that "Simon's non-existence can be evaluated from Simon's point of view in that state of affairs in which Simon does not exist" (163). But, according to Elliot, this claim is false. All I require to be true, however, is that "Simon's non-existence can be evaluated from Simon's point of view in that state of affairs in which Simon exists" (163), a claim that Elliot has no objection to. On the view I suggest, all wrongful life evaluations take place relative to a world in which the subject *exists*; and the question is always whether the subject has *there* been wronged. There is no need, ever, on my account of either wrongful life or the nonidentity problem to assign a value, *even a value of zero*, to nonexistence for an individual who never exists in the world that is subject to appraisal. Even N*, which provides that those who never exist are never wronged, need not be interpreted to quantify over those who never, in the world to be evaluated, exist. N*, rather, provides the foundation for the extremely useful point that, *had* such-and-such *existing* person never existed at all, then that person would never have been wronged.

Dasgupta also objects to the notion that nonexistence can be assigned a zero value. "It makes no sense to attribute a degree of well-being, low or high or nil, to the 'state of not being born.' Non-existence is like nothing for us, not even a very long night, because there is no *us* to imagine upon" (*An Inquiry Into Well-Being and Destitution* [Oxford: Clarendon, 1993], 383). See also David Heyd, *Genethics: Moral Issues in the Creation of People* (Berkeley: University of California Press, 1992), 30.

35. Cohen, "The Morality of Knowingly Conceiving Children with Serious Conditions, 35. *"A 'wrongful life' standard, when applied to possible children, will not be restricted to a life of devastating illness, but can also include conditions that are less severe"* (35).

36. Some theorists suggest skepticism about the kind of netting procedure I describe. See, e.g., Clark Wolf, who writes that "[c]lassical utilitarians assume . . . that pains and pleasures are commensurable so that they can balance one another in a grand utilitarian aggregate. But it is far from obvious that pains and pleasures are commensurable in this way. . . ." ("Person-Affecting Utilitarianism and Population Policy Or, Sissy Jupe's Theory of Social Choice," in *Contingent Future Persons*, ed. Fotion and Heller, 100).

37. Juries should not struggle anew with the question of the value of nonexistence each time they decide a wrongful life case. Rather, the value of nonexistence, according to the view I propose, does not vary from case to case. It could thus be viewed as matter of judicial notice. The jury is then left with the task of determining whether the plaintiff's level of well-being is in the negative range. But there is no reason to assume that the task must be presented to the jury under this particular description. The query presented to the jury might, for instance, be phrased in terms of the balance between the burdens that the plaintiff shoulders and the benefits that he or she enjoys, with some indication of the *kinds* of burdens and benefits that the law of negligence recognizes.

38. Feinberg identifies this problem in, among others, his case of the two "schoolyard bullies" and his airplane crash case ("Wrongful Life," 150–51). I return to his analysis in part 4.6.

39. Feinberg, "Wrongful Life," 147.

40. Feinberg, "Wrongful Life," 147.

41. Feinberg, "Wrongful Life," 146–48.

42. Feinberg, "Wrongful Life," 147.

43. Feinberg, "Wrongful Life," 149.

44. Feinberg, "Wrongful Life," 149, emphasis added. Feinberg frames the test as part of a test of *harm*. Feinberg's fuller account provides that *A* harms *B*, only if *B*'s "personal interest is in a worse condition . . . than it *would be* had

A not acted as he did" (Feinberg, "Wrongful Life," 149, emphasis added). At another point Feinberg suggests a revision to this test: *A* harms *B*, only if "*B*'s personal interest is in a worse state than it *would be* had *A* acted as he should have instead of as he did" (Feinberg, "Wrongful Life," 150, n.5, emphasis added).

45. E. Haavi Morreim makes this point. See "The Concept of Harm Reconceived: A Different Look at 'Wrongful Life,' " *Law and Philosophy* 7 (1988): 28.

46. Feinberg, "Wrongful Life," 150–53. See also Morreim, "The Concept of Harm Reconceived," 10–23.

47. Feinberg, "Wrongful Life," 150–52.

48. Feinberg, "Wrongful Life," 150–52.

49. Feinberg, "Wrongful Life," 153.

50. Feinberg, "Wrongful Life," 153.

51. Morreim's proposal for identifying the plaintiff's baseline, for purposes of determining harm in the wrongful life context as well as in other legal and moral contexts, as what the plaintiff's condition "should have been" at the time in question is one to which my own proposal owes a clear debt. At least, there is a common structure to that proposal and my own, according to which the plaintiff's baseline is the plaintiff's maximal state ("The Concept of Harm Reconceived," 23–27). Morreim speculates that the notion of what "should have been" might be filled out with notions of a "decent minimum of well-being" (25).

52. The idea that the test of harm should bear less analytical weight is suggested analogically by the insight that thorny issues of causation can be better addressed within the analysis of the duty element rather than as causation per se. For an introduction to causation in negligence, see H. L. A. Hart and Tony Honore, *Causation in the Law*, 2d ed. (New York: Oxford University Press, 1985), and Robert E. Keeton, *Legal Cause in the Law of Torts* (Columbus: Ohio State University Press, 1963).

The modal test that I suggest is intended to identify harm that is legally or morally significant. It is not intended to capture the ordinary language sense of the term "harm"—a term that is, of course, highly ambiguous. Thus, on the modal test that I suggest a meteorite's striking the Earth and causing tremendous pain and suffering does not *harm* anyone, unless some agent could have pulled some victim out of "harm's way" and failed to do so. Unavoidable diminutions in well-being thus would never constitute harm under the modal test, and are (and should be) likewise irrelevant to questions of culpability.

53. *Schroeder v. Perkel*, 87 N.J. at 63–64.

54. Hanson, "Suits for Wrongful Life," 7.

55. Hanson, "Suits for Wrongful Life," 7.

56. Thus, for example, the child-plaintiff in *Turpin v. Sortini* is permitted to recover on the basis of a hereditary hearing affliction. 31 Cal. 3d at 220, 643 P.2d at 954, 182 Cal. Rptr. at 337.

57. *Procanik v. Cillo*, 97 N.J. at 351, 478 A.2d at 762.

58. In those few jurisdictions in which wrongful life is a recognized cause of action, courts routinely limit damages to, for example, special damages for

extraordinary medical expenses. *Procanik v. Cillo*, 97 N.J. at 352, 478 A.2d at 762. For another view, see *Procanik v. Cillo*, 97 N.J. at 363–66, 478 A.2d at 768–70 (Handler, J. dissenting). My claim in this chapter is that courts are perfectly free to, and should, pursuant to comfortable, old, unreformed negligence theories, recognize wrongful life claims. But it does not follow that there is no room for courts or legislative bodies to recognize *new* torts in the form of, e.g., "wrongful impairment." Such an alternative theory is described by Hanson, "Suits for Wrongful Life, 1–24.

59. Much of the jury's work in tort cases involves similar guesswork. "If the jury is capable of making this comparison in wrongful death suits, there is no reason to doubt their ability to make the same comparison in wrongful-life suits" (Steinbock, "The Logical Case for Wrongful Life," 17, quoting Dawn Currier, "The Judicial System's Wrongful Conception of Wrongful Life," *Western New England Law Review* 6 [1983]: 493, 505).

60. Feinberg, "Wrongful Life," 158.

61. Heyd, *Genethics*, 30–31, emphasis added.

62. Heyd, *Genethics*, 32, emphasis added.

63. *Gleitman v. Cosgrove*, 49 N.J. at 63, 227 A.2d at 711. Though Tedeschi and Heyd each seem at points to accept the worsening requirement and to reject wrongful life on the grounds that it fails to meet that requirement, it is quite likely that each is, as well, concerned with this independent point. See G. Tedeschi, "On Tort Liability," *Israel Law Review* 1 (1966), at 528–30, and Heyd, *Genethics*, 26–35.

64. Feinberg addresses this inconsistency by refocusing from the issue of whether the infant-plaintiff would have been "better off" never existing at all to the issue of what the infant-plaintiff's "rational preference" is ("Wrongful Life," 158–59), revising the test of harm accordingly ("Wrongful Life," 162–66). But I find the latter proposal extremely difficult. For one thing, it seems to assume well-being to be a matter of preference satisfaction. Although I have generally left the analysis of well-being open, I do note that analyzing well-being in terms of preference satisfaction seems to deny that we make morally relevant distinctions among all those possible "rational preferences" we might have. For another thing, there are special problems, when the plaintiff is a severely disabled infant, with ascertaining—through the vehicle of a "proxy chooser" or otherwise—what that infant's "rational preference" is. We should, rather, go straight to the heart of the matter and inquire whether never existing at all would have been better for *this child*.

65. I note, however, that at other points Heyd suggests that his basic concern is independent of the issue of reference (*Genethics*, 36).

66. See generally Saul Kripke, *Naming and Necessity* (Cambridge: Harvard University Press, 1980).

Chapter 5

Human Cloning

5.1 The New Reproductive Technologies

We have witnessed during the last two decades a tidal wave in the development of new reproductive technologies. In 1993, scientists at George Washington University Hospital in Washington, D.C., announced that they had successfully cloned human embryos in their very early, undifferentiated stages.[1] In this form of cloning, the four to sixteen cells that constitute the very early human embryo are genetically identical; each contains the full complement of genetic material necessary to construct the differentiated organism. Technicians simply divide an eight-cell embryo, thereby producing two four-cell embryos, each of which continues to grow normally to the point at which the cells begin to differentiate into cells of, for example, the nervous system and the heart. Just recently, this technological feat was, unexpectedly, trumped when a Scottish embryologist, Ian Wilmut, announced that he had successfully cloned an adult mammal—a sheep.[2] This latter form of cloning had previously been considered the domain of science fiction writers and nervous ethicists. The belief had been that cloning from differentiated bodily (or somatic) cells of the adult organism remained, for the foreseeable future, a medical impossibility. That belief has now been entirely dispelled.

Technologies in addition to cloning have also flourished. Less remarkable only because it has become increasingly commonplace, in vitro fertilization (IVF), coupled with embryo transfer (ET), is now considered an effective treatment for infertility. IVF/ET can help a woman whose fallopian tubes are damaged or who is otherwise having difficulty becoming pregnant to give birth to a child who is genetically her own. It also permits a woman who is not able to produce her own egg cells, or a woman concerned about the risk of transmitting to her child a hereditary disease detected in other members of her own family, to

179

become pregnant by way of egg donation. In this procedure, the woman or a donor is placed under general anesthesia, and egg cells are retrieved from the ovary and fertilized in vitro, perhaps but not necessarily with the sperm of the woman's spouse or partner. One or more fertilized eggs are then transferred to the woman's uterus where they, with luck, develop in the usual way to one or more full term fetuses. Often more than a single embryo transfer will be needed for pregnancy to be achieved. Thus the treatment, if it succeeds at all, may take months. The cryopreservation, or freezing, of human embryos has been found to be an effective way of storing excess or donor embryos and egg cells until needed for additional transfers, thereby saving the woman the inconvenience and risk of further egg retrievals and the need to rely on donors.

IVF/ET can, moreover, be used in conjunction with hormonal therapies to allow women well past menopause to become pregnant. Thus, it was reported in 1993 that a fifty-nine-year-old woman had given birth to twins after achieving pregnancy with the help of doctors at a private fertility clinic in Rome.[3]

In 1987, the trials of "Baby M" brought commercial surrogacy arrangements into the news.[4] In one form of surrogacy, the so-called "surrogate" mother is impregnated using the sperm of the man who seeks to raise a genetic heir. Once the child is born, the agreement— declared unenforceable in New Jersey in the *Baby M* decision— provides that the surrogate mother will transfer her parental rights to the "contractual" parents—that is, to the genetic father and his partner, who may herself be infertile.

But other forms of surrogacy also exist. The surrogate mother need not, for example, be the genetic mother of the child she gestates. This result is made possible when the technologies of IVF and ET are combined with surrogacy, allowing the contractual mother to contribute her own egg cells to the process, which might be fertilized either using the sperm of the contractual father[5] or, alternatively, using the sperm of a donor, and then transferred to the surrogate (now a mere "gestational") mother. These techniques also allow a couple or an individual to arrange for an egg donated from a woman who is neither the contractual nor the gestational mother to be fertilized in vitro using the sperm of the contractual father or, alternatively, donor sperm.[6]

Insemination by sperm donor is now a common and legally recognized strategy for addressing male infertility,[7] and advertisements routinely appear in national newspapers for the immediate availability of donor eggs.

Finally, new drug therapies designed to treat infertility are regularly introduced to the market and, in all likelihood, account for more new lives than any of the other new technologies.[8]

5.2 The Question of Harm to Children

5.2.1 Who Matters?

Perhaps the most worrisome moral issues regarding the new reproductive technologies spotlight the children these new technologies help to create. This is not to say that concerns about the needs and interests of individuals other than the children are unfounded. Subtle pressures on women to undergo intrusive, risky, and expensive infertility therapies (such as IVF/ET) should be brought to light and examined. A community that expects women to have children implicitly objects to women who do not have children. A community that makes it nicer for women to have children and stay home with them than to pursue aggressively a profession is, nicely, insisting that this expectation be fulfilled. A community that considers women who do not have children a sort of "third sex" is really doing just about all that it can to force women to live a certain kind of life. It seems to me that women who have been put into such a bind have been wronged. But the question is a controversial one. The claim that a woman has undergone infertility treatments because she has been put into an unjust bind, held up against her own testimony that she freely and in her own best interests *chose* to undergo the treatments, might seem paternalistic.

Other potential claimants against the new reproductive technologies might be thought to include the early-stage, undifferentiated human embryos sacrificed in the context of research and development of the new reproductive technologies, including IVF, ET, embryo cryopreservation, and cloning. After all, no one intended that the second generation of the many embryos cloned during the early stages of laboratory research would ever be transferred to the uteruses of their genetic mothers or any other woman and permitted to develop into full term fetuses. And even after the new technologies become old hat, concerns might be raised regarding the respect and dignity accorded to human embryos. Extras are simply discarded or frozen indefinitely—or perhaps indiscriminately donated, by their own genetic "parents" for the "use" of infertile couples. Anyone who thinks that the human *potential* of human embryos entitles them to a certain level of respect and dignity will be appalled. We will delve into this issue further in part 5.3.1. But here too the issues are unclear. For the claim might be made that the human potential of the human embryo entitles it to nothing at all and has no moral significance.[9] And it might be claimed that the contrary view constitutes untethered metaphysical speculation the inevitable result of which is a baseless insinuation of power and control over the most fundamental aspects of the lives of all women—and ultimately decreasing the levels of well-being these woman might otherwise enjoy.

But the children! If the new reproductive technologies harm the children they help create, those who market the new technologies have a problem. Maybe the risks the new technologies impose on infertile women can be justified by reference to the women's own informed consent. But we obviously cannot make this move in the case of the children. Possibly we can justify destroying large numbers of human embryos under the argument that the embryo, for purposes of morality, does not matter. But we cannot make this claim in the case of children, whose status as persons is unquestioned. Children *do* matter and are entitled to have their interests count *alongside our own*.[10]

Even theorists who defend the new technologies do not rule out that these technologies carry with them certain risks to the child. Thus, regarding what he calls "collaborative reproduction" generally, Robertson writes:

> Radically new reproductive techniques . . . pose risks to offspring. Laboratory manipulation of embryos, the splitting of gestational and genetic parenthood, and prenatal screening risk producing children who are physically or psychologically injured by the techniques in question. Of special concern is the impact on children of several sets of genetic and social parents, some of whom the child will never know, which arise in the collaborative use of gamete donors and surrogates.[11]

In particular, human cloning, according to Robertson, "could . . . lead to unrealized parental expectations, invidious comparisons with the cloned individual, or simply identity confusion."[12]

But although Robertson concedes that the new technologies, including cloning, impose a risk of a negative psychosocial effect, he at the same time argues that any negative effect, or *hurt*, that is felt by the children of these new technologies does not amount to a genuine *harm*.[13] In chapter 4, a number of different ways of thinking about harm were sketched. In the end, I proposed a "modal" test of harm according to which harm is an essentially comparative matter and can be understood in terms of the level of well-being a person has in one situation versus the level of well-being that person has in another situation (part 4.6). The adequacy of the modal test will not be a point of dispute in this chapter, and thus Robertson's point can be restated in its terms.

What Robertson is saying, then, is that the new technologies do not a whit diminish, and are, rather, essential to the promotion of, the child's well-being. As such, they do not harm, or genuinely harm, the child.

It seems that if Robertson is correct and the new technologies pose no risk of genuine harm to the children they help to create, then our moral worries evaporate. At least, an account of any residual worries we might have will involve the very difficult notion that, though the child has not been harmed and though by hypothesis no one else has been harmed, application of the new technologies remains morally objectionable. As we have seen, some theorists have accepted the notion of wronging without harming.[14] In what follows, however, I will argue that even given that a person cannot have been wronged without having been harmed (in the sense of there being some diminution in his or her well-being), our worries about cloning remain well-grounded. In particular, I will argue that we can identify respects in which the offspring of cloning in various contexts have been harmed in the sense of there being some diminution in their well-being. It will not necessarily follow, however, from the fact that the children have been harmed in this sense that they have been wronged. Whether for legal or moral purposes, harm is simply one "element" of wrongdoing. The issue of when cloning actually constitutes wrongdoing—that is, the wronging of people—will be separately explored in part 5.4.3.

One other point that I will make in what follows is that the emphasis on the psychosocial effect of cloning tends to understate the potential total negative effect. Thus, I will argue in part 5.5.3 that there are more serious negatives that we should focus on. In particular, we should focus on how cloning affects the child's interest in avoiding the unconsented duplication of his or her genome. It is not that I think that the lives of children produced by application of cloning and its related technologies are not worth living or that it would have been better for these children had they never existed at all. Rather, I believe that whether cloning is unlikely to produce a life that is truly wrongful does not exhaust the moral issue. We must also ask whether imposing an effect that is *less* than the truly horrible can be justified, or excused, in some way.

5.2.2 Robertson's Defense of the New Technologies

Robertson's defense of the new technologies is in some instances compelling. A quick sketch of that defense—which we will examine more closely in part 5.3.2—reveals its broad scope. Suppose that the new technologies will predictably lead to psychosocial distress and other forms of ill-being in the children those technologies help to create. Suppose, then, that on the basis of this fact agents decline to apply the new technologies or the community prohibits their application by law. Then, no psychosocial distress is imposed, but neither is the child produced. For the new technologies make possible a life that, despite its flaws, is well worth living. Thus, it makes no sense to argue that it is in the *child's* interest to prohibit the new technologies. Vaccinations, after all, may hurt, but no one thinks that the properly administered vaccination genuinely harms the child. By analogy, the new reproductive technologies may impose certain negative effects on the children they help to produce, but they cannot, according to Robertson, genuinely harm those children.

Robertson's defense of the new technologies can be expressed in person-affecting terms. Indeed, Robertson sometimes comes very close to using those terms himself. He even refers to the nonidentity problem in connection with his example of a woman who chooses to conceive and give birth to a child with a withered arm.[15] But, contra Parfit and others, Robertson seems not to consider each and every formulation of the nonidentity problem a *problem*. Indeed, I credit my own reevaluation of certain forms of the nonidentity problem—and, correspondingly, of person-affecting consequentialism—to Robertson's work. As I argued in chapter 3, the type 2-alt nonidentity cases seem not to pose problems that demand a solution—a solution that might include the disavowal of person-affecting principles in favor of totalism—but rather to form the basis of perfectly sound arguments.[16] Thus, regarding the child born with the withered arm, Robertson suggests that, since "there is no way this *particular* child *could* have been born normal," this *particular* child seems not to have any sort of legal or moral claim against the woman for making the choice that she has made.[17] Nor does her choice seem otherwise to be morally objectionable. Assuming, as Robertson does, that (1) the flaw is a "mild" one, so that the child's life remains worth living, (2) the child *could* not have been born without the withered arm, and (3) no one else suffers a diminution in well-being as a result of the child's condition, the argument for the permissibility of the woman's choice to have the child seems very persuasive.

Recall, then, the person-affecting M*:

M*: *s* is not wronged by agents in *X* if, for each world *Y* accessible to such agents, *s* has at least as much well-being in *X* as *s* has in *Y*.

On the assumptions that only two alternatives are accessible to the child—never existing at all and coming into existence with the withered arm—and that the child's life would be worth living despite the defect, M* implies that bringing the child into existence does not wrong the child. Recall, as well, P*:

P*: *X* is permissible for agents at *t* *if and only if* no person who exists at or after *t* in *X* is wronged at or after *t* in *X*.

Since the child has not himself been wronged, given that no one else has been wronged P* implies that no wrong has been done at all. Bringing the child with the unavoidably withered arm into existence thus may be a morally permissible choice.

It seems to me that Robertson's argument is compelling with respect to many of the new reproductive technologies, each of which is uniquely designed to bring new people into existence and none of which appear to impose so much damage that the lives they produce would be less than ones worth living.[18] And without IVF, without egg and sperm donation, without the new drug therapies, many children could not have existed at all. Even if these technologies cause the children they bring into existence to experience some degree of psychosocial distress or give rise to even more serious forms of ill-being, the children's lives remain well worth living. The choice to use these technologies thus makes the children they help to create as well off as these children can be made. Assuming the choice does the same for others, personalism has no objection to it. In contrast, the totalist needs more information before evaluating the choice and may come to a different conclusion. According to the totalist, if agents could have produced other, healthier children who would have achieved a higher level of well-being over a lifetime in place of the flawed children they in fact produce, then agents have done something wrong though they have wronged no one. But it is unclear that this totalist account is correct.

Robertson's defense cannot, however, be extended to the full range of new reproductive technologies. Among the technologies for which it fails is human cloning. My objection to Robertson's defense of cloning is not aimed at what I take to be the theory of his argument—that is, at M* or P*. My objection, rather, is to his *application* of the principles to defend cloning.[19] The form of cloning I will focus on first is *embryonic* cloning. However, as we shall see, many of the same points may be made regarding the newer, *somatic* form of cloning.[20]

I do not ultimately conclude that human cloning *always* wrongs the child who is its product. I reach, rather, a more limited conclusion: that the ethical issues regarding the children of cloning are much more complicated than Robertson's analysis reflects and that in some instances considerations of such murky matters as fairness must be taken into account. More than a quick and clean incision with M* will thus be needed to vindicate cloning.

5.3   Human Embryonic Cloning

5.3.1   Defining the Issues: Abortion and the "Dignity" of the Human Embryo

Why are so many people made uneasy by announcements of dramatic technological advances in human reproduction? Are the masses overly emotional and insufficiently analytic? Or could the concern rather be grounded in some significant moral insight that those theorists who are so clear on the essential *rightness* of the new technologies have not yet attended to?

Some theorists have, of course, expressed concerns about cloning and other new technologies. Thus, Richard A. McCormick argues that efforts to perfect the technique of human embryonic cloning and the application of the technique once perfected will inevitably result in the significant waste of human embryos and thus will represent a failure to accord these entities the "profound respect" that they are due.[21] McCormick is far from alone in his view.[22] But McCormick himself, at least, does not appear to be an absolutist. Rather, in his view "the potential of the embryo for personhood makes powerful *prima facie* demands on us not to interfere with that potential."[23] Thus, in McCormick's view, the embryo's potential imposes obligations on us that may be disregarded if compliance with them would violate other, more fundamental, ethical principles.

Robertson, in contrast, provides a broad defense of human cloning. But Robertson's defense of cloning includes no sustained effort to demonstrate that the "prima facie demands" against interfering with human potential are, in fact, illusory, or that they must bow to more fundamental values.[24] Robertson does not expressly explain why he does not debate this point. Perhaps he supposes that the research and development of human cloning ought to be permitted if it generates a likely benefit for (or at least does not burden) those beings whose claim to our respect, concern, and aid is fairly clear. According to this view, what counts, ethically, in the cloning debate is the effect of cloning on flesh-and-blood human beings whose moral status is uncontroversial, including infertile couples and any children that the new technologies enable them to produce. Amorphous concerns regarding subtle indignities experienced by entities whose ethical status is at best unclear would not, according to this view, weigh in at all.[25]

This approach to the ethics of human cloning particularly and the new reproductive technologies generally is not obviously flawed. Perhaps we *should* set aside amorphous concerns in favor of pursuing a course of action that seeks to resolve the real problems of real people. Infertility is a real problem. It can seriously constrain an individual's or a couple's ability to live the kinds of lives they want to live. More to the point, infertility can cause a substantial diminution in the level of well-being they would otherwise enjoy. Reasonable efforts designed to address infertility therefore seem well justified.

Robertson acknowledges that from this fact it does not follow that any and every tactic for curing infertility can be justified. There are limitations; and the test for legitimacy, Robertson suggests, is whether the "interests of *couples* and *offspring* are well served [by human cloning]."[26]

If we are willing to set aside amorphous concerns in favor of pursuing a course of action that seeks to resolve the real problems of real people, then Robertson's plan of action seems a sound one. *If* it can be shown that the interests of the infertile individual or couple, any children produced by application of cloning, and (I would add) any third-party donor or other participant are well served by cloning, then it would seem that, as Robertson suggests, by that very fact the ethical issues raised by human cloning will have been resolved.[27]

But has Robertson effectively demonstrated that the interests of children produced by cloning will be well served? I will argue that Robertson does not achieve that feat and that in many instances it seems that children *will* be harmed by cloning, in the sense that they will suffer a perfectly avoidable diminution in the levels of well-being they could otherwise enjoy.

My argument may be of interest to those who believe that abortion is sometimes a morally permissible choice. Suppose that we have moral doubts about cloning *and* that we take the view that early abortions can be undertaken without *any* concern for the developing embryo—that is, without *any* weighing of the competing interests held by the woman on the one hand and the developing embryo on the other. If this is our position, then we—unlike McCormick—clearly cannot make sense of our doubts about cloning by appealing to claims regarding the "profound respect" due human embryos or "*prima facie* demands" regarding their treatment. Thus, we must instead either rid ourselves of these doubts or else understand them to have some alternative foundation. It seems to me that we can do the latter. Thus, I will argue that there is reason to be concerned about the effect of cloning, not on early human embryos, but rather on the flesh-and-blood children that cloning produces. Thus, the account I will provide sorts out,

on the one hand, concerns about cloning and, on the other, the view
that the early human embryos themselves have some moral significance. We can explain the former and discard the latter.

5.3.2   Robertson's Defense of Embryonic Cloning

We turn, then, to Robertson's defense of embryonic cloning. It will
be sufficient to examine, with Robertson, the cases of cloning that are
most likely to arise. These can be sorted into two groups:

> **Group I**: Cloning, coupled with embryo transfer, is used in the
> treatment of infertility for the purpose of increasing the
> number of embryos transferred to the uterus, on occa-
> sion resulting in the *simultaneous birth* of genetically
> identical twins, triplets, or quadruplets,[28]

and

> **Group II**: Cloning, coupled with embryo transfer and the cryo-
> preservation of the cloned embryos, is used in the treat-
> ment of infertility for the purpose of avoiding
> subsequent egg retrieval, on occasion resulting in ge-
> netically identical siblings being *"born years apart*, in the
> same or different families."[29]

Robertson argues in general terms that:

> there is [a] problem with assessing harm here that goes beyond the psy-
> chosocial and familial problems of a child who is a clone of another. The
> problem—a recurring one with engineering of offspring characteris-
> tics—is that the potentially harmful effects of cloning cannot truly harm
> the clone, because there is no unharmed state, other than nonexistence,
> that *could* be achieved as a point of comparison. If cloning did not occur,
> the cloned individual would not exist. If she had been given a different
> genome, that is, not been cloned, she would not be the same individual
> [citation omitted]. Thus even if the clone suffers inordinately from her
> replica status, *there is no alternative for her* if she is to live at all. Unless the
> life of a clone were so full of unavoidable suffering that her very existence
> were a wrong (an unlikely scenario) cloning would then—whatever its
> psychological effects—not harm the offspring.[30]

In discussing the group I cases, Robertson emphasizes that this general
point holds whether the clones born into the same family at the same

time are twins, triplets, or even quadruplets. According to Robertson, even if the genetically identical individuals suffer

> unique or inordinate psychological problems because they have identical siblings . . . [a]t the very least, it would appear difficult to argue that these disadvantages are so great that the triplet [or quadruplet] should never have been born. Given that this is *the only way for this individual to be born,* its birth hardly appears to be a wrongful life that never should have occurred.[31]

Turning, then, to the group II cases, Robertson argues that whatever the "special problems" faced by the youngest child resulting from the fact that he or she has genetically identical older siblings born into the same or different families, and whatever the oldest child's feelings that

> he is deficient because his parents wanted a newer version of him . . . it is difficult to conclude that later or earlier born twins or triplets are likely to have such serious psychological problems that they should never be born at all.[32]

Thus, Robertson concludes that cloning "would be ethically permissible."[33]

Robertson's supposition that any negative effects of cloning will likely not be so extreme as to make life not worth living seems reasonable. I am therefore more interested in the part of Robertson's argument that attempts to draw the inference, from the fact that the child's life *is* worth living, to the conclusion that cloning, even if it causes "inordinate" suffering or other forms of ill-being, does not genuinely harm the child. When we think in the abstract about the test of harm that Robertson suggests, it seems a peculiar one: the child is harmed *only if* the child is so badly harmed that the child's life is rendered not worth living. In ordinary life, it is quite easy to see how a person might be harmed yet still have a life worth living. Why does Robertson think that the test he proposes works to defeat a claim of harm in the case of cloning?

Robertson's argument to this conclusion depends on two premises. (A) If being brought into existence by application of cloning and certain related technologies (including embryo transfer and, perhaps, cryopreservation) as one of a number of genetically identical individuals is the "only way" for a given child to be brought into existence at all, then causing the child to so exist does not harm, or wrong, the child. And, (B) being brought into existence in that way—by application of those technologies, and as one of a number of genetically identical individuals—*is* the "only way" for that child to exist.

How is premise A to be construed? We might understand the sufficient condition that A establishes to be counterfactual in form—of the "what would have been" variety. We might, that is, understand A to provide that the child is not harmed *if* the child *would* not have existed had the cloning and other technologies not been used as they were. At times, Robertson suggests that this is his intended interpretation.[34] But construed in this way A is an instance of CF, a principle that we have already found ample reason to reject.[35] That the child *would* not have existed or *would* otherwise have been worse off does not by itself imply that no harm or wrong has been done. Even if it is true that, had I not shot the preacher in the arm, I would have shot him in the heart, I still harm, and probably wrong, him when I shoot him in the arm.

Premise A is better understood as appealing to the more plausible M*. If agents have done the best anyone could have done for a child, then agents have not wronged that child. And, on the assumption that existence is better for the child than never having existed at all, agents *have* done the best that anyone could have done for that child if that child *could* not have existed (exists in no accessible world) other than as one of a number of genetically identical individuals. And, thus, A: no wrong is done the child if the child *could* not have existed other than by the cloning technologies and as one of many.

My aim here will not be to scrutinize A, understood in light of M*, nor, as noted earlier, will I revisit M* or P*. Rather, I want to point out that the second premise, premise B, is false in the case of cloning. Since the condition set out by premise A is not satisfied, the argument collapses.

5.4   The Critique

5.4.1   Who Needs Cloning?

Premise B states that being brought into existence by application of the cloning technologies and as one of a number of genetically identical individuals is the "only way" for the cloned offspring to exist.[36] Consider, then, whether B is true in the group I cases, in which genetically identical twins, triplets, quadruplets, or etc. are born at the same time in the same family. Cloning in this context is intended to make it more likely that a pregnancy will be achieved. The transfer of more than one embryo to the uterus makes it more likely that *some* embryo will develop into a full term fetus. Consider the child who develops from the *original embryo*. Does B hold for *that* child? No. It seems that that very child *could* have existed even had the cloning operation not been performed. *Not* cloning, and instead transferring the original embryo as a singleton, was a clearly defined alternative for the agents. Thus, B does not hold, and Robertson's defense fails for the child who develops from the original embryo.[37]

Consider, then, the child who develops from the second (third, fourth, etc.), duplicate embryo. Clearly, this second child could not have achieved existence in the absence of the cloning procedure itself. But this point gains Robertson no ground. For the psychosocial distress and other forms of ill-being that A and B purport to justify is the ill-being produced by the cloning *in combination with* the subsequent transfers of the cloned embryos and development of those cloned embryos into two (three, four, etc.) genetically identical, full-fledged human beings. In other words, the harm of cloning arises not from the cloning per se but rather from existing as one of many rather than as one of one. But is B true for this second child? Is it true that this second child cannot exist except by application of the cloning technologies and as one of many? To see that B does not hold for this second child, we need just observe that the second child could have existed even had none of the embryos other than the one that develops into the second child ever been transferred at all. Discarding those others and transferring the one as a singleton was an option well within reach of the agents. Thus, the second child could have existed, after all, without finding himself or herself one of a number of genetically identical individuals. Here, as well, B does not hold and Robertson's defense fails. The point also holds for the third child, the fourth child, and so on.

Robertson's defense likewise fails in connection with the group II cases. In these cases, genetically identical individuals are born at different times and perhaps into different families. As before, the issue under B is whether one child—say, the first-born—could exist without existing as one of a number of genetically identical individuals. Here, the psychosocial distress that Robertson concedes includes feelings of displacement resulting from having younger siblings who are genetically exactly like oneself. Whether or not we limit our concern to psychosocial distress, with respect to the first-born the failure of B is particularly vivid. Before the second, third, and fourth duplicate embryos are thawed and transferred, the first-born *already* exists. It follows trivially that this child *could* exist without existing as one of a number of genetically identical individuals.

A parallel analysis shows that B fails for the case of any younger child as well. Consider, for instance, the second-born child. Of course, if the first child is already "on the ground" at the time the second embryo is thawed and transferred, the only practical means of bringing the second child into existence is by imposing on her (say) the condition of having a genetically identical older sibling. Considerations of fairness would prohibit our eliminating the older child since doing so would cause a dramatic decrease in that child's level of well-being. Nonetheless, *prior* to the transfer of the *original* embryo—that is, the embryo that develops into the first-born—agents might easily have avoided harming the second-born by simply refraining from transferring, and instead discarding, the original embryo. The agents might likewise then have refrained from transferring, and instead discarded, the remaining embryos other than, of course, the second. Thus, in the case of the second-born also, B is false and Robertson's defense fails. And again the point also holds for the third, fourth, fifth, etc. child.

5.4.2   A Person-Affecting Statement of the Critique

The point of dispute with Robertson can be represented graphically. For convenience, we will consider a composite of the group I and group II cases. Suppose that in alternative *A* multiple clones have been produced from a single human embryo and transferred, and suppose that at least some of these embryos eventually develop into full-fledged people: s_1 and s_2, born into a certain family at a certain time, s_3, born into the same family at a different time, and s_4, born into a different family at a different time. We suppose with Robertson that each child enjoys a net positive level of well-being—say, 5 units of well-being, with it being understood that this level of well-being reflects the depressing effect of any psychosocial distress or other form of ill-being. Suppose that in *B* agents refrain from the suspicious enterprise—the combined application of cloning, embryo transfer, and cryopreservation that causes each child to exist as one of a number of genetically identical individuals rather than as one of one—with the inevitable result, according to Robertson, that none of s_1, s_2, s_3, and s_4 exist at all. In other words:

Case 12/Cloning, Robertson's View

	A	B
s_1	5	
s_2	5	
s_3	5	
s_4	5	

On these facts, M* implies that none of s_1–s_4 have been wronged in A, their well-being having been, in each case, maximized. N* is also applicable.

N*: *s* is not wronged by agents in *X if s* never exists in *X*.

N* implies that none of s_1–s_4 have been wronged in *B*. P* implies, finally, that both *A* and *B* are permissible alternatives.

Using, as before, "*n**" to record these person-affecting implications, we may sum up:

Case 12/Cloning, Robertson's View, Annotated

	A	B
s_1	5*	*
s_2	5*	*
s_3	5*	*
s_4	5*	*

But I have argued that none of the cloned offspring need, in order to exist, to be brought into existence as one of a number of genetically identical individuals. For each child, the agents might have refrained from the initial transfer of the genetically identical embryos other than the transfer of the cloned embryo from which *that* child develops. Since Robertson's version of the facts fails to take into account these better-for-each-s_m alternatives, it is mistaken. For example, consider alternative *C*, in which only the first of the cloned embryos is transferred and permitted to develop into a flesh-and-blood child. This alternative is better for s_1 than *A* is since s_1 in *C* does not exist as one of many. Other, better, alternatives exist for s_2–s_4 as well. Supposing that the difference in the levels of well-being conferred on each child in the better alternatives is, though small, significant, we can sum up:

Case 13/Cloning, Revised

	A	B	C	D	E	F
s_1	5		8			
s_2	5			8		
s_3	5				8	
s_4	5					8

Construed in this way, the cloning case invites an appeal to D*:

D*: *s* is wronged by agents in *X if s* exists in *X* and there is some world *Y* accessible to such agents such that:
  (i) *s* has more well-being in *Y* than *s* has in *X*;
  (ii) for each person *s'* who ever exists in *X*, *either s'* has at least

as much well-being in Y as s' has in X *or s' never exists in Y; and*

(iii) for each s' who ever exists in Y, s' exists at some time in X.

Given these facts, D* implies that each cloned subject is wronged in A. M* and N* resolve some other issues. Now using "$n!$" to record the implication that the indicated person has been wronged at the indicated world, we write:

Case 13/Cloning, Revised and Annotated

	A	B	C	D	E	F
s_1	5!	*	8*	*	*	*
s_2	5!	*	*	8*	*	*
s_3	5!	*	*	*	8*	*
s_4	5!	*	*	*	*	8*

Construed in this way, the cloning scenario parallels a type 3-alt nonidentity problem, not, as Robertson seems to suppose, a type 2-alt nonidentity problem. But the cloning scenario, looked at as a nonidentity problem, is actually much easier to "solve," from a person-affecting point of view, than the original type 3-alt nonidentity problem.[38] In the slave child case, for example, the questionable conduct—the signing of the contract—occurred *prior* to conception. And it was not, as we noted, initially clear (though it became so later) how the couple might have refrained from this questionable conduct but at the same time gone about producing the very same child *as a nonslave* whom they in fact produced *as a slave*.

In the cloning scenario just described, it is easy to say just how agents could have gone about making things better for any one of the multiple, genetically identical children in fact produced. Thus, agents might have produced just *one* of those children without producing the others. They might have achieved this result by transferring one of the cloned embryos to *one woman* at *one time*. (Or perhaps *two* or even *three* embryos could be transferred to one woman at one time, depending on trade-offs for the woman. We turn to this issue in the next part.) The remaining genetically identical embryos might have then been frozen. If the woman had become pregnant and given birth, the remaining embryos could then have been destroyed rather than transferred either to this same woman when she later decides to have another child or to some other woman. If she had not become pregnant, some of these embryos could have been thawed and the procedure just described repeated.

5.4.3   Benefits to Infertile Couples and the Question of Fairness

A critic might note that I have failed to take into account the extent to which cloning, *even if it does harm the cloned offspring, benefits* infertile couples. A critic may argue, in other words, that cloning represents a *trade-off* situation and as such does not meet the conditions of D*. And if the conditions of D* are not satisfied, the implication of wrongdoing may be avoided.

Right off the bat, we can think of two hypotheticals in which cloning may be considered to *benefit* the woman who seeks to become pregnant. Both cases involve an infertile woman who has gone through a single laparoscopy, under general anesthesia and after suffering the discomfort, inconvenience, and expense of the hormonal injections necessary to stimulate egg production. Suppose that in each of the two cases the doctor has collected, say, three egg cells. These egg cells are fertilized in vitro, producing three, genetically distinct human embryos. But this number of embryos is just appropriate to give the woman a reasonable chance of pregnancy in a *single* hormonal cycle. To avoid the necessity of additional egg retrievals in the event that the woman does not become pregnant during the first cycle, the embryos are cloned. Some of the cloned embryos are immediately transferred to the woman's uterus and others are frozen for potential future use. The woman is lucky and gets pregnant right away. She has the baby.

It is at this point that the two hypotheticals diverge. In the first hypothetical, knowing that she will want another baby at a later date and still wanting to avoid additional egg retrievals, the woman does not have the extra, now frozen embryos destroyed. From this batch of embryos she eventually has a second baby. And, though the odds may be (barely) against it, it turns out that the second baby is genetically identical to the first. Because the woman has been able to have the number of children she wants—two—at minimal risk to herself, the bringing into existence of the two genetically identical cloned offspring has benefited her. At the same time, each of the cloned offspring experiences— let us suppose—a diminution in well-being, relative to what each might have enjoyed, in view of their status as clones.

In the second hypothetical, the woman, after having the first baby, decides that she has no further need for the embryos and donates them to an infertile couple. They then have a baby who, again, turns out to be genetically identical to the first baby. Since they wanted a baby and now have one, the couple have benefited from the production of multiple, genetically identical offspring. And again we suppose that each of the cloned offspring is harmed.

Both of these hypotheticals involve trade-offs. Let us consider how this fact affects the moral evaluation of the first hypothetical. Suppose that in *A* the woman gives birth, at distinct times, to two genetically identical children. In *B*, the woman gives birth to the first child. But instead of producing a second baby from what remains of the original batch of embryos, the woman undergoes a further round of hormonal injections, laparoscopy, and IVF/ET. Thus, in *B* she has a second child who is genetically distinct from the first. Making a set of suppositions regarding the levels of well-being to reflect the fact that the case involves a trade-off, I let s_m name the woman, understand s_1 and s_2 to be genetically identical to each other and s_3 to be genetically distinct, and use "$n*?$" and "$n!?$" to indicate those issues with respect to which D* is silent yet we *think* we know what is fair. Then:

Case 14/Cloning Problem with Parent, Annotated

	A	B
s_m	8*	7*?
s_1	6!?	8*
s_2	6*	*
s_3	*	8*

At a glance, considerations of fairness may seem to suggest that *B* is permissible and *A*, in which s_1 is treated unfairly, i.e., unequally, is not. But a critic will observe that the suppositions I have made regarding well-being are somewhat arbitrary. Perhaps it is the parent who will suffer substantially and the child who will suffer minimally if cloning is permitted.

This point is perfectly correct. But it hardly lends support to Robertson's defense of cloning. Rather, it shows very clearly that issues of the likely effect of being brought into existence as one of a number of genetically identical individuals versus the likely effect of hormonal therapies and laparoscopy must be addressed *before we can morally evaluate cloning in a given kind of case.* For one thing, before we can even determine whether (1) personalism proper will resolve the case on its own or (2) considerations of fairness will need to be introduced, we must have at hand a certain amount of information regarding the expected distribution of well-being if cloning is selected and the range of alternative distributions of well-being if cloning is not selected. But once this call is made, whether the case involves a trade-off or not, we are again at a loss to proceed in the absence of information regarding the expected distribution of well-being if cloning is selected and the alternative distributions of well-being that are possible if cloning is not selected.[39]

This way of looking at cloning suggests a profound departure from the defense that Robertson supplies. According to Robertson, issues regarding harm to offspring are fully resolved by the fact that cloning "well serves" the offspring it produces, being the "only way" those offspring can exist. According to the approach I suggest, things are more complicated. For one thing, it will not always be the case that existence as one of many *is* the "only way" each of the cloned offspring can exist. For another, trade-offs can arise, and when they do considerations of fairness will be critical. On Robertson's view, fairness need never enter the picture, since the trade-offs are not there.

In the two hypotheticals just described, the trade-off arises out of the fact that cloning provides a woman with a less risky and more convenient way to address infertility than the alternative, which may involve additional retrievals of her own egg cells via laparoscopy. But suppose that the rationale for cloning has nothing to do with infertility and rather with the desire to produce a child of a certain sort—a child just like, say, some already existing child whom one has had the opportunity to examine carefully or to have examined carefully, perhaps at the genetic level. Perhaps a man wants a child genetically identical to a child whom he regards as superior to any child he might produce naturally. Or perhaps he wants a child who has been screened and certified genetically healthy when his or his partner's family has a history of hereditary disease. The distributions of well-being on each of these two scenarios may well vary from the trade-offs we think are likely in the context of infertility. Thus, perhaps the option of having a naturally selected, more or less average child rather than a genetically superior child would not be so bad, from the man's point of view, after all. Perhaps he would end up enjoying the average child who is genetically his own as much as he would any other child. And perhaps the risk of having a child afflicted with a hereditary disease is—again from the man's own point of view—serious enough to justify, under a theory of fairness, a diminution in the well-being of the child. (This last assumes, of course, the availability of no third alternative that both addresses the man's concern and does not lead to a diminution in the well-being of some child.)

Variations in well-being can be expected to occur on the child's side as well. Thus, perhaps ordinarily it is a bad thing for a child to find himself or herself one of a very large number of genetically identical individuals, born into different families and at different times. At the same time, cases will arise in which it is better to be a clone than not.

Thus, when the Ayalas decided to have another child on a one in four chance that such a child could donate bone marrow to an older sibling who had myelogenous leukemia, they were very lucky.[40] The new baby girl was tissue compatible with the older daughter, and when the baby was old enough, the cancer treatment was completed. But other families may not be so fortunate. Clearly, the Ayala strategy would be more likely to succeed and the older child's life saved if the new baby were not just a sibling but a genetically identical twin.

These facts suggest yet another distribution, one in which it is much better for the older sibling to be a clone than not, and better as well for the parents who want that child to survive. Would it have been better for the younger child not to have been born as the second of two genetically identical individuals and not to have been made to donate bone marrow at a young age? Perhaps; but, if so, the slight diminution in well-being for the younger child—the trade-off—might well be justified as one that is fair.

5.5   *Are* Children Harmed by Cloning?

5.5.1   The Implications of the Harm Issue

As we think about cloning, it is evident that we must come to a good understanding of the consequences of producing multiple, genetically identical children for the children themselves. If being brought into existence as one of a number of genetically identical individuals does not at all harm any of these individuals, then, on the person-affecting view I have described, the choice whether to clone will be evaluated entirely in terms of its effects on others—on, for instance, the woman who wants to avoid laparoscopy or the man who wants to avoid the risk of hereditary disease. There is, in other words, no need to think about fairness. On the other hand, suppose that cloning in some contexts does involve a diminution in the child's level of well-being while generating some benefit for others. Suppose, in other words, that cloning in some contexts involves a trade-off. Then, on the person-affecting view I have described, the choice whether to clone can only be evaluated by appeal to considerations of fairness. Thus, we must assess harm to offspring before we can even begin to evaluate the choice whether in a specific instance to clone—before, that is, we know whether to turn to fairness or not. But fairness itself will be judged by reference to the relative burdens and benefits different possible choices create for the affected persons. To evaluate these choices, we must know what the expected burdens and benefits are.

Clearly, not all cloning choices will necessarily be evaluated in the same way. Where the trade-off does not significantly burden one of the cloned offspring but significantly benefits the other—as in cases like the Ayala situation—then we might think that the cloning choice is permissible, indeed, obligatory. But where the burden to the cloned child is significant—where, for example, the child has been brought into existence as one of a very large number of genetically identical individuals, perhaps born into different families at different times— and the benefit to others unclear, we might think that the cloning choice has wronged the child and is, therefore, itself impermissible.

A convenient thing about Robertson's defense of cloning, had it proved tenable, is that we would not have to think very hard about the ill effects of cloning on the offspring of cloning. Robertson suggests that moral qualms are appropriate only if so many clones are produced that some of them, at least, have lives that are less than worth living. *That* many clones it seems impossible to produce! But, as I have argued, Robertson's defense is not tenable.

5.5.2   The Issue of Psychosocial Distress

What is the likely effect of being brought into existence as one of some number of genetically identical individuals? What is the risk?

It seems reasonable to assume that there is no serious question of the cloning procedure inflicting bodily damage on the multiply cloned children. Robertson thus shifts to the question of whether cloning causes psychosocial distress in the children whom it creates. He argues that it is simply unclear whether identical twins, triplets, or even quadruplets suffer any "unique or inordinate psychological problems because they have identical siblings."[41] "[W]e can only speculate," he writes, whether the intentional production of genetically identical individuals will "lead to unrealized parental expectations, invidious comparisons with the cloned individual, or simply identity confusion."[42] In his view, the water is further muddied by the fact that clones may experience certain special benefits, including the satisfaction of having been "given a desirable genome by loving parents, and even the special bond, akin to the genetic bond of identical twins, of being the clone of a living individual."[43]

Robertson may be correct that we merely speculate when we worry that the children produced by cloning may experience psychosocial distress and that we can equally speculate that these same individuals may enjoy offsetting benefits as a consequence of their status as clones.

But maybe he is wrong. My own view is that we should not be speculating about this truly critical issue one way or the other. Instead, we should make the issue a subject of serious study by theorists and practitioners of psychology and sociology.

It seems to me, however, that even lay people can recognize one factor that seriously complicates the issue of psychosocial distress and will make it far more difficult for us to accept the view that a child will not be significantly harmed by his or her status as a clone. We do not face simply the issue of whether one is likely to experience psychosocial distress when one finds that one has been brought into existence as one of many. There is also the issue of whether one is likely to experience psychosocial distress—and other forms of ill-being—when one finds that one has been brought into existence as one of many *in a world in which genetic identity and the control thereof is, in general, highly valued and, indeed, legally protected*. I will say more about the high value we place on genetic control in the following part. For the moment, it is enough to note that the losses of self-esteem and of the sense of being a full and equal member of society—of both pride and status—may be profound, at once multipliers of any psychosocial distress one might otherwise feel and perhaps forms of ill-being in their own right.

5.5.3   The Control Issue; or, What Is Good for the Goose . . .

In any event, we seem already, de facto, in the clearest possible terms to have conceded that the reproduction of multiple, genetically identical children is likely, in some way or another, seriously to harm those children. The evidence of this lies in the fact that we firmly believe that *we* have an interest in genetic control. Thus, to take one example, we have an interest in not having our gametes contributed, without our consent, for use in treating the infertility of others. Clearly, we would resist, indeed, be horrified by, any such loss of control over our own reproductive capacity. We believe that such a loss would make things *worse for* us and would lead to a diminution in our overall level of well-being. Perhaps we are worried only about the potential psychosocial effects. Perhaps we are just anticipating the angst we might feel upon such a loss of control. Or perhaps it is the loss of control itself—not just our reaction to that loss—that we believe threatens our well-being.[44]

It is not merely that we want to control whether we have children, for it is unlikely that any children produced by the unconsented contribution of our gametes will be—or should be—deemed, years after the fact, ''ours.''[45] Rather, we think it is good for us to retain, where we can, control over the extent to which our gametes are made use of in the production of future people. Thus, we want both to control whether someone else produces *our* child but also, more importantly for purposes here, to control whether *their* child is created by way of an unconsented contribution of *our* gametes.

This seems to be precisely the ground on which the Tennessee Supreme Court gave Junior Davis the authority to destroy the frozen embryos his sperm had been used to create once those embryos became a matter of controversy within the context of divorce proceedings:

> We conclude . . . that an interest in avoiding genetic parenthood can be significant enough to trigger the protections offered to all other aspects of parenthood. The technological fact that someone unknown to these parties could gestate these preembryos does not alter the fact that these parties, the gamete-providers, would become parents in that event, at least in the genetic sense. The profound impact that this would have on them supports their right to sole decisional authority as to whether the process of attempting to gestate these preembryos should continue.[46]

But if we have an interest in genetic control, then so must the person who *will* exist. So must the person produced as one of many genetically identical individuals by way of embryonic cloning. Indeed, that person's interest in control would seem to be more gravely jeopardized by cloning than our own interest would be by the unconsented use of our gametes. For that person will have suffered the unconsented duplication of his or her *entire genome* for the purpose of treating another's infertility. It should be noted that the duplication of the genome remains unconsented even if the individuals whose sperm and egg are used to produce the original embryo give their consent both to the initial cloning of that embryo and to the subsequent transfer of multiple cloned embryos. Consent would not seem theirs to give when the cloning and transfer procedure duplicates not their genome but their *child's*. Whatever precisely the harm that is imposed by the loss of control over one's own genetic identity, the cloned child, more clearly than his or her genetic forbears, suffers that harm. And it is the child's interest in avoiding that ill-being that is more clearly disregarded when multiple, genetically identical embryos are unconsentedly produced and transferred.

In short, what is good for the goose *is good for the goslings.*[47]

Somatic cloning will be discussed separately in the next part. But it is of interest here because it underlines a certain important ethical intuition. In somatic cloning, the genome of the adult organism is replicated by fusing one of that organism's somatic cells with an egg cell previously emptied of its genetic contents. The fused cell, once it commences the process of cell division, is then transferred to develop in utero into the full term organism. In the first reported case involving this form of cloning, the offspring—Dolly, a lamb—was the genetic duplicate of the nameless, unsung sheep individual whose somatic cell contributed the genetic material. Now suppose, hypothetically, that the cell of an adult human being is taken in the course of a routine biopsy and that, without that individual's consent, the genome from that cell is used to produce, via somatic cloning, another human being. Would we consider this conduct to make things worse for the adult human being? It seems that we would. But if we think that the loss of genetic control would make things worse for the adult, then there is no basis on which to say that it would not equally make things worse for the child who is, temporally speaking, heading our way.

But *how, precisely*, does the loss of genetic control impact well-being? I think plausible answers can be given to this question. But I note first that the argument I have just given—an estoppel argument—does not depend on this question being answered. We *concede* that the loss of genetic control is harmful when we insist on having that control for ourselves. Maybe we should rethink (with our psychiatrist) this need for control (though I am not so sure that it is not a good thing). But the point here is that unless and until we take the view that genetic control is a matter of indifference *to us*, we cannot, reasonably, take the view that it is a matter of indifference *to someone who does not yet but will exist*.

Nonetheless, though we need not, we can identify some of the interests that a loss of genetic control may threaten. For one thing, the intentional, unconsented, multiple reproduction of one person's genome in others deprives the one person of the unique capacity to produce offspring whose own genetic make-up reflects that person's genome. A number of people becoming able to reproduce those particular genetic characteristics diminishes the value of the one person's being able to do so. For another, one's genetic inheritance *seems* one's own. Like our kidneys or our inner-most thoughts, we do not want it summarily shared with the world. Finally, it seems that well-being, however conceived, must be understood as interlocking. Moreover, one's genetic inheritance is a partial repository of many of the characteristics of many of the people one has ever known and loved. One's own well-being may thus plummet when one understands that, for instance, a little boy, produced by the unconsented use of one's gametes and so like, say, a grandfather, may be misunderstood and consequently less well cared for than he might otherwise be. The same kind of familial concern may arise when one's entire genome, rather than simply the gametes, are put to unconsented use.[48]

Is the interest that we have in retaining control over our own genetic identities an interest that trumps all other considerations, forcing the conclusion that the use of cloning should *never* be permitted since we can never obtain the appropriate consent from the affected parties? Not necessarily. To the extent that we think our own interest in controlling our genetic identity is not so strong that it demands absolute respect, we might think that the same holds for future people. Imagine that the *Davis* case had been complicated by the Ayala facts. Suppose that the reason Ms. Davis wanted the embryos she and her husband had produced during their marriage to be brought to term as one or more full-fledged human beings was that the Davises' had an older daughter whose life might be saved just as the life of Anissa Ayala was saved—by a bone marrow transplant from a sibling. On these facts, the Tennessee Supreme Court might have described Mr. Davis's interest in avoiding "genetic parenthood" as less than absolute.

Thus, perhaps our interest in controlling our genetic identity must sometimes bow to other interests. Still, it seems clear that we would not want control over our own genetic identity taken from us altogether. And there is no reason to extend to future people less protection than that which we think it correct to provide to ourselves.

As noted earlier, any choice to respect the interest in control that we take ourselves to have in the case of existing people—adults—but not future people—initially, children—may come back to haunt in the form of psychosocial distress. Coming into existence as one of multiple, genetically identical individuals may, in and of itself, create psychosocial distress and threaten one's interest in control. But, in addition, one wants and *should* want not simply to avoid psychosocial distress and to maintain control but also to be treated as others are. It is, in part, a matter of pride and status.

Thus, the potential for harm to offspring mounts. A critic might note that it is better to suffer some loss of psychic health and control, pride and status, than never to exist at all. I agree; but better still to exist with one's psyche, genetic control, and pride intact and one's status up. And this alternative exists, as we have seen, for *each* (though, as we have seen, not all) of the multiple, genetically identical offspring of cloning.

5.6   Human Somatic Cloning

Somatic cloning produces the same kinds of risks for the children it helps to create as embryonic cloning.[49] Like embryonic cloning, the risk increases with the number of genetically identical individuals created. Moreover, as in the case of embryonic cloning, any diminution in well-being that somatic cloning imposes is, as a general matter, avoidable.

Thus, for each cloned individual there exists the alternative of bringing that individual into existence but not as one of ten, or a hundred, or a thousand genetically identical individuals. To bring about this alternative, all agents need do is to produce, via somatic cloning, the one individual and refrain from producing the others. Have agents *wronged* those remaindered individuals whom they never, in the end, bring into existence? Clearly not, and N* implies this obvious result.

There is, however, a caveat. Though Robertson's defense does not seem to work in connection with embryonic cloning, we can define a narrow range of cases of somatic cloning with respect to which his defense is effective. Consider the case in which somatic cloning has been used to bring into existence not one of many genetically identical individuals but rather one additional person who is genetically identical to an already-existing person—an adult, we may suppose, who has properly consented to act as, and has acted as, a genome donor. Could that additional person have been brought into existence other than as one of *two* genetically identical individuals? I do not see how. I suppose that the cloning could have been from a somatic cell taken from the differentiated embryo from which the adult donor eventually develops, and I suppose that that embryo might then have been aborted. Then, the additional person would have been brought into existence as one of *one* rather than as one of *two*. But in these circumstances it is not at all clear that the person brought into existence by way of somatic cloning on the differentiated fetal cell would be *the same person* as the person brought into existence by way of somatic cloning on a cell taken from the adult.

Perhaps, then, the only route into existence (short of murdering the donor) for the latter person *is* to be brought into existence as one of two genetically identical individuals. If this is correct, then as long as the life remains worth living we can conclude that bringing the additional person into existence as one of two neither genuinely harms, nor under M* wrongs, that person. In this narrowly defined context, Robertson's defense of cloning is effective.

Others have mentioned this same kind of defense in connection with somatic cloning. Thus, Silver describes the case of Jennifer, who, a few decades hence, gives birth to a baby, Rachel, whom Jennifer has created by cloning herself. To address the question of whether Jennifer has done anything wrong, Silver asks another question: "Has [Rachel] been harmed in some way so detrimental that it would have been better had she never been born?"[50] The test of harm that this question suggests is appropriate only if Rachel's alternatives are limited to existing as a clone of Jennifer and never existing at all. In this context, the defense succeeds since existing as a clone of Jennifer is the "only way" for Rachel to have an existence that is, from her own point of view, a good thing.

However, in other contexts the defense fails. Thus, suppose that Jennifer produces by somatic cloning not one child but, say, four children to be raised by herself or others. Then, each child is such that, though she cannot exist except as clone-of-Jennifer and thus cannot exist except as one of *two*, she nonetheless can exist as one of two rather than as one of *many* (i.e., *five*). It is necessary, in other words, for each child to exist as clone-of-Jennifer to exist at all. But for no child is it necessary for her existence that the other children be produced as well.

Perhaps Silver intends his argument to be restricted to the case in which Jennifer produces just one child, which child must exist as Jennifer's clone if she is to exist at all. But the restriction is an important one and bears mentioning expressly.

Ruth Macklin makes a point similar to Silver's:

> Evidence, not mere surmise, is required to conclude that the psychological burdens of knowing that one was cloned would be of such magnitude that they would outweigh the benefits of life itself.[51]

Oh why wait for the evidence! We already know that cloning will not be *that* bad for the cloned offspring. So the condition imposed by Macklin's test is satisfied. But is it the right test? It is the right test only if it is restricted to a context in which somatic cloning is used to produce exactly one additional child. In contrast, if the "psychological burdens" derive from being one of three, or ten, or a hundred, then agents clearly might have done better for the one than they in fact have done simply by never bringing all those others into existence to begin with.

For all of the reasons noted above in connection with embryonic cloning, the evaluation of somatic cloning also requires a factual inquiry into the likely psychosocial distress involved in finding oneself brought into existence as one of a number of genetically identical individuals. Moreover, the control argument that I outlined in connection with embryonic cloning applies equally to somatic cloning. Just as we want to see our interest in controlling our own genetic identity carefully protected, we *must* understand that future people—the children we create—will predictably have the same interest in controlling *their* own genetic identity.

Macklin herself notes that it is an "uncontestable ethical right" that adults must give their consent before being cloned.[52] She perhaps thinks this because she recognizes that it would be a loss to us, a diminution in well-being, to be cloned without our consent. As noted earlier, perhaps we should think further about this desire for control; perhaps it is pathological. But as long as we think that it is good for us to have control over our genetic identities, it is hard to fathom why we should not extend the courtesy to the next generation. Again, what is good for the goose. . . .

5.7   Cloning and the Constitution

In the preceding parts, I have associated cloning with various diminutions in the well-being of the cloned offspring. From a moral point of view, this is the correct way to proceed. If there is no diminution in well-being from a subject's maximal level of well-being, there can be no harm and no moral wrong done to that subject. But when we turn to the law, particularly to constitutional law, we need to talk about rights, particularly about rights under the Fourteenth Amendment of the U.S. Constitution.

Two constitutional points need to be made. The first concerns the right of procreative liberty—the right that accords to the individual, rather than the state, choices relating to procreation, for example, choices relating to birth control and abortion. It is an extension of this right that Robertson suggests protects individual choice regarding the use of the new reproductive technologies "to beget and bear children."[53] The second concerns a privacy right relating to genetic control. It is this right that would protect the various interests that we believe we have in keeping others from using our own gametes or genome without our consent—the interest in, we might say, protecting one's status as one of one. It is this right that we would assert in the face of a state law that, e.g., gave fertility clinics the authority to contribute our gametes, or, in coming years, our genome, without our consent to enable others to achieve pregnancy. As suggested in *Davis*, it is certainly plausible to believe that we have such a right under the Fourteenth Amendment.

I note that either of these constitutional points could be literately discussed under the other's heading. Privacy is, after all, itself a form of liberty; and procreative liberty is, we think, a matter of constitutional privacy. But the two points are distinct, one pertaining to the adult, the other to the child. To keep the distinction clear, it will be convenient to regiment the constitutional language in the way described.

5.7.1   The Adult's Right of Procreative Liberty

The first constitutional point is that the right of procreative liberty— the right that we take to protect the choices that we make regarding whether and when to have children—is generally limited by the "harm to others" principle. Thus, the state violates a woman's right of procreative liberty by requiring that she have a child, or requiring that she not have a child. But a state law that criminalizes the woman's kidnapping someone else's baby so that she might herself have a baby to raise when otherwise she would have none is perfectly legitimate. Robertson, as constitutional law scholar, concedes this point when he notes that the test for the legitimacy of the claim of procreative liberty is whether the "interests of couples and offspring are well served [by human cloning]."[54] And he proceeds to argue, as we have seen, that cloning and other new reproductive technologies cause no significant or genuine harm to the offspring they function to create.

But in fact, as we have also seen, the technologies of cloning, together with the related technologies of embryo transfer and cryopreservation, *do* present a risk of harming the very offspring they produce. Being brought into existence, via the cloning technologies, as one of many may pose a risk of avoidable psychosocial distress. It is the reality of this risk that requires empirical investigation. Moreover, being brought into existence, via the cloning technologies, as one of many in a world in which genetic identity is highly valued seems likely to threaten serenity by depriving one of a certain pride and status, and may impose other forms of ill-being as well. Finally, and most clearly, being brought into existence, via the cloning technologies, as one of many is something we as adults concede to be harmful at any point at which we insist on, for ourselves, the "uncontestable ethical right" to consent to losses of genetic control.

Moreover, whatever the harm to offspring, it is *genuine* harm. Thus, this is not one of those situations in which agents *cannot* do any better for a particular child than they have in fact done or in which the child's existence is flawed in some *unavoidable* way. If the harm exists and is genuine, if it is definite, and if we do not simply (and without justification) deem the child's interests to be whatever the parents' in fact are, then the claim of procreative liberty will, as a matter of constitutional law and sound liberty analysis, fail.

5.7.2   The Child's Right of Privacy and Equality

Plausibly, we have a constitutionally protected right of privacy—a right that protects the various interests that we believe we have in controlling the unconsented use of our own gametes or genome. If this is correct, then it seems that there is no reason not to extend the same right to future persons, individuals who are, temporally speaking, heading our way.

Of course, once these cloned offspring exist, they will be, for a very long time, legally disadvantaged; they will be children. Perhaps this fact alone makes us think that we need not worry very much about their constitutional rights. Since children are generally accorded much less in the way of constitutional rights than adults, it might be thought that they lack constitutional rights in this context. But this is a line of thought we should eschew. Perhaps we could get away with it, but a better approach is to understand that:

> [i]t is revolting to have no better reason for a rule of law than that so it was laid down in the time of Henry IV. It is still more revolting if the grounds upon which it was laid down have vanished long since, and the rule simply persists from blind imitation of the past.[55]

We know better, now, than to presume that parents will always act in the interests of their children. We know better than to presume that children are not susceptible to profound psychological injury or that they will always find the strength to overcome any burden we place on their shoulders. If the parent has an interest in controlling his or her own genetic identity that rises to a constitutional level, then so, it seems, does the child. As we have seen, it is not as though this right must somehow be waived on behalf of the child if the child is to come into existence to begin with. As we have seen, a child brought into existence as one of many genetically identical individuals could also have been brought into existence as one of simply one. Thus, the "better to exist" argument does not provide a basis, in this context, on which to decline to recognize the child's right.

At the moment, states are not generally threatening to infringe our privacy right as adults to genetic control. The privacy issue will more likely arise when a legislature or a court puts law into place that protects the adult's interest in avoiding, as an adult, the unconsented duplication of his or her own genome but fails to protect the child's, that is, the future person's, like interest. Thus, for example, we can imagine a court fashioning a tort law claim in a case in which the adult's genome has been unconsentedly duplicated by somatic cloning, but considering consent unnecessary in the case in which the individual cloned was merely future at the time the cloning of his or her genome was effected. Alternatively, a legislature or a court may put law into place that deems legally unprotected the child's, that is, the future person's, interest in genetic control. Thus, we can imagine doctors and clinics who wish to use cloning technologies to treat infertility urging a state legislature to immunize them from any legal claims that multiply-cloned offspring might bring against them at some future date.

One argument for deeming the child's interest unprotected might be that the adult's constitutional right of procreative liberty *requires* that the child's interest be left unprotected. But we have already discussed, in the preceding part, the deficiencies of this assertion. Still, doctors and clinics might argue for immunization on other grounds as well.

State or federal action of either form would seem an infringement of the child's right of privacy to be the one who controls his or her own genetic identity. Moreover, attempts to fashion a body of law that protects the adult's interest in control but not the child's would raise equal protection issues as well. Normally, of course, the law is not required to treat adults and children in precisely the same way, since in many respects their situations are profoundly different. But in this context the rationale for different treatment is not clear. This particular privacy interest is more like the interest we all have in, e.g., life than it is like the interest we all have in, e.g., keeping the company we please. And we countenance different treatment for children only in the latter, and not in the former, case. In any event, this child will grow up.

5.7.3 Policy Implications

The policy implications of the preceding discussions can be summarized. There is no reason that research on human cloning should not proceed. And there is no reason to think that the use of cloning to bring a human being into existence should be banned in all circumstances. Thus, bringing someone into existence by way of somatic cloning—such that that person will exist as one of one or even as one of two genetically identical individuals—does not seem, in itself, problematic. Nor does bringing someone into existence as one of one, by way of embryonic cloning, in itself, seem problematic. The moral objection, if any, against cloning in these contexts will derive from considerations regarding the costs of these technologies and whether funds can be better spent.

At the same time, we have dispelled the notion that the adult's right of procreative liberty *requires* unregulated access to cloning. Moreover, there is every reason to think that some uses of cloning—for example, the use of embryonic or somatic cloning to produce any significant number of genetically identical individuals—should be as a matter of policy prohibited. For one thing, there may be risks of psychosocial distress, including the distress of finding oneself one of many in a world in which genetic identity is highly valued. For another, there is the conceded harm of depriving a person of control over his or her own genetic identity. Finally, there is the constitutional dimension that will need to be taken into account. Not only may giving legal legitimacy to cloning harm future people, but it may also violate the child's—the future person's—constitutional right of privacy. Still, trade-offs that work against the child may be justified (indeed, may be compelling), depending on how in a specific situation (e.g., in an Ayala-type situation) cloning distributes well-being across the population—including the children—whom it affects.

5.8 Commercial Surrogacy and Other New Technologies

Commercial surrogacy, like cloning, is a case in which the argument has been made that the child of surrogacy, to achieve existence, must simply put up with any ill effect caused by the surrogacy arrangements. Posner is one theorist who has made this argument.[56] If we construe Posner to be reasoning by appeal to person-affecting principles, then it is clear that his argument is problematic. In the case of commercial surrogacy, the source of any ill effect for a given child arises from a court's enforcing a commercial agreement that decides who shall have custody of, and parental rights with respect to, that child. The issue then is whether the child can exist without being subjected to this ill effect. But clearly the child can exist without being subjected to this ill effect. At the time the enforcement decision is made, the child is already, so to speak, on the ground. A court's decision to do better for the child—to declare the commercial agreement unenforceable and order the child placed in accordance with the usual "best interests" standard—will not jeopardize that fact.

If a court's enforcing the agreement wrongs the child, we need look no further to declare that act wrong. But what about the couple's choice, *prior* to the child's conception, to enter into a surrogacy contract? This choice imposes a risk on the child since courts may, either mistakenly or pursuant to state law, enforce such a contract. At the same time, this choice causes the child to exist; it is part of the causal sequence of events that leads ultimately to the child's existence. But this fact alone hardly vindicates the choice. Just as in the slave child case, there are other, better things, from the child's own point of view, that the couple could have done at the critical time.[57]

The implication of this fact is that issues of surrogacy must be addressed by way of the same analyses that we have given above in the case of cloning. Thus, as in the case of cloning, we need to recognize the harm associated with the technology and understand that that harm is, in fact, avoidable. Moreover, we need to recognize that trade-offs will need to be resolved by a balancing of well-being between child and childmaker, in accordance with doctrines of fairness. Though we will not try to find this balance here, we are on firm ground, I think, when we speculate that it will not do to distinguish two classes of children and treat them differently with respect to matters most fundamental to their well-being.

Because the new reproductive technologies are uniquely designed to produce new people and because those new people will predictably have lives worth living, with respect to each technology the issue arises whether the harm to offspring that that technology gives rise to, if any, can be excused by the kind of defense that Robertson sketches in connection with embryonic cloning. As we have just seen, the issue arises in connection both with somatic cloning and with commercial surrogacy. The issue equally arises in connection with donor insemination, egg donation, infertility drugs, and postmenopausal pregnancy.[58] What I hope to have shown in this chapter is that the new reproductive technologies cannot be treated as all of a piece. The choice to make use of one technology in one context may be evaluated differently from the choice to use that same technology in another context. And the choice to use one technology in one context may be evaluated differently from the choice to use some other technology in that same context. Thus, we are left with the challenge of facing up to the potential our choices have for creating well-being and ill-being for all those who do, and will, exist.[59]

Notes

1. G. Kolata, "Scientist Clones Human Embryos, and Creates an Ethical Challenge," *New York Times*, 24 Oct. 1993, A1.

2. G. Kolata, "With Cloning of a Sheep, the Ethical Ground Shifts," *New York Times*, 24 Feb. 1997, A1. See also G. Kolata, "Scientist Reports First Cloning Ever of Adult Mammal," *New York Times*, 23 Feb. 1997, A1.

3. At about the same time, Rossana Dalla Corte, sixty-one, was reported to be expecting a baby through the efforts of the same clinic. W. E. Schmidt, "Birth to 59-Year-Old Briton Raises Ethical Storm," *New York Times*, 29 Dec. 1993, A1. For further discussion, see Melinda A. Roberts, "A Way of Looking at the Dalla Corte Case," *Journal of Law, Medicine & Ethics* 22 (1994): 339–42.

4. *In re Baby M*, 217 N.J. Super. 313, 525 A.2d 1128 (Sup. Ct. Chanc. 1987); *rev'd in part*, 109 N.J. 396, 537 A.2d 1227 (1988).

5. See *Johnson v. Calvert*, 5 Cal. 4th 84, 851 P.2d 776, 19 Cal. Rptr. 494 (1993).

6. See *Jaycee B. v. Superior Court*, 42 Cal. App. 4th 718, 49 Cal. Rptr. 2d 694 (1996). In this case, the contractual father, in the context of the divorce, argued that the child who had been produced within the marriage by combining agents and technologies in this particular way was not, in fact, his child and that he need not make payments in support of this child.

7. State statutes, many of which incorporate aspects of the Uniform Parentage Act, define the relationships and obligations of the various parties to sperm donation.

8. For a riveting account of the new reproductive technologies, see Lee M. Silver, *Remaking Eden: Cloning and Beyond in a Brave New World* (New York: Avon Books, 1997).

9. Thus, Silver points out that the technology of somatic cloning seems to suggest that any old somatic cell—scraped from the mouth, scratched from the arm—has the potential for human life. And we surely do not think that all these cells are entitled to respect or dignity (*Remaking Eden*, 46).

10. Courts occasionally mistakenly suggest that children do not matter *as much* as adults. Consider, e.g., the case of "Baby Richard," the four year old whom the Illinois Supreme Court ordered transferred to the custody of a biological father whom the child had never before seen. Prior to the transfer, from just a few days after birth, the child had lived with a couple under an order of adoption. *In re Kirchner*, 164 Ill. 2d 468, 649 N.E.2d 324, 326–29 (1995); see also *O'Connell v. Kirchner*, 513 U.S. 1303 (1995), and *O'Connell v. Kirchner*, 513 U.S. 1138 (1995). For further discussion, see Melinda A. Roberts, "Parent and Child in Conflict: Between Liberty and Responsibility," *Notre Dame Journal of Law, Ethics & Public Policy* 10 (1996): 485–542.

11. John A. Robertson, *Children of Choice: Freedom and the New Reproductive Technologies* (Princeton, N.J.: Princeton University Press, 1994), 13.

12. Robertson, *Children of Choice*, 168.

13. One might define *any* negative, or hurt, as a "harm." In this sense of the term, even the momentary pinch of a properly administered vaccination counts as harm. In this sense of the term, if the new technologies cause psychosocial distress, by that very fact they harm. In response to one who insists on using the term "harm" in this broad sense, Robertson might put his point differently. Though in this broad sense the new technologies impose *harm*, they do not impose, Robertson might say, any *genuine* harm or any morally or legally *significant* harm. For reasons suggested in part 4.4.1, I will, as I think Robertson does, avoid using the term "harm" in this broad sense.

14. Kavka, for example, suggests this view. See part 3.9 ("A Deontic Solution to the Nonidentity Problem"). If one accepts the modal account of harm that I proposed in part 4.6, then M* implies that one cannot be wronged unless one has been harmed. For to be harmed one must have a level of well-being that is less than it might have been. If one is not harmed at all by any agent, and thus enjoys a maximal level of well-being, then one cannot, under M*, have been wronged. I note that, since harm itself is defined in terms of maximal well-being, and well-being is, though left unanalyzed for purposes of this present work, a potentially broad notion (see note 6, chap. 1), there is no reason to think that the view that wronging requires harming sets inappropriate limits on wronging.

15. Robertson, *Children of Choice*, 76.

16. It is the type 2-alt arguments that seem to me not to be problematic. See part 3.3.3.

17. Robertson, *Children of Choice*, 76, emphasis added.

18. Robertson himself takes the scope of his argument to be quite broad. See generally, *Children of Choice*, 13, 75–76, 120–22, 169.

19. The defense also fails in other contexts. See part 5.8 ("Commercial Surrogacy and Other New Technologies").

20. See part 5.6 ("Human Somatic Cloning").

21. Richard A. McCormick, "Blastomere Separation: Some Concerns," *Hastings Center Report* 24 (1994): 14–15. In the absence of regulation, it is surely correct to anticipate that in the next few years vast numbers of human embryos will be split, frozen, and discarded in labs all over the country. For an account of the procedure by which human embryos are cloned to produce additional embryos, each capable in theory of producing a complete organism, see Robertson, "The Question of Human Cloning," *Hastings Center Report* 24 (1994): 6–7.

22. McCormick catalogues a number of well-respected boards and commissions that have reached this conclusion ("Blastomere Separation," 15).

23. McCormick, "Blastomere Separation," 15.

24. He writes merely that "[o]ne can only point to the prevailing moral and legal consensus that views early embryos as too rudimentary in neurological development to have interests or rights. On this view, splitting embryos can no more harm them than freezing or discarding them can" ("The Question of Human Cloning," 10).

25. Similar grounds might be used to defend the view that abortion is morally permissible as long as it is performed early in pregnancy.

26. Robertson, "The Question of Human Cloning," 13, emphasis added.

27. This approach accords well with some of the constitutional claims that Robertson makes. According to Robertson, the "right of married and arguably even unmarried persons to procreate is a fundamental constitutional right that cannot be restricted unless clearly necessary to protect compelling state interests" ("The Question of Human Cloning," 13). See generally Robertson, *Children of Choice*, 22–42. But no one thinks that a constitutional right, even if fundamental, entitles one to bring harm to another person. It is rather the choices that do not harm others, though they may harm the agent, that plausible theories of liberty typically protect. Put another way, the avoidance of harm—particularly, of harm to children—*is* a compelling state interest.

The ethical issue of whether infertility therapies receive more than their fair share of scarce medical resources is put aside altogether for the purposes here. The cost issue is one that can be addressed only in a broader context that considers the many alternative uses that may be made of our health care dollars. Moreover, the cost issue arises only if human cloning, examined on its own terms, otherwise survives ethical scrutiny.

28. Robertson, "The Question of Human Cloning," 11, emphasis added. See also Robertson, *Children of Choice*, 167–70.

29. Robertson, "The Question of Human Cloning," 11.

30. Robertson, *Children of Choice*, 169, emphasis added. The citation omitted is to Derek Parfit, *Reasons and Persons* (Oxford: Clarendon, 1984).

31. Robertson, "The Question of Human Cloning," 10, emphasis added.

32. Robertson, "The Question of Human Cloning," 11.

33. Robertson, "The Question of Human Cloning," 13.

34. Robertson, *Children of Choice*, 122.

35. See part 3.4 ("A Counterfactual Interpretation of the Nonidentity Problem") and part 4.6 ("The Problem of the Baseline").

36. Other theorists have noted that B, as understood here, is a critical component of Robertson's argument. See, e.g., Cynthia Cohen, " 'Give Me Children or I Shall Die!' New Reproductive Technologies and Harm to Children," *Hastings Center Report* 26, no. 2 (1996): 21. Robertson also appears to accept this point.

37. In this paragraph, I am assuming that a child in fact develops from the original embryo. In any real transfer procedure, however, a certain number of embryos may very well *not* result in live births. I also assume that the original embryo *survives* the cloning as one of some number of later-existing genetically identical embryos. We do not need here to make the assumption that we can *identify* any one of the later-existing embryos as the original embryo. The issues of identity that arise at this juncture are fascinating (see also chap. 1, note 62). We cannot without contradiction say that *each* of *multiple* later-existing embryos is identical to the *one* original embryo. See, among many other discussions of this point, David Wiggins, *Identity and Spatio-Temporal Continuity* (Oxford: Oxford University Press, 1967), 53. But what we should say about such cases remains unclear. One possible account is the one I have assumed, according to which the original embryo survives as one of a number of later-existing genetically identical embryos. An alternative account is that twinning destroys the original embryo and brings into existence two new embryos that constitute a second generation, and that twinning a second time destroys both second generation embryos and brings into existence four new embryos that constitute a third generation, and so on. *If* this account is correct, then none of the children who develop from the third-generation embryos could have existed in the absence of the cloning procedure. But this consequence does not bolster Robertson's position an iota, since *not one* of these four children depends, for his or her own existence, on the *other three* third generation embryos being transferred and permitted to develop rather than, say, destroyed. Since *each* child could thus have existed without existing as one of a number of genetically identical individuals, B remains false on this alternative set of assumptions about personal identity.

Whether any of these four individuals *would* have been brought into existence if the legally permissible options included only transferring a single embryo (or perhaps, to the same woman at the same time, two or three embryos) is an open question. Perhaps the transfer of the embryo under these restrictions would simply not be worth doing. However, as argued earlier what *would* happen, were the questionable act avoided, is not a satisfactory test of genuine harm or of personal wronging.

38. See generally part 3.3. For the type 2-alt case, my position has been, following Robertson, that no "solution" is necessary—that is, that personalism's implication of no wrong done in the type 2-alt case is plausible.

39. See part 2.7.4 ("Theory of 'Fair Distribution' ") and, generally, chap. 2.

40. Silver's argument in favor of somatic cloning is stated especially persuasively in the context of his discussion of the Ayala case (*Remaking Eden*, 110–16). Gina Kolata also describes a number of scenarios in which somatic cloning seems to offer clear benefits. See Kolata, *Clone: The Road to Dolly and the Path Ahead* (New York: William Morrow, 1998), 229–48.

41. Robertson, "The Question of Human Cloning," 10.

42. Robertson, *Children of Choice*, 168.

43. Robertson, *Children of Choice*, 168–69.

44. See chap. 1, note 6 for a discussion of the range of possible theories of well-being. Amartya Sen's suggestion seems especially suited to explaining how a loss of genetic control might constitute a diminution in well-being. See Sen, *Inequality Reexamined* (Cambridge, Mass.: Harvard University Press, 1992), 1–55 and especially 4–5 (sketching his notion of well-being as a "person's capability to achieve functionings [which] can vary from most elementary ones, such as being well-nourished, avoiding escapable morbidity and premature mortality, etc., to quite complex and sophisticated achievements, such as having self-respect, being able to take part in the life of the community, and so on").

45. It is conceivable that courts will take themselves to be required by the U.S. Constitution to sever affiliative relationships between children and those whom they take to be parents years after these relationships have been firmly established. See *In re Kirchner*, 164 Ill. 2d 468, 649 N.E.2d 324. Nonetheless, such an analysis would seem questionable from both a legal and a moral point of view.

46. *Davis v. Davis*, 842 S.W.2d 588, 603 (Tenn. 1992).

47. One might argue that any consent that is impossible to obtain—such as in the case of the cloning of the embryo—is unnecessary. But this argument fails. A potential egg donor's comatose state does not negate the need for consent; nor does the newborn's inability to consent to the donation of some vital organ or tissue exonerate the surgeon who excises it.

Naturally occurring twinning—that is, unintentional twinning—must be given a distinct ethical analysis. When the twinning occurs naturally, one twin's argument must be that the pregnant woman should have undergone selective abortion of the other twin. But this argument fails, not because there necessarily would have been any wrong done to the aborted twin but rather because requiring the woman to have an abortion she does not want would wrong her. In contrast, in the case of cloning each of multiple genetically identical offspring can argue that reasonable steps could have been taken early on to avoid the existence of other offspring.

48. The interest in genetic control that I have just described might be considered a *privacy* interest. I avoid the term "privacy" in this part, however, since I do not mean to suggest that the harm of cloning itself *depends on* a "right of privacy" having been violated. A "right of privacy"—a constitutional right that arguably protects our interest in genetic control—comes to the fore in part 5.7.2. For purposes of this part, however, I am suggesting that the interest in

genetic control is connected to well-being in the same way that, say, protecting one's health, or the cash in one's cookie jar, is connected to well-being. Indeed, the *having* of such interests—like having an interest in learning or in other people—is likely to promote well-being. Thus, in my view the loss of genetic control would either itself constitute or alternatively give rise to a diminution in well-being, that is, to a harm. I do not, in other words, see cloning as a matter of a wrong being done without any harm (any diminution in well-being) being imposed. Indeed, as argued in note 14, personalism is committed to the contrary view, according to which there are no wrongs without harms.

49. I have briefly described the technology of somatic cloning in part 5.5.3. For a much richer description of the somatic form of cloning, along with an extensive history of cloning, see Kolata, *Clone*, 120–208. See also Kolata, "With Cloning of a Sheep, the Ethical Ground Shifts," A1, and Kolata, "Scientist Reports First Cloning Ever of Adult Mammal," *New York Times* (23 Feb. 1997), A1.

50. Silver, *Remaking Eden*, 120.

51. Kolata, *Clone*, 20 (citing Ruth Macklin, testimony before the National Bioethics Advisory Commission, 14 March 1997).

52. Kolata, *Clone*, 20 (citing Macklin, testimony).

53. Robertson, *Children of Choice*, 29, 38–42.

54. Robertson, "The Question of Human Cloning," 13. See also Robertson, *Children of Choice*, 15–42, and John Stuart Mill, *On Liberty* (New York: Appleton-Century-Crofts, 1947), 78 ("Acts injurious to others require a totally different treatment"); and, generally, *On Liberty*, chap. 4.

55. *Bowers v. Hardwick*, 478 U.S. 186, 199 (1986), Blackmun, J. dissenting (citing Oliver Wendell Holmes, "The Path of the Law," *Harvard Law Review* 10 [1897]: 457, 469).

56. For arguments that defend the enforcement of surrogacy contracts, see Richard A. Posner, "The Ethics and Economics of Enforcing Contracts of Surrogate Motherhood," *Journal of Contemporary Health Law and Policy* 5 (1989): 22–23; Louis M. Seidman, "Baby M and the Problem of Unstable Preferences," *Georgetown Law Review* 76 (1988): 1829–36, 1832; and Robertson, "Embryos, Families and Procreative Liberty: The Legal Structure of the New Reproduction," *Southern California Law Review* 59 (1986): 939–1041, 1013. See also Robertson, *Children of Choice*, 120–23.

57. See part 3.2 ("Three Nonidentity Cases") and part 3.5 ("A Probabilistic Interpretation of the Nonidentity Cases").

58. See Roberts, "A Way of Looking at the Dalla Corte Case," 339–42.

59. For further discussion of commercial surrogacy, see Roberts, "Good Intentions and a Great Divide: Having Babies by Intending Them," *Law and Philosophy* 12 (1993): 287–317.

Conclusion

The person-affecting intuition, as I have interpreted it, implies that all people who exist now or will exist in the future matter morally. Moreover, even if they do not exist now, they matter now, in the sense that the fact of their future existence places constraints on how we now conduct ourselves.

At the same time, the existence of future people is itself, in many cases, a choice. When it is a choice it is a moral choice. For it is a choice that affects people who matter—that is, people who exist now or will exist in the future. And for each of these individuals we ought, with restrictions, to do the best for him or her that we can. Suppose, however, that we mistakenly choose to bring someone new into existence. There is no basis for holding our choice *against* the person whom we have brought into existence—for treating that person less well than we treat anyone else. That person, just as much as anyone else, matters morally.

The "baseline" obligation that we have as agents with respect to those who matter is to do the best we can for each of them. But we often cannot do our best for each one of a group of people. When we cannot, an appeal to doctrines of fairness is in order. I have said virtually nothing about *who* is responsible—about *who* the culpable party is, in a particular case. By implication from what I have said, obligations fall on anyone who has acted, or might have acted, in such a way as to increase well-being for anyone who matters. It is fairness that allows us to make the judgment that we should not focus our energy and resources on making sure that the first baby born in the year 2100 has his or her diapers properly changed on some particular occasion (by way of setting up a trust, appointing a trustee, etc.), and make sure instead that our own child, wailing upstairs, is properly diapered now. Thus it probably would be *unfair* to the child upstairs to expend the enormous resources that would be necessary to *guarantee* some slight increase in well-being for this future child. We ought instead count on the future child's own parents to see to that child's future diapering needs.

But contrast the case of my chopping down a tree in my own woods today (or polluting a river or an ocean; commercializing wilderness lands; or depleting natural resources). Perhaps this choice increases my own well-being. But it also affects my children, my neighbors, and other members of my community. Perhaps the choice to destroy the tree increases, on a net basis, my own children's well-being—their well-being being closely linked to my own—while decreasing the well-being of my neighbor and other members of the community. If it is the kind of tree that will live for more than several more years, then the choice to destroy it will also affect people who will but do not yet exist. According to personalism, the interests all of these people have in my preserving the tree must be taken into account alongside my own interests and my children's in destroying it.

Does personalism err by failing to discount the needs of future people? My aunt says that she wishes she knew now when, exactly, she would die. For then she would know now whether to adopt a lavish or a conservative style of life. In the absence of this knowledge, she must make lots of guesses. But the guesses she makes should be reasonable ones—she should not, for example, make the supposition that she will still be alive a hundred years from now. Similarly, it would be a mistake for us to suppose that there will always be people or that our acts will all have, in perpetuity, consequences of moral significance. Things change; meteorites strike; viruses run rampant; wars break out. Moreover, for the benefit of those who now or will imminently exist, we can always, if necessary, take steps to reduce the numbers of distant future people. But the suppositions that we now make about the future should reflect a recognition of how often our own past predictions and plans have failed. Thus, how much we save now should be based on our best, tempered, understanding of what the future is likely to bring.

Perhaps it seems that virtually *every* choice we make involves a trade-off—that we can virtually never increase one person's well-being without decreasing someone else's. I do not think this is true at all. Many choices that we make are, I believe, local in nature. They are choices in which we as agents have the power either to decrease or increase someone else's well-being without thereby increasing or decreasing the well-being of anyone else. Consider the parent who gives his child a hard slap. Whose well-being would have been decreased had the parent chosen *not* to slap the child? One who thinks that there is a trade-off between the child's hurt and the feeling of control the parent experiences when he or she hits the child may be working with a poor conception of well-being. Though we have left well-being unanalyzed for purposes here, there is no reason in the world to think that the parent's feeling of control increases an iota the parent's own level of well-being.

Bibliography

Arrow, Kenneth J. *Social Choice and Individual Values*, 2d ed. New Haven, Conn.: Yale University Press, 1973.

Brandt, Richard B. *Ethical Theory*. Englewood Cliffs, N.J.: Prentice Hall, 1959.

Brock, Dan W. "The Non-Identity Problem and Genetic Harms—The Case of Wrongful Handicaps." *Bioethics* 9, no. 3/4 (1995): 269–75.

Broome, John. *Counting the Costs of Global Warming*. Cambridge: White Horse, 1992.

——— and Adam Morton. "The Value of a Person." *Proceedings of the Aristotelian Society* supp. 68 (1994): 167–98.

Cassidy, John. "The Melting-Pot Myth." *The New Yorker*, 14 July 1997, 40–43.

Cohen, Cynthia. " 'Give Me Children or I Shall Die!' New Reproductive Technologies and Harm to Children." *Hastings Center Report* 26, no. 2 (1996): 19–27.

———. "The Morality of Knowingly Conceiving Children with Serious Conditions: An Expanded 'Wrongful Life' Standard." In *Contingent Future People: On the Ethics of Deciding Who Will Live, or Not, in the Future*, ed. Nick Fotion and Jan C. Heller. Dordrecht: Kluwer Academic, 1997.

Coleman, Jules and Christopher Morris. *Rational Commitment and Social Justice: Essays for Gregory Kavka*. Cambridge: Cambridge University Press, forthcoming.

Cowen, Tyler. "What Do We Learn from the Repugnant Conclusion?" *Ethics* 106 (July 1996): 754–75.

Curran, Angela. "Utilitarianism and Future Mistakes: Another Look." *Philosophical Studies* 78 (1995): 71–85.

Dasgupta, Partha. *An Inquiry into Well-Being and Destitution*. Oxford: Clarendon, 1993.

———. "Lives and Well-Being." *Social Choice and Welfare* 5 (1988): 103–26.

———. "Population Size and the Quality of Life." *Proceedings of the Aristotelian Society* supp. 63 (1989): 23–54.

———. "Savings and Fertility: Ethical Issues." *Philosophy and Public Affairs* 23, no. 2 (Spring 1994): 99–127.

Dworkin, Ronald. "What Is Equality? Part I: Equality of Welfare." *Philosophy & Public Affairs* 10, no. 3 (1981): 185–225.

———. "What Is Equality? Part II: Equality of Resources." *Philosophy & Public Affairs* 10, no. 4 (1981): 283–345.

Elliot, Robert. "Contingency, Community and Intergenerational Justice." In *Contingent Future People: On the Ethics of Deciding Who Will Live, or Not, in the Future*, ed. Nick Fotion and Jan C. Heller. Dordrecht: Kluwer Academic, 1997.

Feinberg, Joel. *Harm to Others*. New York: Oxford University Press, 1984.

———. "Wrongful Life and the Counterfactual Element in Harming." *Social Philosophy & Policy* 4, no. 1 (1988): 144–78.

Feldman, Fred. "Adjusting Utility for Justice: A Consequentialist Reply to the Objections from Justice." *Philosophy and Phenomenological Research* 55 (1995): 567–85.

———. *Doing the Best We Can: An Essay in Informal Deontic Logic*. Dordrecht: Reidel, 1986.

———. "Justice, Desert, and the Repugnant Conclusion." *Utilitas* 7, no. 2 (Nov. 1995): 189–206.

Fletcher, George P. *Basic Concepts of Legal Thought*. Oxford: Oxford University Press, 1996.

Fotion, Nick, and Jan C. Heller, eds. *Contingent Future People: On the Ethics of Deciding Who Will Live, or Not, in the Future*. Dordrecht: Kluwer Academic, 1997.

Giere, Ronald N. *Understanding Scientific Reasoning*. Orlando, Fla.: Harcourt Brace, 1997.

Grainger, Christopher J. "Wrongful Life: A Wrong Without a Remedy." *Tort Law Review* 2 (Nov. 1994): 164–74.

Green, Leon. "The Palsgraf Case." *Columbia Law Review* 30 (1930): 789–801.

Grey, William. "Possible Persons and the Problems of Posterity." *Environmental Values* 5 (1996): 161–79.

Hackleman, Tricia Jonas. "Violation of an Individual's Right to Die: The Need for a Wrongful Living Cause of Action." *University of Cincinnati Law Review* 64 (1996): 1355.

Hanser, Matthew. "Harming Future People." *Philosophy & Public Affairs* 19, no. 1 (Winter 1990): 47–70.

Hanson, F. Allan. "Suits for Wrongful Life, Counterfactuals, and the Nonexistence Problem." *Southern California Interdisciplinary Law Journal* 5 (1996): 1–24.

Hare, R. M. *Moral Thinking: Its Levels, Methods and Point*. Oxford: Oxford University Press, 1982.

———. "When Does Potentiality Count?" In *Essays in Bioethics*. Oxford: Clarendon Press, 1993.

———. "When Does Potentiality Count? A Comment on Lockwood." In *Contingent Future People*, ed. Nick Fotion and Jan C. Heller. Dordrecht: Kluwer, 1997.

Harris, John. *Wonderwoman and Superman: The Ethics of Human Biotechnology*. New York: Oxford University Press, 1993.

Hart, H. L. A., and Tony Honore. *Causation in the Law*, 2d. ed. New York: Oxford University Press, 1985.

Heyd, David. *Genethics: Moral Issues in the Creation of People*. Berkeley: University of California Press, 1992.

Holmes, Oliver Wendell. "The Path of the Law," *Harvard Law Review* 10 (1897): 457.

Kagan, Shelly, and Peter Vallentyne. "Infinite Value and Finitely Additive Value Theory." *Journal of Philosophy* 44, no. 1 (Jan. 1997): 5–26.

Kavka, Gregory. "The Paradox of Future Individuals." *Philosophy and Public Affairs* 11, no. 2 (1981): 93–112.

Keeton, Robert E. *Legal Cause in the Law of Torts*. Columbus: Ohio State University Press, 1963.

Kolata, Gina. *Clone: The Road to Dolly and the Path Ahead*. New York: William Morrow, 1998.

———. "Scientist Clones Human Embryos, and Creates an Ethical Challenge." *New York Times*, 24 Oct. 1993, A1.

———. "Scientist Reports First Cloning Ever of Adult Mammal." *New York Times*, 23 Feb. 1997, A1.

———. "With Cloning of a Sheep, the Ethical Ground Shifts." *New York Times*, 24 Feb. 1997, A1.

Kripke, Saul. *Naming and Necessity*. Cambridge, Mass.: Harvard University Press, 1980.

Kyburg, Henry E., Jr. *Probability and Inductive Logic*. London: Macmillan, 1970.

Lessing, Doris. *The Fifth Child*. New York: Knopf, 1988.

Lewis, David. *On the Plurality of Worlds*. Oxford: Blackwell, 1986.

Lockwood, Michael. "Hare on Potentiality: A Rejoinder." In *Contingent Future People*, ed. Nick Fotion and Jan C. Heller. Dordrecht: Kluwer, 1997.

Luban, David. "Social Choice Theory as Jurisprudence." *Southern California Law Review* 69 (1996): 521–88.

McCormick, Richard A. "Blastomere Separation: Some Concerns." *Hastings Center Report* 24 (1994): 14–15.

McMahan, Jefferson. "Wrongful Life: Paradoxes in the Morality of Causing People to Exist." In *Rational Commitment and Social Justice: Essays for Gregory Kavka*, ed. Jules Coleman and Christopher Morris. Cambridge University Press, forthcoming.

Medema, Steven G., and Nicholas Mercuro. *Economics and the Law: From Posner to Post-Modernism*. Princeton, N.J.: Princeton University Press, 1997.

Mill, John Stuart. *On Liberty*. New York: Appleton-Century-Crofts, 1947.

———. "Utilitarianism." In *The Collected Works of John Stuart Mill*, ed. John M. Robson. Toronto: University of Toronto Press, 1969.

Moore, G. E. *Principia Ethica*. Cambridge: Cambridge University Press, 1971.

Morreim, E. Haavi. "The Concept of Harm Reconceived: A Different Look at 'Wrongful Life.' " *Law and Philosophy* 7 (1988): 3–31.

Morrison, Tony. *Beloved*. New York: Knopf, 1987.

Narveson, Jan. "Future People and Us." In *Obligations to Future Generations*, ed. R. I. Sikora and Brian Barry. Philadelphia: Temple University Press, 1978.

———. "Moral Problems of Population." In *Ethics and Population*, ed. Michael D. Bayles. Cambridge, Mass.: Schenkman, 1976.

Parfit, Derek. "Overpopulation and the Quality of Life." In *Applied Ethics*, ed. Peter Singer. Oxford: Oxford University Press, 1986.

———. *Reasons and Persons*. Oxford: Clarendon, 1984.

Persson, Ingmar. "Genetic Therapy, Identity and Person-Regarding Reasons," *Bioethics* 9, no. 1 (1995): 16–31.

Posner, Richard A. *Economic Analysis of the Law*, 4th ed. Boston: Little, Brown, 1992.

———. "The Ethics and Economics of Enforcing Contracts of Surrogate Motherhood." *Journal of Contemporary Health Law and Policy* 5, no. 21 (1989): 21–31.

Prosser, William L., and Page Keeton. *Law of Torts*, 5th ed. Minneapolis: West, 1984.

Rawls, John. *A Theory of Justice*. Oxford: Oxford University Press, 1972.

Roberts, Melinda A. "A Way of Looking at the Dalla Corte Case." *Journal of Law, Medicine & Ethics* 22 (1994): 339–42.

———. "Distinguishing Wrongful From 'Rightful Life.' " *Journal of Contemporary Health Law and Policy* 6 (1990): 59–80.

———. "Good Intentions and a Great Divide: Having Babies by Intending Them." *Law and Philosophy* 12 (1993): 287–317.

———. "Human Cloning: A Case of No Harm Done?" *Journal of Medicine and Philosophy* 21 (1996): 537–554.

———. "Parent and Child in Conflict: Between Liberty and Responsibility." *Notre Dame Journal of Law, Ethics & Public Policy* 10 (1996): 485–542.

———. "Present Duties and Future Persons: When Are Existence-Inducing Acts Wrong?" *Law and Philosophy* 14 (1995): 297–327.

Robertson, John A. *Children of Choice: Freedom and the New Reproductive Technologies*. Princeton, N.J.: Princeton University Press, 1994.

———. "Embryos, Families and Procreative Liberty: The Legal Structure of the New Reproduction." *Southern California Law Review* 59 (1986): 939–1041.

———. "The Question of Human Cloning." *Hastings Center Report* 24 (1994): 6–14.

Ryberg, Jesper. "Parfit's Repugnant Conclusion." *Philosophical Quarterly* 46, no. 183 (April 1996): 203–13.

Schwartz, Thomas. "Obligations to Posterity." In *Obligations to Future Generations*, ed. R. I. Sikora and Brian Barry. Philadelphia: Temple University Press, 1978.

Schmidt, Bernard. "Bronson Alcott's Developing Personalism and the Argument with Emerson." *American Transcendental Quarterly* 8, no. 4 (Dec. 1994): 311.

Schmidt, W. E. "Birth to 59-Year-Old Briton Raises Ethical Storm." *New York Times*, 29 Dec. 1993, A1.

Seidman, Louis M. "Baby M and the Problem of Unstable Preferences." *Georgetown Law Review* 76 (1988): 1829–1836.

Sen, Amartya. *Inequality Reexamined*. Cambridge, Mass.: Harvard University Press, 1992.

Sidgwick, Henry. *The Methods of Ethics*. Chicago: University of Chicago Press, 1962.

Sikora, R. I. "Is it Wrong to Prevent the Existence of Future Generations?" In *Obligations to Future Generations*, ed. R. I. Sikora and Brian Barry. Philadelphia: Temple University Press, 1978.

Sikora, R. I., and Brian Barry, eds. *Obligations to Future Generations*. Philadelphia: Temple University Press, 1978.

Silver, Lee M. *Remaking Eden: Cloning and Beyond in a Brave New World*. New York: Avon Books, 1997.

Slote, Michael. *Beyond Optimizing: A Study of Rational Choice*. Cambridge, Mass.: Harvard University Press, 1989.

Steinbock, Bonnie. "The Logical Case for Wrongful Life." *Hastings Center Report* 16, no. 2 (April 1986): 15–20.

Sumner, L.W. "Classical Utilitarianism and the Population Optimum." In *Obligations to Future Generations*, ed. R. I. Sikora and Brian Barry. Philadelphia: Temple University Press, 1978.

Tedeschi, G. "On Tort Liability for Wrongful Life." *Israel Law Review* 1 (1966): 513–38.

Temkin, Larry S. *Inequality*. New York: Oxford University Press, 1993.

———. "Intransitivity and the Mere Addition Paradox." *Philosophy and Public Affairs* 16, no. 2 (Spring 1987): 138–87.

Vallentyne, Peter, and Shelly Kagan. "Infinite Value and Finitely Additive Value Theory," *Journal of Philosophy* 44, no. 1 (Jan. 1997): 5–26.

Wiggins, David. *Identity and Spatio-Temporal Continuity*. Oxford: Oxford University Press, 1967.

Wolf, Clark. "Person-Affecting Utilitarianism and Population Policy Or, Sissy Jupe's Theory of Social Choice." In *Contingent Future Persons*, ed. Nick Fotion and Jan C. Heller. Dordrecht: Kluwer Academic, 1997.

———. "Social Choice and Normative Population Theory: A Person Affecting Solution to Parfit's Mere Addition Paradox." *Philosophical Studies* 81 (1996): 263–82.

Woodward, James. "The Non-Identity Problem." *Ethics* 96 (July, 1986): 804–31.

Comments

"A Cause of Action for Wrongful Life: A Suggested Analysis." *Minnesota Law Review* 55 (1970): 58–81.

"Park v. Chessin: The Continuing Judicial Development of the Theory of 'Wrongful Life.' " *American Journal of Law & Medicine* 4 (1978): 211–232.

Court Opinions

Anderson v. St. Francis-St. George Hospital, 77 Ohio St. 3d 82, 671 N.E.2d 225 (1996).

Becker v. Schwartz, 46 N.Y.2d 401, 413 N.Y.S.2d 895, 386 N.E.2d 807 (1978).

Berman v. Allan, 80 N.J. 421, 404 A.2d 8 (1979).

Bowers v. Hardwick, 478 U.S. 186 (1986).

Curlender v. Bio-Science Laboratories, 106 Cal. App. 3d 811, 165 Cal. Rptr. 477 (1980).

Davis v. Davis 842 S.W.2d 588 (Tenn. 1992).

In re Baby M, 109 N.J. 396, 537 A.2d 1227 (1988).

In re Baby M, 217 N.J. Super. 313, 525 A.2d 1128 (Sup. Ct. Ch. 1987).

In re Kirchner, 164 Ill. 2d 468, 649 N.E.2d 324 (1995).

Gleitman v. Cosgrove, 49 N.J. 22, 227 A.2d 689 (1967).

Harbeson v. Parke-Davis, 98 Wash. 2d 460, 656 P.2d 483 (1983).

Jaycee B. v. Superior Court, 42 Cal. App. 4th 718, 49 Cal. Rptr. 2d 694 (1996).

Johnson v. Calvert, 5 Cal. 4th 84, 851 P.2d 776, 19 Cal. Rptr. 494 (1993).

Nelson v. Krusen, 678 S.W.2d 918 (Tex. 1984).

O'Connell v. Kirchner, 513 U.S. 1303 (1995).

O'Connell v. Kirchner, 513 U.S. 1138 (1995).

Palsgraf v. Long Island R. Co., 248 N.Y. 339, 162 N.E. 99 (1928).

Park v. Chessin, 60 A.D.2d 80, 400 N.Y.S.2d 110 (N.Y. App. Div. 1977).

Procanik v. Cillo, 97 N.J. 339, 478 A.2d 755 (1984).

Schroeder v. Perkel, 87 N.J. 53, 432 A.2d 834 (1981).

Speck v. Finegold, 497 Pa. 77, 439 A.2d 110 (1981).

Turpin v. Sortini, 31 Cal. 3d 220, 643 P.2d 954, 182 Cal. Rptr. 337 (1982).

Zepeda v. Zepeda, 41 Ill. App. 2d 240, 190 N.E.2d 849 (1963).

Index of Names and Subjects

Index of Principles

P: Broome's principle of moral permissibility, 47

BPAR: Broome's person-affecting ranking principle, 49

PAR*: An alternative person-affecting ranking principle, 52, 71–72

P*: A person-affecting principle of moral permissibility, 33, 64

N*: A person-affecting principle governing personal wronging and the nonexistent, 62

M*: A person-affecting principle governing personal wronging and the maximization of well-being, 62

D*: A person-affecting principle governing personal wronging and the diminution of (failure to maximize) well-being, 63

CF: A counterfactual principle governing personal wronging and what would have been, 102

ME*: A person-affecting principle governing personal wronging and the maximization of expected well-being, 104

Index of Graphs

About the Author

Melinda A. Roberts is an associate professor of philosophy at the College of New Jersey, with doctorates in philosophy from the Five-College Ph.D. Program in Amherst, Massachusetts, and in law from the University of Texas at Austin. Ms. Roberts is the author of several articles on ethics and the law and is currently working on a book on children, ethics, and the Constitution. She lives in Princeton, New Jersey.

SUNY BROCKPORT

3 2815 00815 0537

RG 133 .5 .R62 1998

Roberts, Melinda A., 1954-

Child versus childmaker

DATE DUE

APR 0 5 2006		
MAY 0 2 2006		

DRAKE MEMORIAL LIBRARY
WITHDRAWN
THE COLLEGE AT BROCKPORT

GAYLORD   PRINTED IN U.S.A.